DISCOVERING
North Carolina's
Mountains-to-Sea Trail

DISCOVERING
North Carolina's
Mountains-to-Sea Trail

A Companion for Hikers
and
Armchair Explorers

Jerry Barker

Enjoy the beauty of NC & the MST

Jerry

THE UNIVERSITY OF NORTH CAROLINA PRESS

Chapel Hill

This book was published with the assistance of the Wells Fargo Fund for Excellence of the University of North Carolina Press.

A SOUTHERN GATEWAYS GUIDE

© 2024 Jerry Barker

Designed by Jamison Cockerham
Set in Scala, Alegreya Sans, and Noto Sans Cherokee
by Jamie McKee, MacKey Composition

Cover photographs: *Background:* A hiker on the Cape Hatteras National Seashore, photo by Pamela Ireland. *Insets, left to right:* The Ocracoke Lighthouse, photo by Jerry Barker; Brinegar Cabin along the Blue Ridge Parkway, photo by Jerry Barker; the observation tower on Clingmans Dome (Kuwohi), photo by Kyla Marie Keever.

Opposite: Kate Dixon at Topsail Beach. Photo by Dan Wilkerson; used by permission.

Maps by Curtis Belyea.

Manufactured in the United States of America

LIBRARY OF CONGRESS CATALOGING-IN-PUBLICATION DATA
Names: Barker, Jerry W., author.
Title: Discovering North Carolina's Mountains-to-Sea Trail :
    a companion for hikers and armchair explorers / Jerry Barker.
Other titles: Southern gateways guide.
Description: Chapel Hill : The University of North Carolina Press, 2024. | Series:
    A Southern gateways guide | Includes bibliographical references and index.
Identifiers: LCCN 2023045909 | ISBN 9781469670096 (paper ; alk. paper) |
    ISBN 9781469670102 (epub) | ISBN 9798890886996 (pdf)
Subjects: LCSH: Hiking—North Carolina—Mountains-to-Sea Trail—
    Guidebooks. | Mountains-to-Sea Trail (N.C.)—Guidebooks. |
    BISAC: TRAVEL / United States / South / South Atlantic (DC,
    DE, FL, GA, MD, NC, SC, VA, WV) | NATURE / Regional
Classification: LCC GV199.42.N66 B34 2024 | DDC 796.5109756—dc23/eng/20231018
LC record available at https://lccn.loc.gov/2023045909

Dedicated to

KATE DIXON

Executive Director

Friends of the

Mountains-to-Sea Trail

2008–22

Friends of the Mountains-to-Sea Trail was formed in 1997 and in 2008 was still a volunteer organization, with sixty-seven members. It was time for full-time leadership. Kate Dixon, with extraordinary nonprofit and conservation experience, was named the executive director and for fifteen years helped build a strong organization and community.

Over 200 miles of off-road trail were added during Kate's tenure. One of her greatest achievements was the development of the Coastal Crescent route in southeastern North Carolina. No trail had been built in that part of the state for thirty years.

Membership grew to 1,750 as guidebooks and digital platforms served the hiking public. Partnerships were formed with land managers, towns, and landowners. Annual gatherings steadily outgrew their venues. A key figure in forming the North Carolina's Great Trails State Coalition, Kate helped secure the 2021 passage of the Complete the Trails Fund for the twelve official state trails, and helped have 2023 celebrated as NC Year of the Trail.

At the fortieth anniversary of the MST, Kate was honored with the Order of the Long Leaf Pine. In the fall of 2021, the Kate Dixon Legacy Campaign honored Kate and her extraordinary leadership of the MST and for conservation in North Carolina.

Contents

COASTAL PLAIN AND OUTER BANKS REGION

DISCOVERING
North Carolina's
Mountains-to-Sea Trail

A sunset from the Linville Gorge Chimneys makes you pause to admire.
Photo by Adam Paashaus; used by permission of Friends of the MST.

INTRODUCTION

Exploring the Mountains-to-Sea Trail

History, Culture, and Interesting Sites Nearby

A few years ago, our family flew to Denver for a vacation to visit all the big national parks and iconic sites out west. Just a couple hours up the road my granddaughter yelled, "Look at those sunflowers! Grandpa, can we stop?" Of course, we turned around at the next exit to go walk in and take pictures of the fifty-acre sunflower field.

The next day our destination was Mount Rushmore in South Dakota. After an hour-long tour, we moved on to lesser-known Custer State Park, where we got stuck amid 400 bison crossing and recrossing the highway. We all loved it, awed by the bison size, babies, and protective moms—one even rubbed its beard on the hood of our rental car. When the vacation ended, what were the subjects of most of our stories and photos? You guessed it—sunflowers and bison.

As you hike the Mountains-to-Sea Trail (MST), you'll come across many historical and cultural sites that are not in any guidebook. For example, when hiking Linville Gorge, you can admire the big views and soaring cliffs, but if you're out in the hot sun, you will appreciate knowing the location and history of a small spring near Table Rock where you can cool off. In Segment 10, about 500 yards east of Old Oxford Road, the MST crosses abandoned railroad tracks, but did you know they lead to a trestle over the Eno River that was built in 1909? If you're enjoying a hike or ride along the Blue Ridge Parkway, you wouldn't want to miss a favorite overlook or nearby town where you can get dinner. While near Greensboro you can experience the Civil Rights Museum or the Guilford Courthouse National Military Park. In addition to walking the beaches of Topsail Island, why not visit the nearby turtle hospital?

It's often the unplanned side trips and the surprises we encounter along the MST that make for the most vivid memories. A hiker guidebook is, of course, essential, but it can't mark every story or place along our journey. As Terry Russell put it in his travel memoir *On the Loose*, "Adventure is not in a guidebook and Beauty is not on the map. Seek and ye shall find."

Whether we're hiking, exploring by car, or reading in an armchair, most of us like to find and learn about new sites to visit. This book is not just for experienced or even beginner hikers; it is for anyone who would like to learn more about the 1,175-mile MST corridor across North Carolina. It points out historical, cultural, and other noteworthy sites—some that you can hike to and others that require a short drive—along this serpentine corridor across the mountains, Piedmont, and coastal regions of North Carolina. Its purpose is to motivate us to go exploring. Of course, you can explore on the page with a cup of coffee in hand while sitting in your favorite chair, but you'll miss the sunshine, fresh air, exercise, and conversation.

Along the MST, North Carolina's full diversity can be seen, from some of the oldest mountains in the world, hilly Piedmont farms, sea-level wetlands, and barrier islands, to the state's textile towns and colonial outposts steeped in history. Likewise, there is diversity in the local stories and cultures of Black Americans, Indigenous peoples, and people of color, though they are seldom mentioned in hiking materials. It is time to tell both old and current stories; advance racial and cultural inclusion and diversity in our outdoors; and promote harmony, respect, and community on our shared lands and on the MST. Celebrate diverse organizations—we all belong outdoors. The policies and practices of Friends of the Mountains-to-Sea Trail, in the organization's own words approved by its board of directors, "will reflect our commitment to promote access, equity and inclusiveness, and to discourage discrimination that denies the essential humanity of all people." The MST is an "MST for All."

The Beginnings of the Mountains-to-Sea Trail

The MST is a 1,175-mile trail that crosses North Carolina, from Clingmans Dome (the peak is called Kuwohi in Tsalagi, the Cherokee language) in Great Smoky Mountains National Park on the Tennessee line to Jockey's Ridge State Park on the Outer Banks. It passes through thirty-seven counties, four national parks, three national forests, two national wildlife refuges, twelve state parks, four state game lands, one state forest, one state historic site, and numerous local parks and protected areas. The MST

MST pioneers Howard Lee and Doris Hammett at the 2017 MST Annual Gathering in Elkin. *Photo by Carolyn Meija; used by permission of Friends of the MST.*

passes three lighthouses, including the nation's tallest, and includes two ferry rides. It also offers a 170-mile paddling trail along the Neuse River, from Smithfield to the Neusiok Trail.

The MST is more than just a walk in the woods. More than 715 miles of footpath are now completed, with temporary routes on backroads, bicycle paths, and paddling trails, allowing hikers to follow the MST on an adventure across North Carolina.

Howard Lee is credited as the initiator of the MST. He was the first Black mayor of a majority-white southern city (Chapel Hill), a state senator, and the North Carolina secretary of natural resources and community development. In 1977, he set the MST in motion when he spoke at the Fourth National Trails Symposium and proposed "a trail that would give North Carolina and national visitors using it a real feel for the sights, sounds, and people of the state." "I think it would be a trail that would help—like the first primitive trails—bring us together," Lee said. Jim Hallsey, who was working as the North Carolina trails manager at the time, immediately began work on a feasibility report and proposal for the MST corridor.

Like Benton MacKaye's 1921 vision for the Appalachian Trail, the vision for the MST was that it would be not just a footpath but a corridor surrounded by fields, farms, forests, rivers, towns, and historic sites. Beyond the trail is a realm of wild and conserved lands, and sometimes small towns and urban development.

The nonprofit organization Friends of the Mountains-to-Sea Trail was founded by Allen de Hart in 1997. He is credited as the trail's visionary and champion; he was also one of the first to thru-hike the entire MST. Jeff Brewer served as the first president of the Friends of the MST, from 1997 to 2009, and together Brewer, de Hart, and Hallsey did wonders to plan, construct, organize, and promote the MST in its earliest days. Kate Dixon became the first executive director of the Friends in 2008, and she helped amplify the work of an ever-growing group of MST advocates and volunteers.

North Carolina's natural wonders, history, and culture draw over 50 million visitors to the state each year. Some segment of the MST is within a day's drive of twenty-two states and 161 million people, 48 percent of the US population. The North Carolina Division of Parks and Recreation manages forty-one state parks, fourteen state trails, and numerous natural areas, lakes, scenic rivers, and recreation areas, encompassing the state's diverse environments. From the mountains to the coast, we're blessed to have a state trail to showcase the "variety vacationland" and the "great trails state." The MST is part of the Great Trails State Coalition, which celebrated 2023 as the "Year of the Trail."

Some Fun Facts about the Mountains-to-Sea Trail

- The MST was proposed in 1977 and added to the state park system in 2000; is North Carolina's flagship trail and longest marked footpath; and is the second-longest state trail in the United States (of twenty state trails nationally, only the Florida Trail is longer).
- The trail takes approximately 2,683,874 footsteps to complete; climbs North Carolina's tallest mountain peak (Mount Mitchell, 6,684 feet); is at sea level at Cape Hatteras National Seashore; and scales the highest sand dune in the eastern United States.
- In 2003 Asheville residents Nadja Miller, age nineteen, and Katie Senechal, age twenty, hiked the entire trail from April 3 to June 27, carrying heavy packs and finishing at Jockey's Ridge as the first female completers, and fourth and fifth completers overall. "We endured soaking rain, followed by snow then more rain along the parkway. Linville Gorge with colorful rhododendron was a favorite location and highlights were the interesting and kind people we met across the entire state."
- Diane Van Deren, from Colorado, set the fastest known time (FKT)

Allen de Hart, seventy-six, celebrates the 2003 thru-hike completion by Katie Senechal, twenty, and Nadja Miller, nineteen. De Hart had a celebratory cake waiting in the Visitors Center. *Photo by Allen de Hart; used by permission of Friends of the MST.*

for completing the trail (when it was 935 miles). Diane reached the dunes at Jockey's Ridge in June 2012 in a record twenty-two days, five hours, and three minutes. She was tested with days of rain in the mountains, and forty-mile-per-hour winds and eight inches of rain during Tropical Storm Beryl.

- Tara "Candy Mama" Dower set a new FKT for the 1,175-mile trail in September 2020: twenty-nine days, eight hours, and forty-eight minutes. "It's beautiful, it's hard, it's a constant roller coaster of emotions and feelings," she told the Facebook group Women of the Mountain. "And that's why I'm here."
- On July 1, 2022, Brandon Stapanowich set a new men's FKT of twenty-three days, thirteen hours, and twenty-eight minutes, averaging 50.2 miles a day.
- In November 2020, Goldsboro native and psychologist Cedric Turner-Kopa became the first Black American completer: "I loved eating wild blueberries and seeing a bear in the mountains and experiencing the glowing sand with bioluminescent zooplankton at night on the Pea Island beach. [I'm] grateful for the many people that showed me compassion, concern, and assistance."

Tara "Candy Mama" Dower celebrates twenty-nine days, eight hours, and forty-eight minutes of hiking to set a fastest known time for the 1,175 mile-MST in September 2020. *Photo by Megan Wilmarth; used by permission.*

- Trevor Thomas, from Charlotte, is the only legally blind hiker to complete the trail (April 6–June 22, 2013), and his guide dog, Tennille, is the only canine honored.
- As of 2022, 181 known individuals have completed the entire MST (69 women, 112 men). Mary Ann Nissley from Pennsylvania section-hiked the MST from 1992 to 2017 and is the oldest completer at age eighty-four. "I loved the mountains, the Outer Banks and the people I met."
- To celebrate the MST fortieth anniversary on September 9, 2017, 1,735 people spread across the state and hiked or paddled a portion of the trail, so the entire MST was completed collectively in a day. To my knowledge, this is a first on any long-distance trail.
- There are nineteen volunteer leaders across the state coordinating efforts to build and maintain the trail. In 2022, 1,150 volunteers provided 44,023 hours of service. Volunteers work with many land managers, the people responsible for the use and management of public land.

Trevor Thomas and Tennille received thru-hiker awards at the 2014 Gathering of MST Friends from Allen de Hart and Howard Lee. Tennille is the only guide dog so honored. *Photo used by permission of Friends of the MST.*

How to Read This Book

Hiking the Mountains-to-Sea Trail is a wonderful way to get to know North Carolina's beautiful and varied landscapes. With this book, I hope to give you some history of the state's people and culture in what we'll call the MST corridor, roughly a one-mile-wide area around the trail (so it's about 1,175 square miles in total, roughly the area of Rhode Island or 1.5 times the size of Wake County). It's a great way for anyone—a lifelong North Carolinian, a recent transplant, or a tourist—to get to know the history of our state and its people while enjoying its natural beauty.

Every chapter in this book is dedicated to a segment of the MST—nineteen in all—and provides information on a variety of things of interest along or just off the trail. Think of this book as your tour guide, hiking with you and pointing out things you may not know. I will not duplicate much information that can be found in existing guidebooks; instead, I'll seek to shine light on noteworthy topics not often addressed in MST guides. There will be informative stories about history and culture, quirky facts, and a travelogue approach as we geographically progress from the mountains

Scot "TABA" Ward, five-time MST completer (on his fifth hike he skateboarded roads from the Outer Banks to Stone Mountain State Park). Ward authored the 2009 and 2012 editions of *The Thru-hiker's Manual for the Mountain-to-Sea Trail.* Photo by Cynthia Taylor-Miller; used by permission of Friends of the MST.

to the Piedmont to the sea. Along the way I'll shine a spotlight on towns and cities near the trail. I'll also share deep dives into the history of the trail at appropriate segments and relate interesting stories that deserve to be told, along with commentary that people with experiences on the MST and knowledge of the surrounding areas have shared with me. So there is quite a lot of ground to cover—both on the trail itself and about the things you can do near it.

The book is organized from west (mountains) to east (coast), so eastbound (EB) mileage from the start of the trail will be shared to help you identify locations, written as "EB 0.0." EB mileage numbering restarts at each segment and is subject to change because of trail changes and reroutes; the most current mileage will be online at mountainstoseatrail .org. Prepare to depart the western terminus (Segment 1, EB 0.0) and hike 1,175 miles to Jockey's Ridge State Park (Segment 18, EB 81.9).

Further Information and Resources

Because the goal of this book is to show you the often-hidden histories in the MST corridor, it doesn't have much trail description or information about camping and lodging, food and supplies, water and restrooms, hunting, signs and blazing, accessibility, and parking locations. This information is readily available in the MST Trail Guides on the Friends of the MST website (mountainstoseatrail.org).

In 2000, Allen de Hart published the first MST guidebook, *Hiking North Carolina's Mountains-to-Sea Trail*, which is filled with early MST history. Scot "TABA [There and Back Again]" Ward published an updated guide in 2009 when the trail measured 930 miles: *The Thru-Hiker's Manual for the Mountains-to-Sea Trail of North Carolina*. Scot did his first thru-hike in 2008 and followed it with four additional thru-hikes as he updated his guide.

Another excellent guide is *The Mountains-to-Sea Trail across North Carolina: Walking a Thousand Miles through Wildness, Culture and History* by Danny Bernstein (2013). Bernstein was the twenty-first MST completer and has been blogging about hiking and the outdoors since 2008. Heather Houskeeper, a.k.a. the Botanical Hiker, has thru-hiked the MST twice and authored *A Guide to the Edible and Medicinal Plants of the Mountains-to-Sea Trail* (2014). And finally, the 2020 book *Great Day Hikes on the North Carolina's Mountains-to-Sea Trail*, edited by Jim Grode, is a great resource for those who want a day's adventure on the MST.

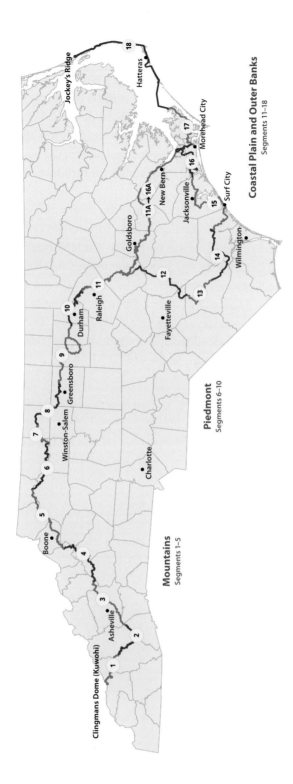

Map of the MST route across North Carolina depicting the nineteen segments. To clearly show where trail segments begin and end, even-numbered trail segments are in brown and odd-numbered segments are in green, while the Neuse River paddle route (segments 11A–16A) are in blue. *Map by Sara Birkemeier, © Friends of Mountains-to-Sea Trail.*

Mountains
Segments 1–5

Piedmont
Segments 6–10

Coastal Plain and Outer Banks
Segments 11–18

Clingmans Dome (Kuwohi)

Asheville

Boone

Winston-Salem

Greensboro

Durham

Raleigh

Charlotte

Fayetteville

Goldsboro

New Bern

Jacksonville

Surf City

Wilmington

Morehead City

Hatteras

Jockey's Ridge

11A → 16A

LEGEND TO MAPS

—— Trails
—— Roads
—— Paddle routes
—— Alternate routes
—— Detours if trail closed

- - - - Additional trails
······ Streams
═══ Highways
—— Roads
• • • Ferry routes

🛶 Paddle endpoints
🥾 Hiking endpoints
⛺ Campgrounds
🗼 Lighthouses
🏛 Historical sites
♿ Accessible point
🅿 Parking
❓ Visitor centers
✈ Airports

County boundaries
Water bodies
Municipal boundaries
Parks
Wilderness area
State boundaries
◎ Tribal and ethnic sites
● Unincorporated places
◉ River-related cultural features
Non-Indigenous name (Indigenous name)

MOUNTAIN REGION

343.3 MILES

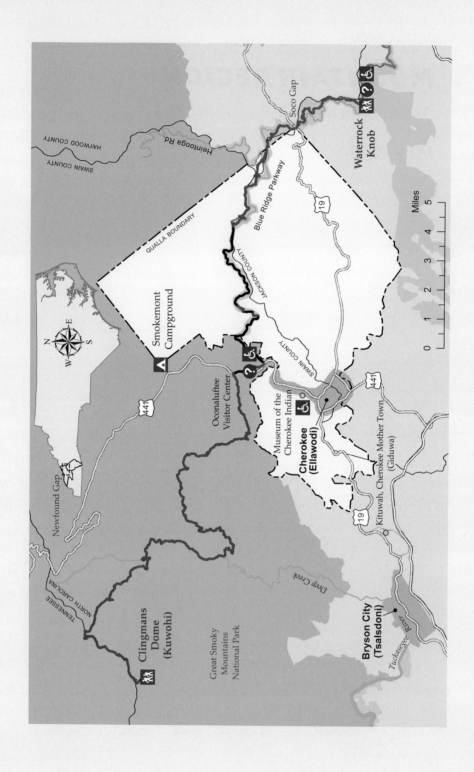

SEGMENT 1

Peak to Peak

Clingmans Dome (Kuwohi) to Waterrock Knob

46.8 MILES

May the warm winds of heaven blow softly upon your
house. May the great spirit bless all who enter there. May
your moccasins make happy tracks in many snows, and
may the rainbow always touch your shoulder.

TRADITIONAL CHEROKEE BLESSING

The Beginning of the Trail

This high-elevation area has natural communities similar to those found in Maine and southern Canada (subarctic ecosystems), but it is also a temperate rainforest. The Great Smoky Mountains National Park (GSMNP)—the nation's most-visited national park—anchors the western end of the MST and, at 816 square miles in size, is known around the world for its biodiversity and natural beauty. The MST also highlights a part of the treasured Blue Ridge Parkway.

Native American history and culture permeate the region. The Qualla Boundary, just south of the park, is a sovereign nation of 57,000 acres, the home of the Eastern Band of Cherokee Indians.

Clingmans Dome (Kuwohi) to Cherokee

The Smoky Mountains are the ancestral home of the Anigiduwagi, or Cherokee. They called these mountains Shaconage, which means "place of blue smoke." The Cherokee name for Clingmans Dome is Kuwohi, meaning "mulberry place." At 6,643 feet, the peak, which straddles the

The Friends' Board of Directors Land Acknowledgment

Friends of the Mountains-to-Sea Trail respectfully acknowledges that the trail traverses traditional and ancestral homelands of Indigenous peoples, whom we honor as the original stewards of the land.

border between North Carolina and Tennessee, is a historically sacred place of reverence. It is the highest point in the Smokies, in Tennessee, and along the Appalachian Trail, and only two mountains in North Carolina rise above it. It is the third-highest peak on the East Coast and the western endpoint of the MST. In 1859, geologist and geographer Arnold Guyot named the peak for Thomas L. Clingman, a US congressman and senator from North Carolina as well as a Confederate brigadier general, ignoring and disrespecting the Cherokee people's long and sacred ties to the place. In July 2022, the Eastern Band of Cherokee Indians Tribal Council petitioned the US Board of Geographic Names to restore the mountain's original name, Kuwohi.

The road to the summit is open from April 1 to November 30 but can be closed in poor weather, so check accordingly. From a parking area, it is a steep 0.6-mile hike, with a gain of 332 feet to the fifty-four-foot circular observation platform, built in 1959, which is accessed by a spiral ramp.

The MST begins at the Clingmans tower, EB 0.0, hiking "east" concurrent with the northbound Appalachian Trail. The views here can be amazing, so the hike is worth the effort. For the first twenty-seven miles, the MST follows ten different Great Smoky Mountains National Park trails that are not blazed with the MST three-inch white dot but with wooden signs at trail intersections (150 total trails in the park).

At EB 3.0, you can hike to the summit of Mount Collins (elevation 6,188 feet), named for Oconaluftee resident Robert Collins, who guided Arnold Guyot across the crest of the Smokies in the late 1850s. At EB 3.9 you leave the Appalachian Trail and take the Fork Ridge Trail for the next 5.2 miles, descending 2,800 feet to Deep Creek (EB 9.0–13.4). This is the most remote area of the entire MST, with no road access for 22.8 miles. True to its name, Deep Creek can be deep and dangerous when it floods (there is no bridge). After the MST leaves it, the Deep Creek Trail

The observation tower on Clingmans Dome (Kuwohi), western terminus of the MST. *Photo by Kyla Marie Keever; used by permission.*

continues 3.9 miles to the Deep Creek Campground, and another three miles to Bryson City and the Tuckasegee River.

Deep Creek Trail was one of the first constructed by the Civilian Conservation Corps in the new national park in the 1930s. It is known for abundant wildflowers that bloom from late February through September, with peak season in mid-April, when the spring ephemerals make their appearance. At EB 12.6, you pass the Benton MacKaye Trail (which continues with the MST to EB 20.8). At EB 13.4, you leave Deep Creek on the Martins Gap Trail (EB 13.4–14.9).

In the first fifteen miles, you've already been on five trails! Continuing through the Smokies, you also join the Sunkota Ridge Trail (EB 14.9–19.8), Thomas Divide Trail (EB 19.8–20.1), Newton Bald Trail (EB 20.1–20.8), Mingus Creek Trail (EB 20.8–26.6), and Oconaluftee River Trail (EB 27.4–28). That might seem odd, but it made the most sense to construct the MST by linking existing trails in the Smokies.

The National Park Service (NPS) offers these safety reminders: Be aware of parking lot vandalism at trailheads. In the Smokies, be prepared for swollen streams, bridge washouts, downed trees, and trail erosion, particularly between December and May. Hikers may carry bear spray within Great Smoky Mountains National Park for the strict purpose of protection from aggressive wildlife (it should not be applied to people, tents, packs, or surrounding area as a repellent). Bear safety is important in both the MST mountain region and the coastal region—a good resource is Bearwise.org.

While on the trail, try the Native Land app (https://native-land.ca/), which maps Indigenous lands and peoples, so you can learn the history of where you are. You'll find information on these Indigenous peoples near the MST across North Carolina (from west to east): Cherokee, Sappony, Sissipahaw, Tuscarora, Sugaree/Catawba, Waxhaw, Creek/Saluda/Cherokee East, Coharie, Waccamaw/Lumbee, Neusiok, Croatan, and Roanoke/Hatteras. North Carolina recognizes eight tribes: Coharie Tribe, Eastern Band of the Cherokee Nation, Haliwa-Saponi Indian Tribe, Lumbee Tribe of North Carolina, Maherrin Indian Tribe, Occaneechi Band of Saponi Nation, Sappony, and Waccamaw Siouan Tribe. Some of these tribes, while recognized by the state, still lack federal recognition, but they continue to occupy their homelands despite the marginalization of their peoples' and tribal governments' decision-making roles.

In 2020, Michael Brune, the Sierra Club's executive director, said, "Willful ignorance is what allows some people to shut their eyes to the reality that the wild places we love are also the ancestral homelands of Native peoples, forced off their lands in the decades or centuries before they became national parks." For the 17,000 Cherokee in North Carolina, the 1838–39 Trail of Tears epitomizes a harsh and cruel history of empire building, deceit, and greed, and their consequences suffered by Native peoples.

It's important to know the history of Indigenous people, so we can understand the history of our state, our region, and the MST. The following is a short history of this section of the Mountains-to-Sea Trail and how it was made possible in cooperation with the Cherokee people.

The Buncombe County Register of Deeds, in conjunction with the Eastern Band of Cherokee Indians and the Museum of the Cherokee Indian, has produced a history of Cherokee land cessions and the formation of Buncombe County, "As Long as the Grass Shall Grow." The US and North Carolina governments expanded territory and broke many treaties with the Cherokee, taking land in violation of "everlasting treaties." The Buncombe County Register of Deeds is working to clarify the chain of title showing who owned land prior to the first land grants.

Larry Blythe of the Cherokee Nation recounts his history with the Mountains-to-Sea Trail:

> I got involved with the MST during my tenure as vice chief, when
> proponents of the MST wanted to cross Tribal property. We have
> an extensive trail system on the Tribal land. However, no trails
> were able to be utilized due to their proximity to residences. When
> the parkway agreed to allow its corridor along the roadway to be
> designated as MST, I started looking and we found a perfect fit by

connecting to our system road at Big Witch Gap, a road (BIA 407) through Tribal land, forests, and Mile High Campground (just off Heintooga Road), with no impacts to houses or other development. I presented a resolution to the Tribal Council and it was passed unanimously.

After decades of planning, building, and alternate routes, in October 2018 the MST route was finalized in western North Carolina—346.8 miles from Clingmans Dome (Kuwohi) to Stone Mountain. In 2014, Walt Weber and "The Gang" from the Carolina Mountain Club published the third edition of the popular western North Carolina guide *Trail Profiles and Maps: From Clingmans Dome to Mount Mitchell and Beyond*, complete with topographical maps and trail elevation profiles.

A Brief History of Cherokee and Its People

Cherokee is a Native American town at the eastern entrance of Great Smoky Mountains National Park and a popular vacation destination. It is one mile south of the MST on US 441. The Cherokee people do not live on a reservation, defined as land that the federal government returned to a Native American tribe. Instead, white chief William Holland Thomas, a US citizen (Cherokee people were not allowed citizenship) and adopted son of Yonaguska, a Cherokee leader, purchased 57,000 acres of property in Jackson and Swain Counties in the 1840s and 1850s (land officially surveyed in 1876). Called the Qualla Boundary, this land is now owned by the Eastern Band of Cherokee Indians (incorporated in 1889), which is recognized by both the federal and North Carolina governments and is a sovereign nation with over 14,000 members, making it the largest tribe in the United States. It is also home to a portion of the MST.

To learn about the 11,000-year-old Cherokee history and the ongoing story of the town and its people, visit the Oconaluftee Indian Village and Visitor Center; see *Unto These Hills*, a play first presented in 1950 that tells the story of the Cherokee from the eighteenth century to the twentieth; and explore the Museum of the Cherokee Indian (part of the Trail of Tears National Historic Trail in North Carolina). The Qualla Arts and Crafts Mutual is the oldest Native American cooperative in the country.

The Cherokee believe the ancient settlement of Kituwah (or Giduwa), on the Tuckasegee River, is one of the "seven mother towns" in the Southeast. It is in Swain County, along US 19, near present-day Bryson City, nine miles

> ### *Mountains-to-Sea Trail in Tsalagi (Cherokee)*
>
> In 1821, Sequoyah completed the Cherokee syllabary, distinguishing the Cherokee people as the only group of American Indians with a written language. (Currently, the New Kituwah Language Academy in Cherokee teaches in English and Tsalagi.) Below is the Tsalagi translation of "Mountains-to-Sea Trail," courtesy of Sharron Panther. It means "mountains you have to go through for you to get to the big water."
>
> SOᏳᏦR ᎡᏣᏋᎯᏍᏅ(Ꮧ) ᎠᎣᎯᏒᎸᎪᎯ ᎡᏣᎷᎯᏍᏅᏧ

from Cherokee. The remains of an ancient earthwork mound, built about 1000 CE, survive there, despite the Rutherford Expedition's destruction of the town in 1776. In 1996, the Eastern Band purchased 309 acres around the mound, and a year later an archeological survey uncovered a sixty-five-acre village and verified the settlement's age. Over a thousand years ago, the circular mound, 170 feet wide and 5 feet tall, served as the foundation for the Cherokee council house, a central site for the tribe's most sacred ceremonies. On the opposite side of the road is the Library of the Cherokee. Nearby is a historical marker for Yonaguska (1760–1839), head chief of the Cherokee who helped his followers avoid removal.

The Smokies

Spanning about 135,000 square miles from northern Georgia to western North Carolina, the Appalachian temperate rainforest sits atop the Southern Appalachian Mountains, one of the oldest mountain ranges in the world. Great Smoky Mountains National Park offers one of the best opportunities to experience and explore this humid and diverse biome. The mountain peaks of Great Smoky Mountains National Park, as well as Mount Mitchell and Grandfather Mountain, contain ecosystems and plant life unique to the southeastern United States and more akin to the environment 300 miles north.

Great Smoky Mountains National Park—816 square miles or 522,427 acres in size, with sixteen mountain peaks—is the nation's most-visited national park, with 14.1 million visitors each year, and is known the world over for the variety and beauty of its flora and fauna, in addition to its breathtaking mountains. In 1976, the park was designated an International Biosphere Reserve, and in 1983 it was recognized as a UN World Heritage Site. Where else in the eastern United States can you find bears and elk, 800 miles of trails, ninety preserved historic structures, old growth forests, and 730 miles of fish-bearing streams, even a Western North Carolina Fly Fishing Trail? Route 441 (Newfound Gap Road), thirty-three miles long and the only road across the park, has ample pull-offs, big vistas to enjoy, and no commercial traffic.

Thanks to the efforts of Horace Kephart, George Masa, and hundreds of others, the region was selected from competing sites. Businesspeople, outdoors enthusiasts, and conservationists, with funding from the federal government, North Carolina and Tennessee, the Rockefeller Family Foundation, and a children's penny crusade, made the protection of the Smoky Mountains possible. The park was established in June 1934, and on September 2, 1940, in Newfound Gap, President Franklin D. Roosevelt dedicated it "for the permanent enjoyment of the people."

Part of that enjoyment stems from the bounty of beautiful flora in the Smokies. Before colonists arrived, eastern and Carolina hemlocks reached 150 feet or more into the mountain skies, creating dark, shady understories that cooled streams for trout and nurtured rhododendrons and rare native ferns. The Great Smoky Mountains contained isolated pockets with hemlocks more than 500 years old. Today, these forests are threatened by the hemlock woolly adelgid, an insect that arrived in North Carolina in 1995. It sucks sap from hemlock, ultimately starving them. Most high-elevation mature hemlocks have died from infestation and create a "skeleton" or "ghost" forest; some younger, isolated trees and those chemically protected are surviving. In addition, balsam woolly adelgids on Mount Mitchell and in the higher elevation areas of the parkway have killed Fraser firs since the 1950s.

From 1933 to 1942 approximately 4,000 men served in the Civilian Conservation Corps in twenty-two camps throughout the Smokies. The CCC both offered men desperately needed employment during the Depression and accomplished such necessary tasks as building fire roads and observation towers, and performing major reforestation.

MST Facts

From 2014 to 2018, the MST alternate River Valley Route left Great Smoky Mountains National Park along Deep Creek, into Bryson City, then through Dillsboro and Sylva—with the iconic Jackson County courthouse on the hill and Bicentennial Park—then worked its way to Waterrock Knob. If you're touring the area, there are numerous cultural and historic sites worth visiting, with accommodations in the local communities.

Nearby Wildlife

Would you pay twenty-five dollars to watch a lightning bug? Synchronous fireflies are so popular in May and early June in the Smokies that people enter a lottery for a parking pass to come watch. The swarms of fireflies or lightning bugs are from the nineteen species found within the national park (of about 125 species of bioluminescent beetles worldwide) and the only lightning bug in the Americas that can synchronize its flashing light patterns. They are actually small flying beetles whose abdomen lights up. Their light patterns are part of their romantic mating display. On the North Carolina side of the Smokies, Cataloochee Valley Tours in Waynesville offers synchronous firefly night hikes (for a fee).

Blue ghost fireflies make their appearance in several valley areas near Asheville. They are different from the fireflies of the Smokies because their light stays on continuously and they fly just above the forest floor. When they're active, thousands of fireflies seem to float, glowing, over the forest floor. Night tours are available from Cradle of Forestry in Pisgah National Forest and from Asheville Hiking Tours (both for a fee). And if you're camping anywhere in the Southern Appalachians in the spring, if the conditions are right, you might be fortunate enough to have your own private showing.

From creatures small to great, Great Smoky Mountains National Park has it all. Twenty-five elk were introduced to the park in 2001 to see if they could flourish in the South, and an additional twenty-seven came in 2002. Now, more than twenty years later, the elk have been successfully established in the park. Most are in the Cataloochee Valley area, but their range is spreading. The Smoky Mountain Elk Fest is held in Maggie Valley every September. Elk are also known by their Shawnee name, *wapiti*, meaning "white rear."

Some Literary History near the Trail

Horace Kephart's last camp is memorialized with a historic millstone and the park's Campsite #57 (near EB 13.4, 200 feet down the Deep Creek Trail). Kephart is the author of *Our Southern Highlanders*, detailing his life in the Great Smoky Mountains of western North Carolina, and the classic outdoors guide *Camping and Woodcraft*, published in 1906. He is often called the father of Great Smoky Mountains National Park and is credited with establishing the Appalachian Trail through the state. Of his three years living alone in the Smokies, he wrote, "It is one of the blessings of wilderness life that it shows us how few things we need in order to be perfectly happy. We do not go to the woods to rough it; we go to smooth it—we get it rough enough in town. But let us live the simple, natural life in the woods, and leave all frills behind." His mentor was George W. Sears, pen name Nessmuk, a sportswriter for *Forest and Stream* magazine in the 1880s and an early conservationist. In 1884, Sears published *Woodcraft and Camping*—a very similar title to that of Kephart's classic book.

Some sixty years before the start of the twentieth century, the Smoky Mountains were a wilderness rich in old-growth forests and biodiversity. But the land was stolen from the Cherokee, and by 1900 settlers and big logging companies were moving in to clear-cut the forests and plunder the abundant natural resources. Kephart knew something must be done, and soon, or it would all be gone with no hope of coming back. He took up his pen to advocate for the mountains and a park to protect them. He wrote numerous magazine articles and letters, ultimately persuading both the public and political decision-makers that the Smokies should be a national park to preserve its inspiring vistas and unique natural features for visitors from near and far. "I owe my life to these mountains," he wrote, "and I want them preserved that others may profit from them."

Back on the Trail

Farther along this segment, you'll encounter the Mingus Mill (EB 26.6). In 1790, John Jacob and Sarah Mingus and their five children were some of the first settlers in the Oconaluftee River valley. Jacob built a waterwheel on Mingus Creek to power his corn mill. Nearly 100 years later, in 1886, Abraham Mingus, grandson of John Jacob, and John Leandus Floyd built a two-and-a-half-story wooden gristmill, which runs the machinery in the building using a water-powered turbine instead of a waterwheel. In the late 1800s and early 1900s, the mill served as a gathering place for nearby communities. During the week, families tended to their chores, crops, and livestock, and then they traveled, often a long way, to the mill on Saturday. There they traded goods to meet their basic needs and socialized while having their corn milled. The mill operated on a toll system in which local farmers paid for the milling of their corn and wheat with 10 percent of the finished meal. In 1930, the mill was sold to the national park, but it is still in operation. It is located a half mile north of the Oconaluftee Visitor Center on US 441.

The Minguses were enslavers. To find the enslaved peoples' Enloe Slave Graveyard, locate the gate at the far end of the mill parking lot. This is the trailhead from the Mingus Creek Trail. To the right of the gate is a path. Follow it up a hill about seventy-five feet to the cemetery. There are six graves with only rock grave markers to identify them; the last burial was in 1860. As a whole, the Great Smoky Mountains National Park documents seventy-seven cemeteries with 2,726 graves.

The Oconaluftee Baptist Church, also known as the Lufty Baptist Church or Smokemont Baptist Church, is a historic church near the town of Cherokee (EB 25.5). It is located off US 441, overlooking the Smokemont Campground. The town of Smokemont no longer exists. Lufty Church was organized in 1836, reconstructed in 1912, and became part of the national park in 1935.

The early colonists arrived in the Smokies with very little and worked hard to survive, clearing land for crops, making tools, and building cabins. Most necessities were produced on the farms, and farmers had little contact with anyone other than their neighbors.

There is also a history of Black Americans, enslaved and free, that needs telling. Adam McNeil conducted research from 2018 to 2020, supported by the Great Smoky Mountains Association, searching cemeteries, gravesites, slave census surveys, and oral histories. In 1860, slave surveys of Jackson County showed 348 enslaved African Americans held by forty-seven enslavers, and Haywood County had 317 enslaved people held by sixty-seven enslavers. Enslaved people brought the banjo from Africa to Appalachia, were skilled craftsmen, and were soldiers for the Union army. Cassius Cash, the sixteenth superintendent of Great Smoky Mountains National Park and the first African American to hold that position, said in a press release, "In learning about our past, we open the doors to our future. We hope that even more people will see themselves included and connected to the Smokies through this effort." In a statement in June

Larry Blythe, former vice-chief, and Mike Parker, marketing director and former chair of the Tribal Council, members of the Eastern Band of Cherokee Indians and Friends of the MST, at the Davis Cabin on the Mountain Farm Museum and Oconaluftee Visitor Center. *Photo by Larry Blythe; used by permission.*

2020, Deputy Director David Vela, first Latino to lead the National Park Service, said, "The National Park Service is committed to . . . ensuring equity . . . in the way we welcome visitors to the places in our care. We . . . will do more to make what we do more accessible and relevant to all communities."

Larry Blythe, an elder and former vice chief of the Eastern Band of Cherokee Indians, as well as a forester, tells of his great-grandmother Ada Springer's connection to the Oconaluftee Visitor Center and Mountain Farm Museum.

She grew up in Swain County around the turn of the nineteenth century and married Jim Wiggins around 1910. Jim was killed in a logging accident in 1920, leaving Ada to raise five children, including my grandmother, Laura Wiggins. Ada then married Joe Queen, who had bought the John Davis home on Indian Creek, built in 1902. Joe was a widower and had two children, which gave them a total of seven children, plus soon a new baby son. The house was too small for the large family and according to my grandmother Laura, the children did not get along. Later Joe and Ada "parted" (divorced). Joe Queen lived in the house until the Federal Government condemned the land to create the Great Smoky Mountains National Park. The house was relocated to the Mountain Farm Museum and the MST goes right past the Davis cabin.

The cabin shows the type of material and workmanship put into the construction of the house. American chestnut logs were utilized and it took two years to construct. Rocks for the fireplace were obtained locally at the house's original location. The Mountain Farm Museum is a replica of a mountain farmstead and shows what the settlers and in some cases the Cherokee people would have constructed. I am proud that the house has been preserved. For a time, I had no idea that it held such a part of my family's personal history, but I treasure it more now.

The Oconaluftee River (EB 28) and other rivers in the area were sacred to the Cherokee. Rivers were their source of water and food, as well as places for cleansing, trade, navigation, and celebration. Communities were located beside rivers, always on the west side so they were facing east in their going-to-the-water ritual. *Oconaluftee* is an English interpretation of the Tsalagi word *egwanulti*, meaning "near the river."

Oconaluftee River to Waterrock Knob

The MST travels twenty-eight miles in the Smokies before starting along the Blue Ridge Parkway. At the southern endpoint of the parkway, near Oconaluftee and Cherokee (EB 28, Milepost [MP] 469), is Great Smoky Mountains National Park. From there, the parkway traverses 252 miles through the rugged and scenic Blue Ridge Mountains of North Carolina. The parkway's entire length in both North Carolina and Virginia is 469 miles (Virginia includes miles 0–217). There are 134 overlooks in North Carolina (Oconaluftee, MP 468.4, to Devils Garden, MP 235.7).

Construction on the parkway started on September 11, 1935, during President Franklin D. Roosevelt's time in office. Beginning near Cumberland Knob in North Carolina (not far from the Virginia border), the work was done by private construction companies operating under federal contracts through New Deal public works agencies such as the Works Progress Administration, the Civilian Conservation Corps, and the Civilian Public Service. By the end of 1966, all but one 7.7-mile stretch of the parkway was complete. That last segment, around the Linn Cove Viaduct near Grandfather Mountain, opened in 1987.

There is no entry fee to travel the parkway; some sections are closed in winter, and keep in mind that commercial vehicles are prohibited. In its entirety there are 360 miles of trails, fourteen visitor centers, eight campgrounds, and ninety-one historic buildings. Twenty-five tunnels in North Carolina cut through rock. The highest parkway point is the Richland Balsam Overlook (elevation 6,047 feet, MP 431). It is the most visited unit of the National Park System, with 15.9 million annual visitors (more than the Grand Canyon, Yellowstone, and Yosemite combined). The parkway was on North Carolina's version of the America the Beautiful quarter in 2015. Need to find an overlook? Check https://www.virtualblueridge.com /parkway-milepost-guide/.

According to historian Anne Mitchell Whisnant, in the 1920s and 1930s both North Carolina and Tennessee wanted the parkway route. As she writes in *Super-Scenic Motorway: A Blue Ridge Parkway History,*

> Planning for the Parkway in North Carolina fell largely to the staff at the State Highway and Public Works Commission, through the office of engineer R. Getty Browning. It was Browning's vision of what the Parkway could be that guided the initial design process. Browning was called the "architect of the Blue Ridge Parkway" and "the man who is responsible, more than any other man, for the location of the . . . Parkway in North Carolina rather than in Tennessee."
>
> Robert Doughton arranged for himself, developer Stephens, and Governor Ehringhaus to have a post-hearing audience with President Roosevelt, where they presented him with a red leather album full of "beautiful pictures in natural colors of the scenic spots they hoped the Parkway would include. On November 10, 1934, the long-awaited word arrived. . . . Secretary Ickes adopted North Carolina's route. North Carolina would get nearly 250 miles.

But the parkway was not finished all the way to Cherokee. In the 1930s, Chief Blythe wanted the parkway to bring tourism and much-needed jobs, but the vice chief didn't. There were disputes about the location and width of right-of-way through Cherokee land, and in 1939 a compromise was made to have a ridge route and bypass the fertile Soco Valley for the final fifteen miles. Nine hundred acres—the Boundary Tree tract—were purchased in 1949 to add tourist cabins and other amenities. A new amphitheater was built right into the hills, and the outdoor pageant *Unto These Hills* was created to present Cherokee history and culture.

The MST does not allow biking on natural surface trail due to the damage it can do, especially on wet trail. The parkway does allow biking, and an excellent resource is the book *Bicycling the Blue Ridge: A Guide to Skyline Drive and the Blue Ridge Parkway* (in its sixth edition), by Elizabeth and Charlie Skinner. The book is suitable for people interested in casual rides but more directed to cyclists planning extended tours.

Carolina Mountain Club

The nonprofit Carolina Mountain Club (CMC) started in 1923 and grew into a significant organization in the 1930s, emphasizing trail construction and maintenance, conservation advocacy, and hiking opportunities. In 2023 Danny Bernstein authored *Carolina Mountain Club: One Hundred Years*.

Of the six incorporators of the CMC, two have mountains named for them: Mount Ambler for Chase Ambler and Tennent Mountain for Gaillard Tennent (also the first president of the CMC). Other early CMC members have been recognized: Mount Kephart for Horace Kephart; the Art Loeb National Recreational Trail; Arch Nichols at the Folk Art Center in Asheville; and Masa Knob for George Masa. Masa was born in Japan, came to America in 1901, and settled in Asheville in 1915. His passion for photography from then until his death in 1934 inspired John D. Rockefeller to preserve the Smokies. Masa coauthored the first *Guide of the Smokies*, but his name was removed from the credits because he was Japanese. His legendary motto was "more walk, less talk." Ruth Brothers became the first female CMC president in 1948.

In his 2009 book, *Trail Profiles and Maps: From the Great Smokies to Mount Mitchell and Beyond*, Walt Weber writes that it took fourteen years and fifty-eight days—from September 19, 1983, to November 15, 1997—to build the MST from Great Smoky Mountains National Park to Mount Mitchell. To complete this work, the state, the US Forest Service, and the National Park Service signed an agreement in 1979 to divvy up responsibilities, setting lots of planning and labor in motion. Task forces

Walt Weber and "The Gang": Carolina Mountain Club volunteers
Rich Evans, Bob Beach, Walt Weber, Stuart English, and Les Love.
Photo by Marcia Weber; used by permission.

were given sections of the proposed MST: the Balsam Highlands Task Force, the Pisgah Ridge Task Force, the South Pisgah Task Force, and the Central Blue Ridge Task Force. Today, individual task force members also have responsibility for maintaining specific sections of the Appalachian Trail and MST. While the NPS is responsible for the twenty-eight miles of trail in Great Smoky Mountains National Park, the CMC covers the MST from the parkway (Segment 1, EB 28) to Black Mountain Campground (Segment 3, EB 71.5), for a total of 154 miles. What an amazing commitment and effort by the volunteers of the CMC.

Back on the Trail

After ascending near the parkway corridor for 7.5 miles, a nice 6.7-mile hike is from Big Witch Overlook to Soco Gap Overlook (EB 35.5–42.4). The trail follows a gravel road for the first 4.2 miles, including a stretch through Mile High Campground. A pass, Soco Gap (elevation 4,340 feet), is located at the eastern edge of the Qualla Boundary, sandwiched between the Balsam Mountains to the north and the Plott Balsam Range to the south. The Cherokee call the gap Ahalunun'yi, meaning "Ambush Place," because it was here that they ambushed a group of invading Shawnees in the mid-1700s. Soco Gap separates the counties of Haywood (established in 1808) and Jackson (established in 1851), as well as the French Broad and Little Tennessee river basins. Soco Falls is about 1.5 miles from Soco Gap (MP 455.7), and there may be a blue blaze connector from the MST in the future. The earliest attempt to hike the MST was made by Lee Price, who started at Soco Gap on April 3, 1983, and hiked to Smithfield.

The Heintooga Ridge Road crosses the MST at EB 39.8, near Mile High Campground. Adjacent to this camping area is an area of red spruce, disjoined from any surrounding stands of red spruce, giving a feel of being in a rainforest of the Pacific Northwest. Heintooga Ridge Road starts at parkway MP 458.2, eleven miles from the south end of the parkway. This road is usually open from late May through October. The first four miles are paved and within the parkway boundaries. High-elevation overlooks offer views of the mountain ridges. Later you enter Great Smoky Mountains National Park, where you can find a picnic area and the beautiful Heintooga Overlook. The fourteen-mile, one-lane, unpaved Heintooga Round Bottom Road begins there. "Heintooga" derives from the Tsalagi word *iyentooga*, meaning "hiding place."

At EB 43.9 is Howard's Bridge, named in honor of Howard McDonald, who set the record for most volunteer hours with the CMC, and at EB 46.6 is "Piet's Place," a bench with a view in honor of Piet Bodenhorst, a CMC leader instrumental in completing the MST in the Waterrock Knob area. Along the mile from EB 45.6 to 46.6 are some beautiful rock steps, formed with huge rocks, that required hardworking, skilled trail builders—thank you to the volunteers! Segment 1 ends on Waterrock Knob at EB 46.8.

In the early 1990s, there were only a handful of volunteers building the MST and no momentum to complete it. North Carolina State Parks dispatched a trail manager to meet with folks from the CMC, Central Blue Ridge Club, and the Sauratown Trail. Some suggested that the MST stop at Stone Mountain. Arch Nichols with the CMC said if worked stopped, the CMC would complete a "Peak to Peak Trail" from the Smokies to Mount Mitchell. Allen de Hart said a hiking guidebook was needed, and by 2000 he published the first guide. Allen also knew that positive publicity was needed, so he started planning the first thru-hike with Alan Householder in 1997 and pushed to form a nonprofit Friends organization in 1997.

SEGMENT 2

The Balsams

Waterrock Knob to Pisgah Inn

63.6 MILES

Climb the mountains and get their good tidings. Nature's peace
will flow into you as sunshine flows into trees. The winds will
blow their own freshness into you and the storms their energy,
while cares will drop away from you like the leaves of autumn.

JOHN MUIR

Great views come frequently along this sixty-three-mile segment of the high-elevation MST. It is bookended by the third-highest point on the entire MST and the famous Pisgah Inn. A challenging segment, it includes almost 25,000 feet of ups and downs on rocky trails. It is very remote (only crossing paved roads seven times in a fifty-four-mile stretch), mostly on public forest lands with no resupply opportunity.

Waterrock Knob is home to the highest visitor center on the parkway (MP 251.2) at 5,820 feet. At the peak, visitors can see up to fifty miles of Appalachian Mountains, making it a perfect place for sunrises, sunsets, and dark skies. The visitor center provides useful information on the rugged surroundings and breathtaking views. Take a steep walk from the visitor center to the top of Waterrock Knob, 1.2 miles round-trip. The summit is 6,273 feet in elevation and is the highest point on the parkway! The accessible visitor center contains restrooms, exhibits, and books for sale, but no water. "Camp Rock" was the pioneer name for the area now occupied by the visitor center parking lot, and nearby springs flow over the "Waterrock" where hunters and farmers gathered to rest.

In 2016, with the addition of 5,300 acres, the area became Waterrock Knob Park. This celebrated the centennial of the NPS and the new

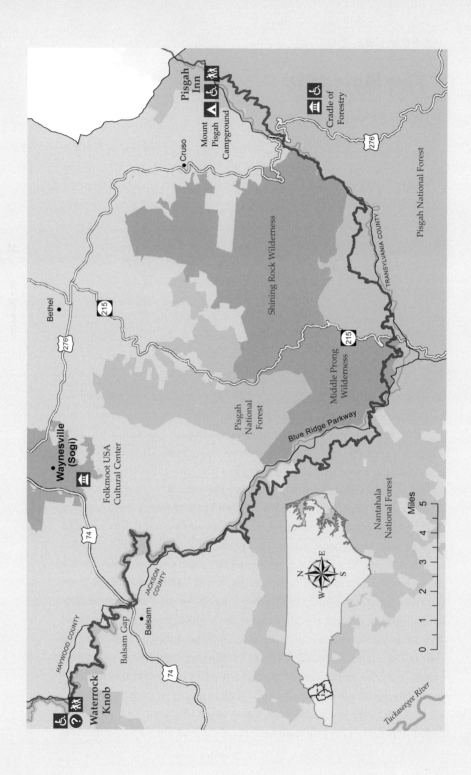

Pisgah
Inn

Cradle of
Forestry

Mount
Pisgah
Campground

• Cruso

Pisgah National Forest

276

TRANSYLVANIA COUNTY

Shining Rock Wilderness

Bethel
•

215

276

215

Middle Prong
Wilderness

Pisgah
National
Forest

Blue Ridge Parkway

Waynesville
(Sogi)

Folkmoot USA
Cultural Center

74

Nantahala
National Forest

Miles

N
W   E
S

JACKSON
COUNTY

HAYWOOD COUNTY

Balsam
•

Balsam Gap

74

Waterrock
Knob

?

0   1   2   3   4   5

Tuckaseegee River

protected lands, habitats, and views. The Conservation Fund, other conservation nonprofits, and private landowners made this expansion possible. In December 2018, Les Love, Larry Blythe, Kate Dixon, and other leaders gathered at Waterrock Knob Visitor Center to celebrate the completion of the route from the Oconaluftee River to Waterrock Knob, which finished the 343.3-mile MST Mountains Region.

Acid rain has contributed to the death of many balsam trees in their habitat above 5,000 feet elevation. The pH of acid rain can be as high as 3.0, the same as common vinegar. Most hemlocks along the parkway have met a similar demise, but rather than acid rain, the hemlock woolly adelgid, a nonnative insect, is to blame. At higher elevations the balsam woolly adelgid has also killed most of the balsam fir and Fraser fir on these high peaks (see more under Mount Mitchell).

Back on the Trail

The South Beyond 6,000 (SB6K) is a CMC-sponsored program aimed at encouraging hikers to climb the forty 6,000-foot peaks in the Southern Appalachian Mountains (in North Carolina and Tennessee, there are over sixty summits above 6,000 feet, but only forty were selected for the SB6K). Mount Washington in New Hampshire is the only other East Coast 6,000-foot peak.

Weather alert! At higher elevations a hiker must be aware of cold temperatures and high winds. On ridgelines, the wind chill factor can cause hypothermia. For example, Waterrock Knob's average temperature in July is 60°F and annual rainfall is sixty inches. Be safe and retreat to lower elevations if you're not adequately prepared.

As you depart the Waterrock Knob Visitor Center, be prepared to descend eighty-five wooden steps, cross many rivulets of water if it's recently rained, enjoy a short stroll along the parkway, walk a relaxing forest service road for a mile or two, and in about eight miles enter the parkway's Orchards Overlook parking lot (EB 7.7). After this mostly downhill stretch of trail comes about a mile of Blue Ridge Parkway hiking. In 2020, about five miles north of Balsam Gap, a couple from Kentucky ran into a trail maintainer who told them they "were the first hikers he had seen in sixteen years." This is not a heavily traveled part of the MST.

Nearby: Waynesville

Waynesville is the largest town west of Asheville, in "Hey Now" Haywood County, about six miles northeast of the MST. Visit its lively Main Street or take part in the Haywood County Quilts Trail, Apple Harvest Daze in October, Folkmoot, or the Museum of North Carolina Handicrafts. The mild summers are a great time to explore these mountains, but the fall is just as good when the leaves change.

There is a highway marker near Waynesville that tells of an early "mountains to sea" traveler, Francis Asbury (1745–1816). Starting in 1771, Asbury did seventy-two horseback rides and walked across North Carolina (and a few other states), covering an estimated 230,000 miles. He was a circuit-riding preacher and missionary among settlements and the first Methodist bishop. Asbury maintained a diary of his thirty-year travels, chronicling hunger, cold, and fevers; slept alongside creeks and in barns, homes, and churches; preached over 16,400 sermons; and ordained over 4,000 preachers. The Shook House in Clyde was a favorite stop (built in 1795, some claim it's the oldest standing frame-built house in western North Carolina). Asbury was known as "The Prophet of the Long Road." In 1764, the pay was sixty-four dollars per year, but this had increased to eighty dollars by 1800, with a horse often provided.

Doris Hammett, MD, was a pioneering leader of the MST. As chair of the State Trails Committee and the American Trails Association Board, she hosted the National Trails Symposium at Lake Junaluska, where Howard Lee, North Carolina secretary of natural resources and community development, gave a speech that changed the trail system in North Carolina forever. It catalyzed the creation of the MST, or as Lee quipped, it "accidently started the mountains to the sea trail." Lake Junaluska, about nine miles from the MST in Haywood County, hosted the trail's forty-fifth anniversary in April 2022.

In 1979, Doris Hammett led the Balsam Highlands Task Force in planning a new MST trail, mapping the route, and acquiring right of way. They started construction in 1982 and dedicated 9.1 miles on May 30, 1987, from Bear Pen Gap (EB 33.8, MP 427.6) to Bubbling Springs at NC 215 (EB 42.3). From 1990 to 1998 they built the MST from Balsam Gap to Old Bald on abandoned logging roads. In 2002 the CMC took over Balsam Highlands work to extend the trail west to Oconaluftee. In 2009 the CMC completed seven miles from Fork Ridge Overlook to Balsam Gap. Dan Pittilo donated records from 1979 through 1998 to the

University of North Carolina Asheville on the work of the Balsam Highlands Task Force, saying they were "one of the earlier groups planning and developing the MST."

Nearby

Balsam is a small community in Jackson County, located near Balsam Gap at 3,307 feet, along US 74 (the Great Smoky Mountains Expressway), with the post office 0.3 mile off the MST at EB 9.6. The town is named after the nicknames for red spruce and Fraser fir trees, which dominate the high elevations of the Appalachian Mountains. Balsam Mountain Inn was a wooden Victorian hotel located in Balsam (just off today's Blue Ridge Parkway) built to serve the highest railway station in the East in 1908. The inn, one of the few remaining grand Southern Railway Resort Hotels, was added to the National Register of Historic Places in 1982. It was restored in 1990 and renamed the Grand Old Lady Hotel in 2019. Enjoy a three-course gourmet American breakfast and a quiet setting with spectacular mountain views from the front porch. Note that small, iron "welcome" signs above room doors mark those that are home to a resident ghost.

From the crossing of US 74 at EB 9.4, the trail is mostly wooded ups and downs until Pisgah Inn at the end of the section (EB 63.6). The parkway overlooks usually have sweeping views of the national forest lands. The flat area around Doubletop Mountain Overlook (EB 19.6) and many other mountain tops will have abundant and beautiful native flowers, but the CMC Friday Crew knows the area from there, around Old Bald, to EB 33.8 near Bear Pen Gap as the "forgotten fourteen on the MST" because the trail is so rocky and difficult.

Dark skies are great for seeing the Milky Way, constellations, and the expansive night sky. There are many great dark skies along the MST such as in the Smokies, Pisgah National Forest, and Linville Gorge (Shortoff to Table Rock), along the parkway overlooks at Graveyard Fields and Craggy Dome, and at Hanging Rock (Moore's Knob). Near Spruce Pine is the Mayland Earth to Sky Park and Bare Dark Sky Observatory, and in 2017 the largest public observatory in the state opened (admission for a fee). Pisgah Astronomical Research Institute is accessible from NC 215.

Nantahala National Forest, established in 1920, encompasses 531,148 acres. *Nantahala* is a Tsalagi word meaning "land of the noonday sun." The MST passes through the Nantahala, EB 20.8 to EB 35.1, and the footpath mostly follows an old roadbed. The combined Nantahala and Pisgah National Forests total 1.1 million acres and are the most visited national forests, with nearly 7 million visitors each year.

At EB 21.6, you will come upon a beautiful, restful, grassy field called Earl Ammons Meadows with a plaque identifying "papaw's hunting stand" (it can be reached from a grassy pull-off on the southside of MP 434.2 with a rusty T-bar marking the trailhead). Chuck Millsaps of Great Outdoor Provisions Company, who supported endurance runner Diane Van Deren on her record-setting hike of the MST, said, "One of my favorite memories from our adventure in 2012 was on Day 2. We were lost but taken in at midnight by a kind couple who had been taking pictures of the starlit night nearby." That's how Chuck and the support team came to camp at Ammons Meadows.

According to the US Forest Service, Pisgah National Forest "is a land of mile-high peaks, cascading waterfalls, and heavily forested slopes. Comprised of over 500,000 acres, the Pisgah is primarily a hardwood forest with whitewater rivers and hundreds of miles of trails. This national forest is home of the first tract of land purchased under the Weeks Act of 1911, which led to the creation of the national forests in the eastern United States. It also boasts two of the first designated wilderness areas in the east." The MST enters Pisgah National Forest at EB 36.0 and straddles the Haywood and Transylvania county lines along the parkway.

Going straight at EB 34.3 rather than turning left to stay on the trail takes you to Charlie's Bald with several campsites, endless wildflowers in the summer, blueberries in season, and views of Nantahala National Forest at the end. The bald is also accessible from Bear Pen Gap at parkway MP 427.6.

From EB 37.7 to 42.3, the MST crosses the Middle Prong Wilderness Area. This area was given wilderness protection in 1984 and covers 7,900 acres in Pisgah National Forest. Because trails in wilderness areas are minimally maintained, with limited signage and few footbridges, come prepared with a high degree of self-reliance.

To get the MST through the wilderness area in 1982–1987, crosscut saws were used to remove trees. Early 1900s logging rail lines were removed for trail construction, and in several locations you can still see railroad ties with spikes and logging cables. It took five years for the Balsam Highlands Task Force to construct just over nine miles of trail. The work was so difficult and agreements so hard to make that in the late

NC State University student Leanh Ta enjoying the Pisgah National Forest view on a seven-day backpacking trip. *Photo by Jerry Barker.*

1990s a proposal was made to terminate the MST at Balsam Gap instead of the high point in the Smokies. Fortunately, that didn't get approved.

A hard hike leaves Haywood Gap on the parkway (elevation 5,225 feet) for seven miles with a 650-foot gain to NC 215 north of Beech Gap (EB 35.8–42.3). This crosses the Middle Prong Wilderness and has three side trip options that are worth your time. First, there is access to Rough Butt Bald Overlook (MP 426.5). Second, the gorgeous Fork Ridge meadows near Mount Hardy (elevation 6,110 feet) can be accessed via the Green Mountain Trail (a north turn off the MST and only one-tenth of a mile to what some consider the best views in Pisgah National Forest and the heart of Middle Prong Wilderness). Third, at EB 42.2 you cross Bubbling Spring Branch, and a short walk upstream brings you to two waterfalls. If traveling along the parkway, at the MP 422.4 overlook, there is a half-mile trail to the top of Devil's Courthouse with magnificent views.

The MST reaches Rough Butt Bald Overlook at 5,300 feet on the parkway. Farther north the MST intersects Big Butt Trail. Why all the butts? The word is really describing how a mountain breaks off steeply, a variation of *butte.*

On November 9, 1969, Art Loeb (1914–68), "industrialist, conservation-ist, and hiker," was honored by the Carolina Mountain Club with a trail named for him. The twenty-eight-mile Art Loeb Trail starts near the Davidson River in Brevard and ends below Cold Mountain at the Daniel Boone Scout Camp in the Shining Rock Wilderness. It follows the MST between EB 45.5 and 46.6. Black Balsam Knob Road (Forest Road 816; EB 46.6) is a heavily used road for hikers and campers. Black Balsam Knob's summit, at 6,214 feet, boasts a 360-degree view and a plaque paying tribute to Loeb. The summit is a 425-foot climb, a half mile north on the Art Loeb Trail, where it and the MST cross FR 816. Almost entirely devoid of trees, the summit is more reminiscent of New England than North Carolina. Black Balsam Knob is the twenty-third-highest of the forty mountains in North Carolina over 6,000 feet. In 1979 the trail was designated a National Recreation Trail.

A mile and a half past FR 816 is an access trail to the Graveyard Fields area. Within this area are thirteen wooden bridges and several convenient parkway access points. Why is it called Graveyard Fields? Because of the clear-cutting of timber that left hillsides of moss-covered stumps, and later the many charred stumps following the massive Thanksgiving fire in 1925 and another in April 1942. The Upper and Second Falls of the Yellowstone Prong are not on the MST but can be accessed from the trail or directly from the Graveyard Fields parking area at MP 418.

Early colonialists lived mostly in the forest and depended on its wood to survive. They felled trees to build things like cabins, barns, outbuild-ings, furniture, fence posts, sled runners, gun stocks, and toys, and to provide heat to stay warm, cook, wash clothes, render lard, make soap, and soften hog hide.

Nearby is Shining Rock Wilderness, North Carolina's largest wilder-ness area, encompassing 18,000 acres. It was designated under the ini-tial Wilderness Preservation Act in 1964. The MST skirts the border of Shining Rock Wilderness between Cherry Cove and Pigeon Gap. There are eleven wilderness areas in North Carolina. These state- and federally protected lands are left to the forces of nature, with little to no human intervention to hinder natural biological and physical processes. There are over 102,000 acres of wilderness in North Carolina's four national forests managed by the US Forest Service (USFS). Of the approximately 1 million acres of national forest in the state, only about 800 acres are logged each year. Overall, the USFS manages 8 percent of US land—over 193 million acres across 154 national forests and twenty national grasslands.

Hussein and Nashua El-Genk's family, the first completers of the Forty-Hike Challenge in 2020, admiring the views along Graveyard Fields.
Photo by Hussein El-Genk; used by permission.

In 2021, Randy Moore was named the twentieth chief of the USFS, the first African American in the agency's 116-year history. Moore previously served with the USFS in North Carolina.

Have your ever heard "Yellowstone" and "skinny dip" in the same sentence? In Segment 2, at EB 51.6, the MST guidebook reads, "Cross Yellowstone Prong just below Skinny Dip Falls," which was largely washed out in August 2021 when Tropical Storm Fred dumped fourteen inches of rain. This area is both gorgeous and popular, with the ice-cold waters of Skinny Dip Falls and a quarter mile away the Looking Glass Rock Overlook on the parkway (MP 417; look for the dragon tree, whose bent trunk is shaped like a dragon head and is adorned with red streamers). According to a popular MST story, a mother and child were swimming in Yellowstone Prong when a volunteer trail builder told her the MST was coming through, and she exclaimed, "Well, there goes our skinny dip falls." Yellowstone Prong is named for the yellowish moss that covers rocks in the creek.

Nashua and Hussein El-Genk of Durham, with their four children, Zakariyya, Ayyub, Kareema, and Rasheed (ages twelve, ten, eight, and six, respectively), were the first to complete the MST 40 Hike Challenge in 2020. Nashua told Friends of the MST that "the kids learned so much about the history of North Carolina as they hiked across the state." The kids' favorites and surprises? Three said they were surprised by how cold the water was at Skinny Dip Falls in the summer and how much fun it was. They also loved Wolf Rock in Stone Mountain State Park because it looks like the moon when you walk on it. One family favorite was the highest peak in the Smokies. Hussein said the family enjoyed discussions and reflections about the hike, historical and environmental.

A couple of miles after crossing NC 215 is a side trail to the top of Devil's Courthouse with magnificent views. It is also accessible on a half-mile trail from the parkway at MP 422.4. At EB 51.9, a side trail (400 feet) leads to the spectacular Looking Glass Rock Overlook (MP 417), a 390-million-year-old granite monolith. A great viewing area for the monarch butterfly migration each September is Tunnel Gap Parkway Overlook at MP 415.6, about seven miles south of Pisgah Inn.

Walt Weber tells of working with the Monday crew led by legendary Dick Roberts in the 1990s.

> On a Saturday scouting trip we found a heavily grown-over passage between two boulders, which led to an excellent route which passed over the 5,056-foot Green Knob summit [marked by a brass benchmark embedded on a large rock; currently EB 55.6]. Just before reaching the summit we found a location to the right of and just below the flag line we were developing that had the potential of providing an excellent view of Looking Glass Rock and the broad surrounding area, but the view was blocked by the tops of some very tall trees that were rooted from an area below this ledge. When we later came back with the Monday Trail Crew to dig in our revised flag line, our sawyer disappeared down over the side at the viewpoint location and took out the offending trees. So, [today] as you are munching away at this excellent spot, take a look down and visualize our intrepid sawyer scrambling down over the side, years ago, to open up the vista you are now enjoying with your snacks.

Walt thinks this is one of the prime views in Pisgah. CMC volunteers named the large boulder steps the "Grand Staircase."

A Bit of History

George Vanderbilt II first visited North Carolina in 1887 and immediately fell in love with the Asheville area. When he returned in 1888, he began buying land, eventually totaling 180,000 acres. His 250-room mansion, Biltmore, was finished in 1895, with four acres of floor space, thirty-five bedrooms, and sixty-seven fireplaces, the largest privately owned home in America (admission for a fee). Later, a dairy and horse barn were added, and in 1983 the Biltmore Estate Wine Company opened. *Biltmore* is a combination of his last name and the English word for rolling hills.

In 1892, Frederick Law Olmsted, Vanderbilt's landscape architect, hired Gifford Pinchot, a trained forester who later became the first chief of the US Forest Service. At the Biltmore Estate, near Asheville, Pinchot started the first forestry management plan in the United States and the first professional, large-scale reforestation project. In 1898 Pinchot departed Biltmore, and Carl Schenck came in to create the Biltmore Forest School, the first forestry school in the United States (he stayed until 1909, and 1913 saw the last graduates). Schenck is considered the father of American forestry.

In 1880, the Western North Carolina Railroad made its first scheduled arrival in Asheville and Biltmore. This paved the way for private rail spurs to reach into smaller communities and then into the forests. When the small town of Canton connected the rail spurs to what is now Pisgah National Forest, it established a paper mill that grew into the largest in North Carolina. The mill bought up and clear-cut thousands of acres and then sold them to the federal government. Two years after Vanderbilt died in 1914, the US government purchased 80,600 acres to form the main portion of Pisgah National Forest. In 1999 the US government stopped building new logging roads.

In 1968, 6,500 acres of Pisgah were designated the Cradle of Forestry in America, located along US 276 about four miles south of the parkway where the MST crosses US 276 at EB 57 (and five miles south of the Pisgah Inn). The area is visible from parkway MP 411.

Back on the Trail

Volunteers who build and maintain the MST often use a Pulaski, a tool with an axe on one side for chopping and a mattock or adze for digging on the other side. The axe was created in 1913 by Ed Pulaski, a US Forest Service assistant ranger. He was inspired to create a better tool after being injured fighting a wildfire in Idaho. A McLeod is another trail builder's friend, also called a rakehoe, along with more common pickaxe, shovel, and lopper tools.

Sliding Rock is a slip and slide adventure for children and adults in Pisgah National Forest, near Brevard, about five miles from the parkway and MST (cross NC 276 at EB 57). It is fed by Looking Glass Creek. One at a time, sliders ride down the sixty-foot flat, sloping boulder, propelled by rushing, chilly water (50–60°F!), to an eight-foot-deep pool at the bottom. Then they swim a few strokes to the shore and do it all over again. Looking Glass Rock (elevation 3,969 feet) and falls are nearby, as is the Cradle of Forestry and the Pink Beds.

On March 4, 1996, when the Pisgah Ridge Section was completed at "Promontory Stump," the Pisgah district ranger spoke a few words and a time capsule containing a golden rock (for the mountains), a golden seashell (for the sea), and a photo of the CMC crew was buried in a stump. In 2012 the materials were placed in a small box. In 2019 the items were moved to an army surplus ammo box and buried just off the trail near EB 58.2 (look for a white metal blaze one foot above the ground and a small pile of rocks on the downhill side).

A Quick Stop at the Pisgah Inn

Car camping in Model T's attracted some of the best-known Americans to the Pisgah Forest area between 1915 and 1924. It may have been George Vanderbilt's interest in riding and conservation that drew Henry Ford, Thomas Edison, Harvey Firestone, and John Burroughs (who called themselves the "Four Vagabonds") to the area near the Cradle of Forestry.

Pisgah Inn is the end of MST Segment 2. When it first opened in 1920 the only way to access it was the rough and rocky Pisgah Motor Road through Candler. World War II about killed tourism, and the inn fell into disrepair. The inn reopened in 1952, a new parkway section opened in 1964, and the new present-day Pisgah Inn also opened in 1964. From 1985 to 1989 funds were raised, the main lodge saved, and the 1920 structures demolished. Today, it is worth making a stop for a meal or a night at the inn. The Blue Ridge Parkway archives have a photo of pioneering African American ranger Willie McDaniel standing at the Pisgah Inn sign in 1973.

The High Peaks and Asheville

Pisgah Inn to Black Mountain Campground

71.5 MILES

This hill though high I covet ascend; The difficulty will not me offend; For I perceive the way of life lies here . . . let's neither faint nor fear.

JOHN BUNYAN, *THE PILGRIM'S PROGRESS*

This segment is closely connected with the Blue Ridge Parkway corridor for most of its seventy-one miles, allowing access to parkway overlooks, ease of shuttles, and convenience to Asheville. The MST ascends from EB 30 to 62 as it climbs to the 6,684-foot summit of Mount Mitchell, and then descends 3,600 feet the last five miles. People love the flowering laurel and rhododendron in early summer and the fall leaf colors displayed along this route.

At the summit of Frying Pan Mountain sits a seventy-foot summit fire tower, the highest elevation fire tower in the entire state. The easiest access is from parkway MP 409.6 at a gravel pull-off, taking FS 450 from the gap (elevation 4,950 feet) 0.75 miles to the summit (elevation 5,450 feet). From Pisgah Campground it is 2.1 miles each way.

Pisgah Inn to Asheville

At EB 1.0, you pass the former site of George Vanderbilt's Buck Spring Lodge. This history is just off the trail and worth investigating. The main lodge, stable, and kitchen–dining building were started in 1896, as were a dam and pump located along a creek. A four-bedroom cottage was added in 1903. In 1910–11 a motor road reached the lodge and a hydropower plant delivered electricity. The honeymoon cottage was added in 1910, making

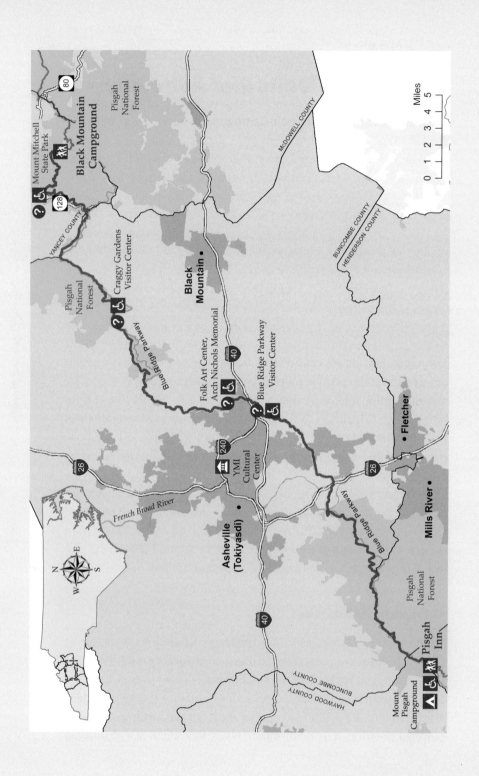

eight buildings. When George Vanderbilt died in 1914, ownership transferred to his wife Edith, and the lodge was closed and fenced off for most of the 1920s and early 1930s. When Edith died in 1958, ownership of the lodge property went to her grandson George Cecil. In the late 1950s the Park Service was exploring routes for the parkway, and in 1959, a 471-acre tract was sold to the state of North Carolina. It was decided best to remove the buildings. In 2004–2008 the CMC, Biltmore Estate, and parkway folks planned and reclaimed the property from vines and trees. *Trail Profiles and Maps: From Clingmans Dome to Mount Mitchell and Beyond* has a more detailed account of the building and use of the Buck Spring Lodge and the Shut-In Trail.

The Mount Pisgah trailhead is at EB 1.4, elevation 5,722 feet, with a 750-foot climb from its parking lot. On a clear day it can be seen from Asheville, sixteen miles away. It is a 2.6-mile round-trip hike. A dozen volunteers from the South Pisgah Task Force worked ten days in 1997 to rework the trail from the MST to the summit. MST thru-hiker Danny Bernstein includes a comprehensive description of the hike at https://www.exploreasheville.com/stories/post/mount-pisgah-trail/. *Pisgah* is derived from the Hebrew word for "summit" and references the mountain from which Moses first laid eyes on the Promised Land.

The Shut-In Trail is 17.5 miles of the MST south of Asheville with an elevation change of 3,611 feet (EB 1.4–18.6). One mile from the Pisgah Inn, at the former site of George Vanderbilt's Buck Springs Lodge, is one end of the old bridle trail he built to connect Biltmore House to this hunting lodge located near the summit of Mount Pisgah. The other end is near the North Carolina Arboretum and the French Broad River. While the MST Trail Guide mentions this trail and generally follows it, Geoffrey Norman published an account in the June 6, 1978, issue of *Esquire* ("Pop Hollandsworth's Secret Hiking Trail"). Around 1896 the Vanderbilts paid men ten cents an hour to clear a tunnel through laurel and rhododendron with axes and saws, lay a rock foundation, then pack a layer of dirt to make it easier for the horses. A 1903 letter from Schenck to Vanderbilt mentions the "Shut In." Vanderbilt owned about 150,000 acres of what is now national forest. Norman said that "the land passed to the government [and] the trail grew over and was cut in several places by the Blue Ridge Parkway."

"Few people had any use for it," wrote Norman, "until James 'Pop' Hollandsworth and his boys (from the Asheville School for Boys) found it and started fixing it up." Pop, who served as dean of boys and assistant

A section of the 17.5-mile bridle trail built in 1896 for George Vanderbilt, resurrected as the Shut-In Trail connecting the French Broad River to Mount Pisgah. *Photo by Jerry Barker.*

director at Camp Sequoyah near Weaverville, said the trail couldn't be found on any map and called it the Shut-In Trail. (A 1941 topographic map identified a trail with no name going up the Shut-In Ridge.) Pop took leave in 1967 to help establish the North Carolina Outward Bound School near Linville Gorge, but he returned to his boys at Asheville School and their work to restore "their secret trail." With its good stone foundation and its shade, it is as fine as any trail in North Carolina.

In 1973, the CMC proposed a scenic foot trail including segments of the Shut-In Trail. In the 1960s the parkway right-of-way included much of the Shut-In Trail and some trail was destroyed in parkway construction. Thanks to tireless efforts by "Pop" Hollandsworth, Arch Nichols, and others, the Shut-In Trail became the first state designated western segment of the MST and was designated a National Recreation Trail in 1981.

Mills River Valley Overlook (elevation 4,085 feet, MP 404.5, EB 4.5) has great views on both sides of the parkway. The namesake of the Mills River was William Mills, a hunter who lived in this area during the late 1700s. His accounts from that time are the last evidence of elk in North Carolina before their recent reintroduction.

At EB 8.4 the MST crosses 4,064-foot Ferrin Knob. Once there was a fire tower on top, but now only the concrete bases remain.

Nearby

At EB 9.7, the MST crosses Bent Creek Road, which leads to the oldest federal experimental forest on the East Coast—Bent Creek Experimental Forest. The forest spans almost 6,000 acres within Pisgah National Forest, not far from Asheville, and got its name around 1795, when European settlers started to inhabit the area, from its horseshoe-shaped bend near the French Broad River. The once-dense forest was logged by 1900. In 1925 the Forest Service preserved 1,100 acres, previously part of the Biltmore Estate, for research on rehabilitating cutover lands and promoting and practicing sustainable forestry management. In 1939 the parkway proposed a segregated Bent Creek Recreation Area for African Americans, but when work resumed after World War II, plans for the facilities were dropped. When Lake Powhatan Recreation Area and Campground opened, it was for everyone (about one mile from the MST as the crow flies).

The North Carolina Arboretum (434 acres, established in 1986) show-cases a variety of trees and botanical gardens, and is located within the Bent Creek Experimental Forest southwest of Asheville near the parkway (admission for a fee). September is the best time of year to see butterflies migrating through the area, and the arboretum hosts a Monarch Migration Day. The MST runs adjacent to the arboretum as it leaves the Shut-In Trail (EB 18.1).

Back on the Trail

The MST crosses the French Broad River—among the oldest in the world—at EB 18.7. The Native American name was *Antokiasdiyi*, meaning "the place where they race." The river runs 218 miles, beginning near Rosman in Transylvania County and heading into Tennessee where it meets the Holston River in Knoxville and turns into the Tennessee River. The French Broad runs through Asheville and the surrounding national forests, so there are opportunities for camping, hiking, biking, and paddling. The river is perfect for tubing and float trips in Asheville. The French Broad River Paddle Trail has campsites along 117 miles, eight to ten miles apart. It is said that North Carolina has 38,000 miles of wild and scenic rivers, and the French Broad is one of the best.

At EB 20.5 the MST crosses over I-26. Urban traffic noise increases as does hiker traffic due to the proximity to Asheville (elevation 2,134 feet). At EB 24.2, Biltmore Village is about four miles away. It is a charming, leafy enclave created to house employees of the sprawling Biltmore Estate, George W. Vanderbilt's home constructed between 1890 and 1895 and the largest private residence in the nation. Remember that there is an entry fee. All roads lead to the beautiful Cathedral of All Souls, an 1896 Romanesque Revival landmark, and to forty shops and ten cafés and restaurants nearby.

Asheville was established in 1797 and is known as the "Land of the Sky." The Grove Park Inn was built from granite boulders mined and moved by mules and wagons from Sunset Mountain. When it opened on July 12, 1913, Secretary of State William Jennings Bryan delivered the keynote address and declared it "a hotel built for the ages." Of course Asheville has many great highlights, including restaurants, a growing craft beer industry, the Asheville Bread Festival, the Thomas Wolfe Memorial, galleries, music, and LaZoom tours. Since 1928 Asheville has hosted the Mountain Dance and Folk Festival, the longest continuously running festival in the nation, featuring mountain music, bluegrass, square dance, clogging, and more.

Just off the trail in Asheville is the Folk Art Center (MP 382, EB 29.8 and 32.2) with the Annual World Gee Haw Whimmy Diddle Competition—a whimmy diddle being two pencil-thin sticks made from laurel or rhododendron, one with notches and a wooden propeller, gee to make it go right, and haw to go left. In the 1960s, a summer camp counselor met local woodcarver Edsel Martin. When asked how he carved the natural-looking cardinal he was working on, he replied, "I just cut off what don't look like a bird." The Southern Highland Crafts Guild was established in 1930, now with over 700 members, and became part of the Folk Art Center in the late 1980s as a cooperative to promote highland handcrafts.

The Arch Nichols Section, from the French Broad River to the Black Mountain Campground, was named by the Carolina Mountain Club (CMC) for its four-time president (1941–42, 1947–48, 1957–58, and 1963), who made a career in the US Forest Service. Even before the MST, Nichols pushed for a trail from Mount Pisgah to Mount Mitchell. He was a major force in initiating the planning of the MST route in the late 1970s, and leading the CMC work to build and maintain the MST. After his death in 1989, he was recognized with a memorial plaque at the Folk Art Center.

Allen Barton, CMC president, said of Arch, "He got things done—he made things happen."

Well worth a stop is the Blue Ridge Parkway Visitor Center (EB 29.8, MP 384, 0.3 mile off the MST), which features a film and exhibits highlighting western North Carolina's natural and cultural heritage and recreational opportunities. We now expect visitor centers and exhibits throughout national parks, but did you know that they were a focus of Mission 66, a ten-year program of the National Park Service intended to expand visitor services by 1966, in time for its fiftieth anniversary? In 1916, when the Park Service was created, there was no national road system and airline travel was in its early days, so trains were the main mode of long-distance travel. After World War II, when the highway system was developed and Americans found themselves with more money in their pockets and more time on their hands, the parks were not ready for the influx of automobile tourists. Mission 66 projects provided high-quality interpretation service and involved a variety of infrastructure projects. The Blue Ridge Folklife Project, conducted in 1978 by Patrick Mullen and a team of cultural specialists, chronicled the history of African Americans along the parkway, covering religion, medical folklore, quilting, agriculture, and foodways. Also nearby is the Blue Ridge National Heritage Area (established in 2003 by the National Park Service, MP 384), the regional steward of living Appalachian traditions, which invites visitors to explore music, craft, the outdoors, and the native wisdom. So are the Botanical Gardens at Asheville, ten acres managed by an independent nonprofit dedicated to studying and promoting the native plants and habitats of the Southern Appalachians; and the Western North Carolina Nature Center, one mile from the MST.

In 1827, the completion of the Buncombe Turnpike brought increased commercial traffic to the mountains of North Carolina. This seventy-five-mile route served settlers and livestock drivers across the state, from the South Carolina line to Tennessee, until the late 1880s. It became a trading route to the Atlantic Ocean at Charleston, generally following the current I-26 corridor, along the French Broad River in Asheville through Columbia and Spartanburg. In Asheville the turnpike went by the County Courthouse, what became Pack Square, continuing to Hot Springs and into Tennessee. In 1889 North Carolina's first electric streetcars started running in Asheville, and Western Carolina University was established.

Several small towns near the MST in South Asheville offer lodging and restaurants. Skyland is about two miles from the MST and Arden about three miles, along US 25 in Buncombe County. The town of Fletcher is located between Asheville and Hendersonville, near the Asheville airport. Fletcher was first settled in 1795 when the Murray family made the difficult journey from South Carolina up Howard Gap Road (later part of the Buncombe Turnpike). The town is home to one of the few limestone quarries east of Knoxville, a valuable resource for agriculture, and the quarry along Fanning Bridge Road still operates today.

Interstates, State Roads, and the MST

Interstate 40 runs east to west from Asheville, to Greensboro and Raleigh, and then continues to Wilmington, a total of 423 miles in North Carolina. This allows quick access across the state for MST hikers. In Asheville, the MST goes under I-40 then crosses over US 70.

US 70 (established in 1926) runs from Arizona to the Crystal Coast of North Carolina. In North Carolina it is a major 488-mile-long highway connecting major MST cities including Asheville, Greensboro, Durham, Raleigh, Goldsboro, and New Bern. Going east from Beaufort, US 70 merges with part of the Outer Banks Scenic Byway (a National Scenic Byway), before ending in the community of Atlantic, near Cedar Island along Core Sound. US 70 was originally Old NC 10—the Central Highway—built in 1911, which connected many of the state's early mill villages, tobacco factories, towns, and railroads as it followed the corridor from Beaufort to Asheville. It began at the brick courthouse in Beaufort and was the first highway to cross the state from the coast to the Georgia state line. The American Automobile Association published its first North Carolina highway map in 1938.

President Barack Obama and First Lady Michelle Obama, while visiting Asheville in April 2010, hiked a portion of the MST. When they encountered another hiker, they stopped for a friendly chat and a photo. They hiked west from Bull Gap (westbound marker [WB] 31.2) toward Craven Gap, to a gravel road pullover for Elk Mountain Scenic Highway (WB 32.2) for a 1.1-mile trek.

At EB 34.8 a spur trail leads fifty yards to the Haw Creek Valley Overlook (elevation 2,780 feet), locally known as "lunch rock," a scenic observation point with picturesque mountain and valley views.

Many say that Elk Mountain / Town Mountain Loop (EB 39.1) is one of Asheville's top one-hour scenic drives. Nearby is Rattlesnake Lodge (EB 41.7), the ruins of a summer home built by Asheville physician Chase Ambler in 1903–4 (1.5 miles from Ox Creek Road parking via the MST, and what is thought to be Ambler's old four-foot-wide carriage road to Bull Gap). A trail leading down to the right is the first of two leading to a parking area on the parkway at Tanbark Ridge Tunnel (MP 374.5) about half a mile away. Ambler first purchased 318 acres and added another 1,300 acres in ensuing years, extending his property from Bull Gap to Lane Pinnacle. He built a toolshed where a water-driven generator produced electricity. All logs in the lodge and other buildings were hand-hewn chestnut. Ambler built about forty-five miles of trails from his property, including a bridle trail to Mount Mitchell, portions of which are used by the MST. The lodge burned down in 1926. The 1,300-acre parcel was sold in 1916 to become part of Pisgah National Forest. The original 318 acres were sold in 1920 and eventually became parkway right-of-way in the 1930s.

Ambler was a strong supporter of the National Forest system and chaired the committee that formed the Appalachian Mountain Club (southern chapter) in 1920, which was replaced by the Carolina Mountain Club in 1923. "Little did he know that after his death . . . the trails he built in order for people to enjoy the mountains would become part of the MST," wrote his grandson, A. Chase Ambler Jr., in his 1994 book *Rattlesnake Lodge: A Brief History and Guidebook*. Walt Weber's book *Trail Profiles and Maps: From Clingmans Dome to Mount Mitchell and Beyond* also contains more history on Rattlesnake Lodge.

Woodfin Watershed is a 1,840-acre property located along the Laurel Fork and Sugarcamp Fork of Reems Creek, north of Asheville near Weaverville. The best view of the property is just past MP 368–71 while heading south on the parkway. Conservation of the tract of old-growth forest protects a public drinking water source (North Asheville), wildlife habitat, and open space. The Southern Appalachian Highlands Conservancy (SAHC; https://appalachian.org/740-2/) purchased a conservation easement on the property in 2005. The SAHC also purchased ninety acres on Snowball Mountain, forever protecting incredible views of the much-loved Craggy Mountains for tourists and residents alike. This tract is easily seen from the parkway and national forest land, and it borders the Snowball Mountain Trail and Camp Sequoyah Trail, both open to the public. All this protected land is near the MST between Lane Pinnacle and Craggy Gardens.

North Carolina is home to five Wilderness Study Areas (WSA) protected by the US Forest Service, totaling 25,816 acres. Nantahala National Forest includes Overflow Creek and Snowbird (no MST trail). Pisgah National Forest has Harper Creek, Lost Cove, and Craggy Mountain (with MST trail). The Craggy Mountains WSA spans 2,380 acres north of parkway land from Bee Tree Gap eastward to Greybeard Overlook. As a WSA, the US Forest Service manages it as wilderness and recommends it for full wilderness protection, which would ban the use of power tools, limit groups of visitors to no more than ten people, and protect it from logging, mining, road construction, and off-road vehicles.

The Craggy Mountains WSA is in Pisgah National Forest. The MST runs for about one mile here, beginning between the Craggy Gardens Visitor Center and Craggy Pinnacle and ending near Greybeard Overlook. There is strong support to establish a Craggy Wilderness and National Scenic Area, nationally protecting over 16,000 acres—the first National Scenic Area in North Carolina. Although Arch Nichols led efforts to establish the Craggy Mountain Scenic Area in 1958, the new proposal would protect more acres from timber harvesting and include better watershed protection.

Craggy Gardens picnic area (EB 47.9) and Craggy Gardens Visitor Center (EB 48.8; MP 364.5) are beautiful places to take a break. Craggy Gardens is a rocky forest covered in rhododendron located on the parkway, with gnarled beech, birch, buckeye, and blueberry bushes and wildflowers lining the path to a stunning rocky summit and panoramic views on Craggy Pinnacle (elevation 5,892 feet; MP 364.1). It is just a 252-foot, 1.4-mile round-trip hike to the top of the summit, not part of the MST. Craggy Dome (elevation 6,079 feet) is trailless, but it is the tallest peak in the Great Craggy Mountains.

Glassmine Falls is visible from EB 53.8 on the parkway overlook (MP 361.2). Years ago, a mica mine sat at the bottom of the waterfall. Miners called mica, or "isinglass" mineral, "glass" for short.

Blackstock Knob (elevation 6,320 feet) and the very rocky Potato Knob (elevation 6,420 feet) are the last obstacles before heading up Mount Mitchell. Part of Potato Knob was covered with rocks and boulders that had broken loose from above due to freezing and thawing. To form a trail, heavy slabs of stone had to be moved, and once again CMC volunteers provided the people power to do the job. If it's been raining, there is a "get wet falls" along the route. The views and wildflowers are spectacular. Native Fraser fir grows beside the trail. Many of the spruces here are not the native red spruce, which once grew in the area, but rather Norway spruce, which came from Europe after logging cleared much of the forests from 1890 to 1920. The Norway is identified by drooping twigs along the main limbs. Still, this area boasts the largest contiguous red spruce forest in the Southern Appalachians.

Which peak could be claimed the highest summit in the eastern United States was a topic of debate in the early 1800s. Some believed the distinction belonged to Mount Washington in New Hampshire, while others argued for Clingmans Dome (Kuwohi) in the Smokies, or Grandfather Mountain. To settle the dispute, the state sent UNC professor Elisha Mitchell to measure the elevation of Grandfather Mountain and the Black Mountains in 1835. At that time, he determined Mount Mitchell in the Black Mountains was higher than Mount Washington, making it the highest mountain east of the Mississippi. Mitchell returned to the Black Mountains in 1857 to verify his measurements. On June 27, on his way to the Cane River Valley, he slipped and fell into a gorge along Sugar Camp Fork, near the waterfall that now bears his name. Eleven days later, the famous mountain guide "Big Tom" Wilson found Mitchell's body.

A year later, in June 1858, his body was interred on Mount Mitchell's peak, identified with only a stone cairn until 1888 when a wooden marker was added. A new memorial was dedicated in 1928. Mount Mitchell's first lookout tower was built in 1916 and replaced by a stone tower in 1927. In 1959, that tower was replaced with another tower, and in 2009 a handicap-accessible observation deck took its place. Today Mitchell's grave and the observation deck are located in Mount Mitchell State Park.

Mitchell's revelation in the 1830s and 1840s that the Black Mountains were the highest in the Appalachian Range and in the eastern United States brought an onslaught of tourists. By the middle of the nineteenth century, a lodge had been built in the southern part of the range and a number of simple cabins dotted the higher slopes. As northern forests were cleared to meet the growing demand for lumber in the late 1800s, logging firms turned their attention to the untouched forests of Southern Appalachia. Between 1908 and 1912, northern lumber companies purchased timber rights to most of the forests in the Black Mountains and started massive logging operations there. In 1915, the North Carolina legislature stepped in and purchased the land that would become the bulk of Mount Mitchell State Park. The Pisgah National Forest, established in 1916, also began buying up and replanting overtimbered lands. In 1922, the first automobile road to the summit was completed, and in 1948, NC 128, which connected Mount Mitchell and the Blue Ridge Parkway, was completed.

Because of its high elevation, the summit ridge of Mount Mitchell is home to a rare collection of plants that can only be found on a few high peaks in the Southern Appalachians, making it similar to a high-elevation cloud forest. While threats from acid rain and air pollution plague the Fraser firs here, a more significant threat is the balsam woolly adelgid. Already weakened by acid rain, the firs may be more prone to the insect's assault than they would be at full strength.

The red spruce and Fraser fir trees that dominate the upper slopes of the Black Mountains look dark from afar, giving the mountain range its name. Six of the ten highest peaks in the eastern United States can be found here (Mount Washington in New Hampshire is the highest in the northeastern United States at 6,288 feet). The crest of the Black Mountains is just fifteen miles long but contains these tall peaks: Mount Mitchell, 6,684 feet in elevation, followed in order hiking north by Mount Craig, 6,663 feet (named for Governor Locke Craig); Big Tom, 6,581 feet (named for Tom Wilson); Balsam Cone, 6,611 feet; Cattail Peak, 6,583 feet; Potato Hill, 6,475 feet (Deep Gap at 5,300 feet), Winter Star Peak, 6,212 feet; Gibbs Mountain, 6,240 feet; and Celo, 6,327 feet. To the south of Mount Mitchell is Mount Gibbes, 6,560 feet, and Clingmans Peak, 6,540 feet with radio towers; don't confuse these with the 6,643-foot Clingmans Dome (Kuwohi) in the Smokies.

Mount Mitchell State Park was the first state park in North Carolina, established in 1915. It encompasses 4,789 acres in Yancey County (EB 63.9–65.8). In 1993, thirty-six inches of snow was recorded in one day. In 1985 the lowest temperature ever recorded in North Carolina was on Mount Mitchell, −34°F. The average temperature in summer is 65.9°F and in winter 17.0°F. Weather can be harsh, with heavy rain and strong winds. Because of its high elevation, some wildflowers bloom in August.

Camp Alice was a logger's camp on the south side of Mount Mitchell from the late 1890s until 1922, and it accommodated tourists after 1914. The camp was named for its cook. A railroad ran from Black Mountain to deliver the logs from the Mitchell area (1915–20). The Mount Mitchell Motor Road (Old Toll Road, three dollars per car) used the old railroad bed for vehicles. Tourists drove to Camp Alice on a one-way road that

Summit observation at Mount Mitchell, highest point in North Carolina.
Photo by Stan Seals; used by permission.

operated coming up to Mitchell from 8 a.m. to 1 p.m. and going down from 3:30 p.m. to 5:30 p.m. Visitors could hike the trails, visit the Mount Mitchell summit, or spend a night in the rustic lodge and enjoy the restaurant. In 1939, when the parkway was completed, Camp Alice was closed and the road abandoned. Remnants of the former toll road remain undisturbed, and the MST follows it in places. Today, nothing remains of Camp Alice, and camping is not permitted on the site (near EB 60.4). The MST follows the blue-blazed Camp Alice Trail and yellow-blazed Old Mitchell Trail.

Commissary Trail is an easy two-mile hike, along Commissary Ridge, beginning at the park office and following an old logging railroad bed from the early 1900s.

Mount Mitchell is the highest peak in North Carolina and east of the Mississippi. The nearest higher peak is Lone Butte in Colorado. One can reach the summit observation tower about 500 feet from the MST, at EB 65.1. (Just north of Mount Mitchell are Mount Craig and Big Tom, peaks with bronze markers thanks to the efforts of Arch Nichols.)

From the Mount Mitchell summit, it is basically six miles down to the Black Mountain Campground (elevation 3,040 feet), for a descent of 3,644 feet. The High Peaks Trail Association maintains that trail and in 2020 helped remove a 48-inch diameter, 100-foot-tall red oak that had fallen across the MST. Its 160 growth rings mean it started growing in 1860, when the Civil War was starting and close to the time Mitchell measured the peak.

Some Nearby History

A state highway historical marker in Buncombe County reads, "André Michaux—French botanist, pioneer in studying flora of western NC, visited Black Mountains, August, 1794." He arrived in America in 1785 and discovered the Southern Appalachians' botanical bounty. He made at least five visits to western North Carolina, studying flora along the French Broad and Catawba Rivers. On later trips he toured Mount Mitchell, Grandfather Mountain, Table Rock, Hawksbill, and Linville Gorge. He is best known for discovering and naming over 250 new plants. Many plants have been named for Michaux, the most spectacular being the rare Carolina lily, *Lilium michauxii*, which was made the state wildflower in 2003. Michaux wrote two books based on his American findings: *The History of North American Oaks* (1801) and *Flora Boreali Americana* (1803).

Other historic visitors include Hernando de Soto and the Spanish who were in the Toe River Valley on the east side of Mount Mitchell. They were the first Europeans to see the Appalachian Mountains and to visit what is now Mitchell County in the 1540s. William Bartram, a Philadelphia naturalist, also explored the North Carolina mountains and visited the Cherokee in 1775. In 1791, he published *Bartram's Travels*, which narrates his journey through the American South and his encounters with Native Americans between 1773 and 1777.

Back on the Trail

Black walnut trees grow in bottomlands and moist fertile hillsides throughout North Carolina. Durable furniture made by pioneers and furniture factories required this hardwood. The nuts are a great way to sweeten brownies or other desserts. Pioneers used the walnut pigment for dying cloth.

You reach the end of Segment 3 at the cold water of the South Toe River at EB 71.5. It's time to cool off those tender toes.

Gorges, Peaks, and Waterfalls

Black Mountain Campground to Beacon Heights

76.5 MILES

I am well again, I came to life in the cool winds
and crystal waters of the mountains.

JOHN MUIR

Segment 4 of the MST has more elevation over its seventy-five miles than any other section. The total ascent is 15,730 feet, and the total descent is 14,517 feet. Remote (only crossing three paved roads) and somewhat wild, its beautiful forests, rivers, streams, and spectacular vistas stretch along the cliffs of Linville Gorge Wilderness Area. Be prepared to wade or rock-hop a dozen or more creek crossings.

Black Mountain Campground to Table Rock

This segment begins at Forest Service Road 472 (South Toe River Road) near Black Mountain Campground. As the MST leaves the campground, crossing FR 2074, look for remnants of the Mount Mitchell Fish Hatchery, on the same site as a 1930s Civilian Conservation Corps camp. At EB 5.4 this segment of the MST first crosses the parkway.

Nearby

If you want to explore the area "near the MST" in this segment, without the extreme elevation and remoteness, you could stay on the Blue Ridge Parkway for stops like Crabtree Falls, Little Switzerland, the Museum of North Carolina Minerals, the Orchards at Altapass, Linville Caverns

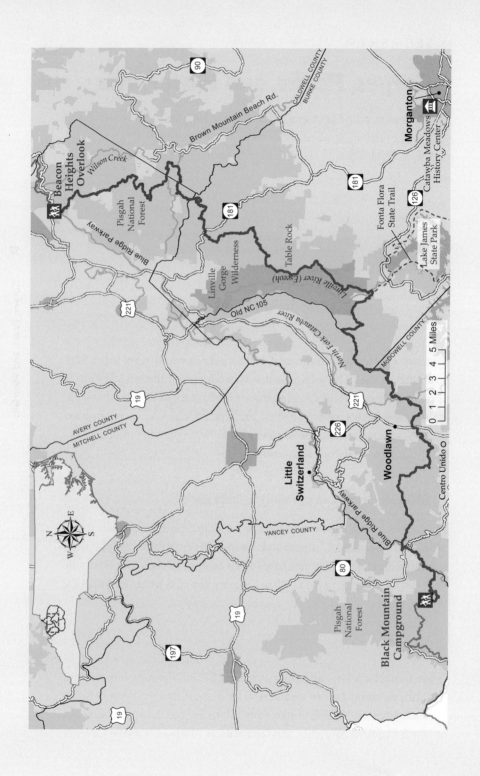

and Falls, and Crossnore. (For the sticklers, this does not count toward completing the MST!)

The MST leaves the parkway corridor near NC 128 (Segment 3, EB 60.3, MP 360), heading up Mount Mitchell, then down to Black Mountain Campground (Segment 3, EB 71.5/Segment 4, EB 0.0), and, except for five miles near NC 80, it doesn't rejoin the parkway until Beacon Heights (MP 305), a total of eighty-one trail miles away from the parkway corridor, reconnecting at Beacon Heights near Grandfather Mountain (Segment 4, EB 76.5).

Back on the Trail

Bob Benner is credited with persistently pushing to get the MST off the parkway and routed through some of the MST's most challenging trail (with steep elevations, creek crossings, and remoteness). Bob published *Carolina Whitewater: A Paddler's Guide to the Western Carolinas* (coauthored with David Benner) in 1996, promoted the North Carolina Scenic Rivers Act, was a member of the State Trails Committee and a Sierra Club conservationist, led regional public meetings, and spent thirty-four years leading the Central Blue Ridge Task Force. He wanted folks to get to know the beauty of the rugged North Carolina backcountry, and the MST is blessed that he persisted in establishing the route we have today.

In November 2020, Mark Rostan and Brian Zimmer completed "Grandell"—Grandfather Mountain to Mount Mitchell. They made this 101-mile run-hike in thirty-seven hours, sixteen minutes, and forty-six seconds.

At EB 7.7 the MST passes over the parkway and briefly over NC 80, entering forests and heading to Woods Mountain. At EB 12.5 the MST begins an ascent of Woods Mountain. At the summit (EB 13.2) it is 800 yards to the remains of the Woods Mountain Lookout Tower that was dismantled in the mid-1960s. The MST descends about 2,000 feet over the next six miles on the old Woods Mountain Trail, until it crosses US Highway 221.

Woods Mountain Bike Trail (contact MTBProject.com) is a classic trail that traverses a long ridge for about five miles and then descends a massive mountain for about five miles before climbing out on a variety of forest roads and trails—a total of 12.5 miles. It is a challenging "expert" trail 1,352 feet up and 3,289 feet down, with an average grade of 7 percent. The bottom of Woods Mountain gets very confusing, as the corridor follows

Bob Benner, Central
Blue Ridge Task Force
leader for thirty-four
years and an MST
Board member. *Photo
by Donnie Williams;
used by permission.*

forest roads and sections of the MST. The end of the bike trail is shared
with the MST until EB 19.5 at US 221.

After crossing US 221 (one of only three paved highways on this seventy-five-mile segment) in about two miles you descend to the North Fork
of the Catawba River (elevation 1,320 feet; *Catawba* means "people of the
river"). In another 2.5 miles (EB 23.3) you reach the 200-foot pedestrian
bridge crossing the river. Allen de Hart had the dream for a bridge to
safely accommodate hikers and even used his home as collateral for the
project. The bridge was built with a Recreational Trails Program grant,
and the USFS helped fund environmental work (a $250,000 project). The
bridge was brought in by helicopter. The bridge and Bald Knob Trail were
dedicated on May 6, 2006, the same day Friends of the MST presented
Bob Benner with the Order of the Long Leaf Pine. Just east of the river
you cross the Clinchfield railroad tracks.

The old MST route to the south of Bald Knob went through Champion Paper Company lands where the Friends had an agreement to use
their property. It was a rough, simple, and often overgrown trail. Allen
de Hart, Jeff Brewer, and Bob Benner flagged a new route in the fall

of 1996 (approved by the USFS) and started new trail construction on Thanksgiving weekend. Jeff Brewer, the sixth MST thru-hiker, tells of the new Friends organization mobilizing volunteers to build new trails on long weekends.

> An area we spent a ton of time on was the trail up Bald Knob (elevation 3,495 feet) outside of Marion and Woodlawn. It was a difficult trail project due to hiking uphill just to start the work. Volunteer support was limited. We built twenty-six switchbacks up that mountain to make that trail happen. We had a hiding spot for all of our tools from spring to fall and then pulled them off the mountain for winter storage. One time we had a bear bite into our stored chainsaw gas can. It took several years to finish and was dedicated in 2006.

Alan Householder started at the western terminus on April 18, 1997, and with Allen de Hart completed the first thru-hike of the then 935-mile MST at Jockey's Ridge on June 12, 1997. Alan helped scout a route up Bald Knob from the North Fork of the Catawba River and shared this report:

> We were told by the NC State Trail Coordinator that there was no way that a trail could go there but obviously it could due to Allen's determination as well as getting the state to put a bridge across the river. On my thru-hike, the trail wasn't there yet and this section was the most challenging as well as the most adventurous! I found a fallen tree that spanned the river and slid me and my backpack across it safely and then had to bushwhack up the mountain to the FS Road on Dobson Knob—an unforgettable experience! My other big challenge was finding campsites along the way that were not on the Parkway land. I backpacked from Clingmans Dome to Blowing Rock where Allen joined me the rest of the way (he had already previously hiked the entire trail in those sections). Mostly we had great weather throughout our journey and received a lot of publicity along the way.

All across North Carolina they wore T-shirts with "Mountains-to-Sea Trail—1997 Expedition" in bold letters.

De Hart said Bald Knob was the hardest section on the entire trail, and Danny Bernstein called it the "toughest climb of the MST." Thru-hikers often journal about their hike. Johnny Massey (the twelfth MST thru-hiker) wrote that he and his cohiker Dave were in bear country near Dobson

Alan Householder and Allen de Hart on the first thru-hike of the MST, in 1997. *Photo used by permission of Friends of the MST.*

Knob. For safety they ate their lunch back-to-back. Johnny said, "Luckily, for the bear, he did not show his face and have to tangle with two tough bear fighters like us."

The Overmountain Victory National Historic Trail (OVT, yellow blaze) is part of the US National Trails System, and 225 of its miles are in North Carolina. The trail was named for the Overmountain Men, a group of Patriots from East Tennessee and Virginia who crossed the mountains into North Carolina before heading to South Carolina to fight the Battle of Kings Mountain during the Revolutionary War. Two groups moved into North Carolina, one crossing Gillespie Gap (a monument stands at the Museum of North Carolina Minerals, MP 330.9) and another at Hefner Gap (segment of trail at MP 325.9), passing near Woodlawn (on US 221) and on Old NC 105 west of Linville Gorge (EB 31.8–34). At EB 31.8 the MST first intersects with the OVT on the deeply rutted Yellow Mountain Road (authorized as a toll road in 1827) and again along Old NC 105.

A Bit of History

On September 30, 1780, more than 1,000 Patriot troops, including Pied-mont militias, camped out and regrouped at Quaker Meadows (in what is now Morganton, near I-40, along the Catawba River) before traveling another 170 miles to Kings Mountain. Named for a Quaker trader, the meadow was owned during the Revolutionary War by Patriot colonels

Joseph and Charles McDowell. Today Quaker Meadows is identified by a historical marker, and Charles McDowell's stately red brick house, built in 1812 and since restored, stands nearby.

Lake James State Park (elevation 1,200 feet) sits at the feet of the Blue Ridge Mountains, between Marion and Morganton. The 6,812-acre lake formed in 1916–23 when Duke Power Company built hydroelectric dams, connected by a canal, across the Catawba River and two tributaries, Paddy Creek and the Linville River. Lake James was named after the power company's founder, James B. Duke, and still serves as a hydroelectric unit today. Circling Lake James for twenty-nine miles is a key segment of the Fonta Flora State Trail, established in 2015, with a 2.7-mile connecting blue-blaze trail along the Linville River to the MST. The trail was named for a local settlement of African American sharecroppers whose homes were flooded when Lake James was created. The North Catawba and Linville Rivers merge to form the Catawba River, known as "the hardest working river in America."

Back on the Trail

The Pinnacle (elevation 2,850 feet, EB 34.3) is "just off the trail," east of Old NC 105 (or Kistler Memorial Highway), with spectacular views in several directions. Local historian Denise Bishop says it is considered a sacred place by Native peoples.

In early March a side trip off the MST will take you to Daffodil Flats, a small valley floor along the Linville River that is filled annually with a bright yellow field of thousands of blooming daffodils. At the Pinnacle continue downward on the MST three-quarters of a mile to a four-way intersection with the Leadmine Trail (EB 35.1, the MST goes right, Leadmine goes left, shortly after a rough wooden sign). Only the MST is blazed; this area is rugged wilderness, requires navigation skills—expect no cell signal.

The first known colonists in the Daffodil Flats area were the Shooks, who obtained a tract of land in the gorge around 1870, and the Dellingers, who lived on another tract for about fifteen years. Joseph Dellinger's wife, Rachel, and their daughter Matilda stayed until 1910. No one knows who planted the daffodils—it may have been Matilda or a flood may have brought them down from the Linville area in Avery County.

On July 15, 1916, 22.22 inches of rain fell in Altapass, a mountain town in Mitchell County. That day broke the record for the heaviest rainfall in a single day ever in the United States, and what followed became known as the Great Flood of 1916. Waterways, already at capacity from earlier days of rain, rushed across low ground at breakneck speed, washing the corpses of livestock, hogsheads of tobacco, bales of cotton, moonshine stills, and entire buildings into the Catawba, Yadkin, and French Broad Rivers. When the Linville River flooded, it broke a large portion off the face of Shortoff Mountain.

Erosion from overlogging was blamed for increased flooding, leaving clear-cut lands with nothing to stop the mighty waters. The federal Weeks Act ensured protection of forests in the East (Pisgah National Forest was the first acreage to secure protection in 1916), but by the time it was being enforced, the Great Flood had already done its damage. Between Statesville and Asheville, barely a mile of railroad track survived the flood. But most rail lines were operating again by September, thanks to the area's out-of-work farmers, mill workers, and laborers. These men traveled to construction camps set up by Southern Railway to work for room, board, and $1.50 a day until the railroad was fully restored.

A Bright Bit of Local History

Since the 1800s, on cloudless nights when the moon is nowhere to be seen, travelers in western North Carolina have spotted mysterious light-filled pinwheels or globes making their way lazily across the dark sky. Sightings of the so-called Brown Mountain Lights are rare and only occasionally reported. According to one folktale, the lights are the spirit of a Native American, likely Cherokee, searching for his lost maiden. Others attribute them to reflections from passing trains, St. Elmo's fire (light created by electrical discharges during stormy weather), moon dogs (when the tricky light of the moon is viewed through haze), fox fire (phosphorescent light produced from decaying wood), or even aliens from outer space. Though the first scientific study was conducted in 1913 to ascertain exactly where the lights came from, no one has ever determined their origin. Even Thomas Edison came to investigate, camping out at the Brown Mountain Lights overlook on NC 181, but he couldn't explain the mystery. Jim Baity, writer for the *Asheville Citizen Times*, investigated and wrote an article on the lights in July 1962, the same year hundreds of cars, packed with curious travelers hoping to catch a glimpse of the enigmatic Brown Mountain Lights, lined NC 181 and Wiseman's View. Author Wade Edward Speer, a native of Marion, wrote *The Brown Mountain Lights: History,*

Science and Human Nature Explain an Appalachian Mystery, published by McFarland in 2017. The best viewpoints are Wiseman's View (NC 105) and the overlook on NC 181.

Around 1971, I met local Ralph I. Lael at a store on NC 181, and I asked him if his accounts of the lights were true. He replied, "Yes, that's what happened to me on Brown Mountain." He was about eighty years old at the time we talked. A friend from Gingercake Acres had given me a twenty-eight-page booklet, *The Brown Mountain Lights*, written by Lael in 1965. In it, he described repeated trips to Brown Mountain dedicated to finding the source of the lights. One night he encountered a light, a sphere about twelve feet across, that beckoned him to follow, and they entered a crevice that led to a crystal ballroom–like place inside the mountain. The lights could converse with him and described being created on their home planet, Pewam, which destroyed itself. Most of them live on Venus, with this small group on Earth here to keep us from destroying ourselves. In October 1962, the lights took Lael to Venus on a "flying saucer" to visit with the "aliens" and then returned him to Brown Mountain. He was instructed to not reveal many details but to urge more brotherly love. The next time I stopped to visit Lael, I was told he had died.

Mike Fischesser (North Carolina Outward Bound School staff, 1972–85) and members of the Brown Mountain Lights Research Team have conducted the most extensive research on the lights and have recorded over forty interviews with people who have seen the lights—and some who have seen the Linville Gorge Lights—between 1920 and the 1980s. Through their exploration of the mountain, they think they located the spot where Ralph Lael first encountered the lights. Appalachian State University professor Daniel B. Caton has studied the lights, has written about them, and maintains a website, brownmountainlights.org.

Back on the Trail

The Linville River, from near Crossnore downriver through Linville Gorge, is considered one of the best waters in the state for fishing brook trout. The native eastern trout is really not a trout but a char, that is, a brookie or speckled trout. The Toe River near Black Mountain Campground is also a highly rated trout stream. A Western North Carolina Fly Fishing Trail is anchored by the Tuckasegee River near the Smokies.

After crossing the sixty-foot-wide Linville River (EB 37.1), a hiker will climb 1,700 feet over the next 1.7 miles to the top of Shortoff Mountain

Thru-hiker Claire "Marmot" Dumont admiring the view northward up Linville Gorge from the Chimneys. *Photo by Larry Dumont; used by permission.*

(elevation 2,883 feet). The hike up from the Linville River offers views of Lake James, including the site of a fort in the 1992 film *The Last of the Mohicans*, much of which was shot in North Carolina. Shortoff Mountain is also a well-known rock-climbing area.

Denise Bishop recalls once seeing a steel cable near the summit of Shortoff and meeting a person who said he used it to haul laurel and rhododendron plants from the gorge for his plant nursery. She hasn't seen the cable recently but has heard from another person that they also saw the cable. Wolf Pit Road gives access to the general area.

The MST passes directly beside a mountain bog on the top of Shortoff Mountain (EB 39.4). It is an estimated one acre in size. The mountain bogs of the Southern Appalachians are one of the rarest and most extraordinary habitats in North America. Known for their nutrient-poor, highly acidic, and very wet soil, bogs are usually found in low-lying areas where water collects. Some rare flora and fauna thrive in these harsh conditions. At one time, nearly 5,000 acres of bogs existed in North Carolina, but only about 500 acres remain today. In the mountains, many have been destroyed by draining, ditching, and development. Mountain bog conservation is critical to preserving and bringing back populations of the bog turtle (the smallest turtle species in the country), the sweet pitcher plant, and other endangered plants.

The Linville Gorge Wilderness Area is home to one of the wildest, rockiest, and most breathtaking gorges in the eastern United States (MST for 8.7 miles; EB 37.1–45.7). Before Europeans inhabited the area, the Cherokee called it Eseeoh, meaning "a river of many cliffs." After colonists arrived, the gorge was named for explorer William Linville and his son John, who were killed by Shawnees there in 1766, in the shadow of Shortoff Mountain. Today it is known by some as the "Grand Canyon of the East."

In the early 1900s, a large portion of the North Carolina mountains were clear-cut for timber by logging companies. The unforgiving steep walls of Linville Gorge made it just too expensive to retrieve the wood. As a result, Linville Gorge contains one of the only old-growth, virgin forests in the state. There are gigantic hemlock trees, hillsides of "rhododendron hell," beautiful tangles and blooms of mountain laurel, rattlesnakes, skunks, black bears, "pothole kettles" along the raging Linville River, and many other natural features and vistas to accent the rocky, steep MST.

Linville Gorge Wilderness Area sits on 11,786 acres within Pisgah National Forest. It is the third-largest wilderness area in North Carolina, and one of only two wilderness gorges in the southern United States. John D. Rockefeller donated funds to purchase the area in 1952, beginning its formal protection. When Congress approved and enacted the Wilderness Act in 1964, creating the National Wilderness Preservation System, Linville Gorge was one of the first federally protected wilderness areas in the country. Today, the Grandfather Ranger District of the US Forest Service manages the land.

The gorge's terrain is steep and rugged, with elevations ranging from 1,280 feet along the Linville River to 4,120 feet at the top of Gingercake Mountain. The walls of Linville Gorge enclose the Linville River for nearly twelve miles as it descends about 1,900 feet before it moves into the wide-open plains of the Catawba Valley. The Cambric Branch Trail (FST 234; junction at EB 42.3) drops into the gorge on an unmaintained trail. Near EB 43.2 a trail to the left drops into the gorge to the Amphitheater area, with the Mummy and the Daddy rock-climbing walls. For the next mile the MST is on top of the climbing cliffs known as the North Carolina Wall, and then the MST has smaller cliffs called the Chimneys on its right. Trails into the gorge may be off limits at times to protect peregrine falcons.

Several rock-climbing sites sit beside or near the MST in Linville Gorge locations, including Shortoff Mountain, the Amphitheatre, the North Carolina Wall, the Chimneys, Table Rock, Little Table Rock, Devil's Cellar, and Hawksbill. These climbs are featured in *The Climber's Guide to North Carolina* by Thomas Kelley and *Carolina Rocks* by Erica Lineberry. Lineberry's book features the world-class climbing area of Moore's Wall (Hanging Rock), the fantastic slabs of Stone Mountain, which is pictured on the book cover, and the incredibly popular cliffs of Pilot Mountain, with 550 climbing routes described.

The "Table Rock Fire" in Linville Gorge Wilderness Area started in the Table Rock picnic area on November 12, 2013. A campfire right beside the MST was not extinguished and quickly grew from 15 acres to 300 acres, threatening the Outward Bound basecamp. A team of 100 firefighters grew to 200; assistance came from multiple agencies and several states; helicopters dropped water. Soon it was 1,000 acres, south of the Chimneys, halfway to the river, and after eight days over 2,000 acres were burning. The authors of the postfire report wrote of burnout, containment lines, road and trail closures, lack of access, and "mop up" hot spots. Two days later, a half inch of rain couldn't stop it. Only after twenty days and 2,579 acres were burned was it 100 percent contained. It was a spectacular fire and a devastating one—except, of course, for the trees and plants that benefit from the effects of forest fires.

Table Rock to Beacon Heights

North Carolina Outward Bound School began in the summer of 1967 at the Table Rock Base. The property (eighty-plus acres), on the east side of Table Rock, is leased and operated under a Special Use Permit from the US Forest Service. Table Rock Base is the school's largest and primary base. During its operating season (March through October), the school serves more than 1,100 students.

Table Rock Mountain (elevation 4,101 feet, named Namonda by the Cherokee) is 9.5 miles from the nearest highway, NC 181, mostly on a rough, gravel road. From the MST (EB 44.9) it is a side trip of only 300 yards to the impressive summit. Until the early 1980s a firefighter's lookout hut at the summit was staffed during dry seasons. A Civilian Conservation Corps crew built a fourteen-foot-square, one-room lookout house with a telephone line in 1935 and then rebuilt it in 1948. A cable ran from the summit to a spring near the saddle between Table Rock and Little Table Rock. By using a crank at the top, a ranger could lower a bucket to the spring, where it stopped under a water pipe, then crank it back to the top—the old fashion way to get "running water." The lookout ceased being used in the 1960s and was burned and removed in the early 1980s. Some the hut's concrete base remains, and the boxed spring is mentioned in the MST guidebook (EB 44.9). As an aside, Table Mountain pine is not named for Table Rock Mountain.

Nearby

From MST EB 45.7, a spur road to the left leads 500 yards to the Table Rock Road and the Spence Ridge Trailhead to the Linville River (2.2 miles). Walking an additional mile gets you to the Hawksbill Trail. Hawksbill is a classic spot for sunsets and meteor showers. The 360-degree views from the top of Hawksbill Mountain (elevation 4,009 feet) are some of the most spectacular you'll find in North Carolina. From the Table Rock Road it is a 1.5-mile round-trip hike to the summit.

A Brief History of Juan Pardo

Well before the United States was formed, Spanish explorer Juan Pardo led two expeditions in the western North Carolina mountains in 1566–67, more than twenty years after Hernando de Soto's journeys in 1540. According to the Appalachian history website digitalheritage.org, Pardo constructed Fort San Juan and two other forts near Joara, one of the largest Native American towns in the region, not far from present-day Morganton. This was the first interior European settlement in the present-day United States. Faced with the threat of Indigenous retaliation near the Smoky Mountains, he abandoned the forts and Spain gave up its quest for a land route to Mexico through the Appalachians. Not long after the retreat of Pardo and the Spanish, the British moved in as the colonial power in Southern Appalachia. The fort site, on private property called the Berry Site, was rediscovered in 2013 after decades of archeological searching. The nearby Catawba Meadows Site is also worth exploring.

Back on the Trail

In 2020, on HikingUpward.com, Zack Robbins reported that Steels Creek Falls is worth a 100-yard detour (EB 49.5). There are five named waterfalls

Kids rock-hopping Harper Creek on a three-day backpacking trip.
Photo by Jerry Barker.

on the extended Steels Creek Trail and on tributaries of the creek. Of particular note are Steels Creek Falls, Beverly Hillbilly Falls, and Rip Breeches Falls. The third edition of *North Carolina Waterfalls* provides a good map of the area. Be warned that this is considered a difficult trail.

The MST crosses NC 181, which connects to the parkway and the town of Linville to the north and Morganton and I-40 to the south. Morganton, in Burke County, boasts a stately 180-year-old county courthouse, a stop on the Ben F. Long IV Fresco Trail, and the Morganton Greenway System. Lake James State Park and South Mountains State Park are short drives from the city. The city motto is "Nature's Playground." As you cross NC 181 (EB 53.7), the trail sign says "Upper Creek 2.1 miles." The MST is not the best access to Upper Creek Falls, a favorite swimming hole of the locals with a rope swing, that is about two miles north on NC 181. Heading east, the MST joins the Greentown Trail, a 7.6-mile out-and-back trail, with the first mile a very steep descent (792 feet), crossing Upper Creek. When this area was booming with logging, there was a Greentown post office.

The Harper Creek and Lost Cove Wilderness Study Areas (WSAs), traversed by the MST, are known for their frequent stream crossings, beautiful waterfalls and cascading streams, and abundant wildlife and wildflowers. These areas protect 7,138 acres and 5,708 acres, respectively. Within the Harper Creek WSA lies a part of the Wilson Creek Wild and Scenic River Management Area.

As you descend from NC 181, you enter first the Harper Creek WSA at EB 58, then the Raider Camp Creek drainage (the name may have originated during the Civil War). Next you follow Harper Creek, and you'll love your detour to the bottom of Harper Creek Falls for a cold swim and picturesque falls. As you gain elevation, you'll follow North Harper Creek and leave Harper Creek WSA at FR 464 (EB 66.6). The MST then enters Lost Cove WSA and goes down to Lost Cove Creek and Hunt Fish Falls. Then you begin ascending again up Gragg Prong, passing beautiful Gragg Prong Falls, and eventually arriving at Roseborough Road, exiting Lost Cove WSA (EB 70.7), for a total of just over twelve miles through these wilderness study areas and over about twenty creek crossings. Only the nimble and lucky get through with dry feet. Gragg Prong may have been named after John Gragg, a Revolutionary War soldier, or Will Gragg, the first community postmaster in 1886.

While attempting a thru-hike in the winter of 2018, Jason Murrell encountered more than wet feet. "I dealt with three back-to-back-to-back ice storms in the mountains, stranding me in my tent for two days. While crossing a creek—in Raider Camp, Harper and Lost Cove Creek area—I got swept off my feet and lost my pack, but thankfully was able to chase it down. I got seriously hypothermic and had to stop for the day, build a fire, and dry everything out. Unfortunately, the next day, I had to cross creeks several more times. It was cold, but thankfully, the sun was out and I was able to continue."

Wilson Creek was named a National Wild and Scenic River in 2000, one of only five in North Carolina. By definition, these waterways must be free-flowing, unpolluted, and generally inaccessible by roads. Wilson Creek's headwaters are on the flanks of Grandfather Mountain, and it runs twenty-three miles to the Johns River in Burke County.

The MST crosses Roseborough Road (FS 981) just 0.4 mile past Gragg Prong Creek. Roseborough is a part of Carey's Flat township, with members of the Gragg family still living there. For the next six miles, the trail generally climbs, with Grandmother Mountain to your left, until you reach Beacon Heights. Take time to absorb the magnificent view from the nearby rocks.

Some Nearby History

Mortimer and Edgemont are like ghost towns in Caldwell County's Wilson Creek township. In the early 1900s, the township was headquarters for a large logging camp and a bustling cotton mill town. The financial crash of 1929 brought a sudden stop to the town's economic life, and by 1930 the entire town was shuttered. Around 1933, the township of Wilson Creek was revived when a man from Lenoir, O. P. Lutz, bought it plus a thousand acres of the mountains that surround it. Lutz brought the old mill back into operation to make nylon hosiery—the latest fashion in high demand at the time—with six machines he had shipped from Germany.

On August 13, 1940, just one week after Lutz's hosiery factory opened, the entire town of about 800 people was wiped away by a tremendous flood that swept through in the middle of the night. All that remains now are foundations and industrial machinery, neglected and covered with vines. Hikers along Harper Creek occasionally find pieces of railroad track left from trains used to haul timber from the mountains.

Built in 1924 at the corner of what are now NC 90 and Brown Mountain Beach Road, Betsey's Ole Country Store still serves the community as a general store and post office. When it was first established nearly a century ago, Mortimer was a booming logging town. Today visitors can peruse the shelves of the store and stay at the campground nestled in the woods of the Wilson Creek area, which has welcomed guests since the 1940s. Owner Bruce Gray is dedicated to keeping the creek clean and estimates he has removed 144,000 pounds of trash. If you're interested in supporting Gray's nonprofit dedicated to river cleanup, check out their website at ACleanWilsonCreek.com. Beginning in 2022 cleanup efforts have been supported by Latino Aventureros. Also make sure to visit the Wilson Creek Visitor Center in Collettsville at 7805 Brown Mountain Beach Road. Although Edgemont is considered a ghost town, Coffey's General Store still operates.

Back on the Trail

Beacon Heights Trail is a short out-and-back side trip at EB 76.4. The trail boasts spectacular panoramic views, especially to the south, east, and north from its summit, making it one of the most popular trails in the area. As we end Segment 4, we're back to the parkway.

The High Country

Beacon Heights to Devils Garden Overlook

84.9 MILES

I do not ask to walk smooth paths nor bear an easy load.
I pray for strength and fortitude to climb the rock-strewn road.

GAIL BROOK BURKET

Starting in the shadow of Grandfather Mountain and following near the Blue Ridge Parkway corridor almost to the Virginia border, this section of the MST is rich with scenic views along a gently rolling trail. It has access to highways, small towns, camping, and a variety of parks, making it convenient to arrange hikes with shuttles and accommodate easy- to moderate-level hikes. This is the last of the five mountain segments before the MST descends into the Piedmont.

Beacon Heights to Blowing Rock

Leaving the Beacon Heights parking lot at parkway MP 305 and beginning the MST hike, you'll see signage for the Beacon Heights Trail, which spans just under a mile round-trip and is worth the effort. To begin an eastbound MST hike, turn left (north) at the Tanawha Trail.

From EB 0.1 to EB 11.7 (from Beacon Heights Parking Area to Boone Fork Trail), the MST follows the Tanawha Trail for fourteen miles. This stretch of trail was completed in the mid-1980s and explores the flanks of Grandfather Mountain. *Tanawha*, the Cherokee name for Grandfather Mountain, means "fabulous hawk," also a fitting name for a trail that offers gorgeous, soaring views, plus shady coves and valleys along the way.

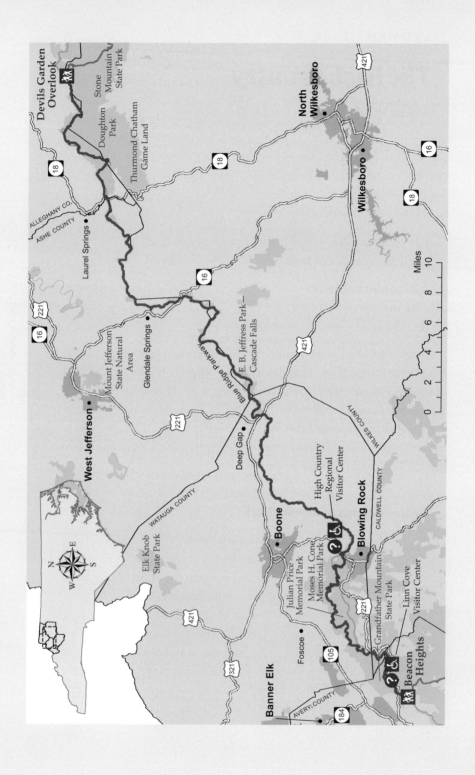

Nearby History

Three miles from the MST trailhead at Beacon Heights Parking Area is the small Avery County community of Linville. As mentioned earlier, the town was named for colonists William and John Linville, who were killed by a Shawnee war party in 1766. Over 100 years later, in 1883, Linville was designed in the shape of a square with charming parks and streets in a grid. Today Linville is a headquarters for summer hiking, and is known for the beautiful fall leaf season, the Linville Caverns, and the breathtaking Linville Falls. The Linville Historic District was listed on the National Register of Historic Places in 1979.

Three miles south of Linville is the town of Newland, the seat of Avery County. The Avery County Courthouse and Avery County Jail are listed on the National Register of Historic Places. The East Tennessee and Western North Carolina Railroad ("Tweetsie," for the sound of its whistle) passed through the town until 1940. The Avery County Historical Museum occupies the historic jail in Newland and has extensive displays on the railroad, as well as a restored caboose.

Back on the Trail

Do you know where Forrest Gump Curve is near the MST? On the Grandfather Mountain Entrance Road (admission for a fee) is a curve that Tom Hanks as Forrest ran in the 1994 film. His curve is about two miles from the Beacon Heights Parking Area. Forrest's saying, "Mama always said you can tell a lot about a person by their shoes, where they going, where they been," is especially true for hikers.

Randy Johnson is the MST task force leader from Grandfather Mountain to Blowing Rock and the author of the award-winning book *Grandfather Mountain: The History and Guide to an Appalachian Icon.* He launched Grandfather's innovative trail management program in the 1970s, reopened the peak's oldest paths, and built new trails. In the mid-1980s, as the Blue Ridge Parkway was nearing completion on Grandfather Mountain, he consulted on the design for the parkway's Tanawha Trail, now concurrent with the MST for the next 14.2 miles. In 2017, he authored *Hiking the Blue Ridge Parkway: The Ultimate Travel Guide to America's Most Popular Scenic Roadway.*

Grandfather Mountain has been an International Biosphere Preserve since 1992. In fact, Johnson claims that "Grandfather is likely Eastern

America's most ecologically significant summit." The Grandfather Mountain Stewardship Foundation operates 720 acres of the mountain as a scenic visitor attraction. The paved road up the mountain provides picnic facilities, restrooms, gift shops, a restaurant, environmental animal habitats, and a nature museum. Families love the Mile-High Swinging Bridge (a 228-foot swaying bridge over an eighty-foot chasm with 360-degree views). Special events on the meadows include Singing on the Mountain in June and the Grandfather Mountain Highland Games and Gathering of Scottish Clans in July. Hugh Morton (1921–2006) was renowned as the Grandfather Mountain developer, conservationist, photographer, and promoter of North Carolina tourism. Spring flowers, summer tourists, and fall leaf colors keep the Grandfather Mountain area bustling year-round.

In 2008, the state of North Carolina turned 3,647 acres of the undeveloped high summits into Grandfather Mountain State Park. Free access to the state park is available along the parkway (MP 298–305) where the MST follows the Tanawha Trail and Boone Fork Trail along the southeastern flanks of the mountain (EB 0.0–16.4) from Beacon Heights to Moses Cone Park. Calloway Peak (elevation 5,946 feet) is the highest point on Grandfather Mountain.

Grandfather Mountain is known for cold, windy weather. A wind speed record was set in 2019 at 124 miles per hour, and it got pretty cold in 1985, at −32°F. Nearby Banner Elk is considered the coldest town in North Carolina, with an average low of 38°F. In October, it hosts the annual Woolly Worm Festival. During the festival, attendees are encouraged to enter their own wooly worm (worms can be purchased there) in "heats" to see which worm races up the hanging string the fastest. The colorful bands on the winning worm are used to predict the cold weeks of winter.

Along the MST at EB 1.4, a stop at the Linn Cove Visitor Center (MP 304.4) gives excellent information on the building of the viaduct, which can be viewed up close from the trail (EB 1.6–2.1). Parkway planners built the Linn Cove Viaduct—153 segments, each weighing fifty tons, stretching for 1,243 feet—to protect Grandfather Mountain's unique and vulnerable habitat. This impressive engineering and conservation project was the last portion of the parkway to be completed (in 1987), at a cost of nearly $10 million.

The MST crosses Wilson Creek at EB 2.5 (the parkway's Wilson Creek Overlook is on the right, MP 303.6). This is the only MST crossing of Wilson Creek, one of North Carolina's five National Wild and Scenic

Rivers. Spectacular views of the summits of Grandfather Mountain and the Linn Cove Viaduct can be enjoyed at a rocky, jagged precipice named Rough Ridge (EB 3.7). Considered one of best short hikes on the parkway, the hike is great for photo ops and fall colors. Parking is at MP 302.8 for the 0.6-mile route up to the Rough Ridge precipice. At the northeast end, the trail passes apple orchards and pastureland, blanketed in spring wildflowers.

Three trails intersect the MST from EB 6.7 to EB 7.2: the Daniel Boone Scout Trail, the Nuwati Trail (*nuwati* means "medicine" in Tsalagi, the Cherokee language), and the Asutsi Trail (*asutsi* is Tsalagi for "bridge"). The Nuwati follows the route of an old logging railroad. The Asutsi is a short, easy trail (0.4 mile) that is used solely as an access trail from nearby US 221 to the Tanawha/MST, mostly in winter when the parkway can be closed due to snow and you cannot drive to the Boone Fork Parking Area. Pay close attention to blazes and signs to stay on the MST.

Boone Fork Trail is a moderate 5.2-mile, heavily trafficked loop trail that is the main MST trailhead on the parkway flank of Grandfather. Along the trail are cranberries in bog landscapes and a twenty-five-foot waterfall. It starts and ends a mile from the MST at the picnic area in Julian Price Memorial Park (4,200 acres of hardwood forest, with a 129-site campground). Price, the founder of one of the nation's largest insurance companies, purchased this land as a recreation area for his employees. When he died in 1946, his heirs gave the land to the Blue Ridge Parkway as a memorial. It is at MP 297, directly adjacent to Cone Park. Price Lake is considered by many to be one of the most gorgeous lakes in the state.

At EB 14.2 you cross the Boone Fork's eighty-foot bridge, constructed between August and October 2016. The $250,000 project was funded by the Recreational Trails Program, with matching funds from the Blue Ridge Parkway Foundation. Volunteers from the Grandfather/Tanawha Task Force, headed by Randy Johnson, and many volunteers from Appalachian State University's Delta Sigma Phi fraternity did most of the site-preparation work. Since the location is 1.2 miles from any road, tools, equipment, and bridge components were delivered to the site by helicopter. At EB 15.6 hikers reach Shulls Mill Road. A hundred years ago Shulls Mills was a busy sawmill town, but it became a victim of the Depression and the Great Flood of 1940.

Moses H. Cone Memorial Park (EB 16) is a 3,500-acre country estate in Blowing Rock, on the parkway between MP 292 and 295, with access at MP 294. In the early 1900s, Moses Cone's textile mills led the world in the production of high-quality denim. Moses and Bertha Cone, the son and daughter of German and Jewish immigrants, built their summer retreat with nature and conservation in mind in the mid-1890s, and in 1949 the land was donated to the National Park Service. Visit Flat Top Manor (established in 1891), an estate with twenty-three rooms (today home to the Southern Highland Craft Guild craft shop, a bookstore, and a park office) and magnificent views. A carriage house and apple orchard are open to the curious. Cone Park played a major role in the growth of Blowing Rock in its early years.

There are interesting side trips at Cone Park on twenty-five miles of winding carriage trails. The MST joins the Rich Mountain Trail at EB 16, meandering along meadows and past grazing cattle. Nearby is the three-mile Deer Park Loop, through beautiful old forests and abundant wildflowers. Go left on Flat Top Mountain Road before reaching the Manor House for a side trip to the Cone gravesites (0.9 mile) and Flat Top Mountain Tower at Cone Park (2.4 miles). It's an easy ramble up Flat Top (elevation 4,469 feet), with wildflowers along the path to the four-story tower.

Blowing Rock to Deep Gap

At EB 23.6 turn right for a relaxed route into Blowing Rock, a tourist-friendly mountain town. With plentiful restaurants, shops, and lodging, most within walking distance of the town center, it's great for pedestrians. It's also an ideal place to take a break from trail camping, with several reasonably priced inns. Jan Karon's best-selling Mitford books got their start as a series in the *Blowing Rocket*, the town's paper. Nearby is the family attraction Tweetsie Railroad, which was a nickname for the narrow-gauge East Tennessee and Western North Carolina Railroad that ran from Johnson City, Tennessee, to Boone in 1882.

The town was chartered in 1889 and is named for the Blowing Rock, a formation overhanging the Johns River gorge. Northwest winds rush through the gorge's walls with so much force that it causes snow to fall upside down. The Blowing Rock is known as North Carolina's oldest travel attraction, drawing visitors since 1933.

The graveyard at the Mount Bethel Reformed Church contains the graves of two Revolutionary War soldiers. Organized in 1886, it's the oldest church in Blowing Rock. In April 2018, over 100 unmarked graves were found at a site now believed to date back to around 1750. The graves are

Fringed phacelias abound along the carriage trail through Deer Park Loop of the Rich Mountain Trail in Moses Cone Memorial Park.
Photo by Mary Bengtson; used by permission.

now marked with small headstones and footstones. First Independent Baptist was once the Blowing Rock Negro Community Church (1949–80) and the first African American church to serve the Possum Hollow Road community.

The Green Park Inn

Chestnut trees play a prominent role at Blowing Rock's Green Park Inn, where the beautiful wood is displayed throughout—chestnut beams, a chestnut mantel, and even on the menu, with meals served on a plank of chestnut in the Chestnut Grill. The Green Park Inn has served travelers seeking the beauty of the High Country, only minutes from downtown Blowing Rock, since 1891. It is the last remaining grand manor hotel in western North Carolina. When it was built, the Appalachian forests were about one-fourth American chestnut—the largest tree in eastern North America—but a chestnut blight appeared in 1904, and by the 1940s most chestnuts had died. The American Chestnut Foundation, based in Asheville, is fighting to bring the tree back to prominence.

Boone: Only a Short Car Trip Away

Boone is a bustling college town located about six miles from the MST at Blowing Rock (EB 23.6, US 221/321). The town was named after Daniel Boone, whose cabin stood just a few hundred feet away from the courthouse when Watauga County was formed in 1849. Fifty years later, in 1899, the Watauga Academy (now Appalachian State University) was founded. At an elevation of 3,333 feet, Boone is a lively place to enjoy the mountains and a hub for outdoor adventures—it's commonly referred to as the "Ski Capital of the South"—with amenities that hikers and families will enjoy, such as Doc Watson Day, Horn in the West, summer concerts at the Jones House, and visits to the Watauga Farmers Market or Mast General Store.

Back on the Trail

There are good sights along this section. A walk through a pasture might bring out the cows to stare you down. There is a large rock shelf between Thunder Hill Overlook and Raven Rock Parking Area (EB 25.7–26.7). Hiking east after the trail enters the woods past Thunder Hill Overlook, when you come to a log bench, the trail goes to the right around a big rock, but if you go left, you go to the bottom of the rock where the rock makes a large overhang. You can see stains from campfire smoke on the roof of the overhang. Just before reaching Raven Rock Parking Area, side trails lead you under more rock overhangs.

At EB 29.5, you follow an old roadbed, a relic mountain road that conveys what travel was like before the parkway. Good photo ops can be found while rock-hopping along and on the bridge over High Shoals Creek, as well as at the Goshen Creek Viaduct. Allen de Hart used to say the "enchanted forest" (EB 32.2–33.2) was the prettiest woods in the area, and at EB 35.7, he identified a heritage apple orchard. At EB 35.8 you walk past Parkway Elementary School.

A "Big Push" in 2011 drew volunteers from across the state to finish the final five miles of the MST with the Watauga Task Force. The fifty-foot High Shoals Creek Bridge opened in 2013 (EB 29.9), made of preformed fiberglass components with wood tread. The construction costs of $47,500 came from the Recreational Trails Program, locally raised funds, and the Friends' cash reserves, with volunteer labor from the Watauga Task Force.

The Junaluska Community

It might surprise you to know that one of Appalachia's oldest Black communities is in Boone, just a few miles from the MST. Many residents of Junaluska are descendants of enslaved people, and the community has historically been segregated from the mostly white town. Located on a hillside near downtown Boone, at the foot of Howard's Knob, Junaluska sits on steep land few white residents wanted. The oldest standing houses date to the late nineteenth century. After Emancipation, many former enslaved people became sharecroppers and received or purchased land. The community became close-knit, with residents knowing that they could depend on each other. Residents survived on subsistence agriculture, family gardens, hogs, and chickens. They made their own entertainment and had their own Black baseball team, known as the Mountain Lions. Prior to 1964, residents were restricted to menial jobs such as working as farmhands and housemaids. The community boasted a small grocery store, a school, a hairdresser, and a one-chair barbershop. Even after desegregation in the mid-1960s, Junaluska residents rarely went into Boone at night because it was unsafe, and racist violence was common.

The 102-year-old Boone Mennonite Brethren Church, one of six Black Mennonite churches in North Carolina, practices a mix of Mennonite theology and African American traditions. The church was the center of Junaluska's community from the 1930s to the 1950s. In 2017, efforts by the Junaluska Heritage Association helped secure a monument in the Old Boone Cemetery dedicated to 165 mostly unmarked graves in the segregated Black section, begun as a cemetery for enslaved people. Junaluska City Park is located at 135 Bear Way in Boone, and nearby is accessible Howards Knob County Park. *Junaluska: Oral Histories of a Black Appalachian Community*, edited by Susan E. Keefe and the Junaluska Heritage Association, is an oral history of the community and a worthwhile read to help understand this small but important piece of Black Appalachia.

Deep Gap to Laurel Springs

These days, it is not uncommon to see wild turkeys in the High Country. In 2021, the wild turkey harvest broke the record as the highest (28,403 birds harvested) during North Carolina's five-week turkey hunting season, according to the North Carolina Wildlife Commission. The eastern wild turkey is a majestic bird with a wingspan of up to five feet and weighing up to twenty-four pounds. Wild turkeys roam most of the state, mostly preferring forests but often wandering into more open areas in search of food (nuts and seeds, leaves, and insects). Despite their size, they are capable and graceful fliers, often roosting high up in the trees to evade predators and find food. Listen for their calls, and if you're lucky, maybe you'll catch sight of a male strutting near the trail. These "tom turkeys" or "gobblers" puff up and strut around, shaking and displaying their magnificent feathers. This turkey trot is most often used to attract a mate ("hens") but may also be done to show dominance.

A marker at the Cascades Recreation Area pullover at EB 45.3 (MP 271.9) describes the park named in honor of native North Carolinian E. B. Jeffress. It reads, "600 acres of mountain, field and forest comprise this memorial to the late E. B. Jeffress. Mr. Jeffress rose to prominence as a newspaper publisher. While Chair of the State Highway Commission in 1934, he was instrumental in routing the Blue Ridge Parkway through scenic North Carolina. Teacher—Journalist—Public Servant— The memory of E. B. Jeffress is honored here on a portion of the land he loved." Much of his life was lived in Greensboro, where he was mayor from 1925 to 1929 and helped establish the Greensboro–High Point Airport.

In addition to the Cascades Recreation Area, the park includes the Cool Springs Baptist Church and Rev. Jesse Brown cabin historic area (EB 44.7). According to the National Park Service informational display for Cool Springs Baptist Church, on summer Sundays of long ago, mountain families gathered to hear circuit-riding preachers expound from the shade of a big maple tree. Later, the reconstructed "church" served as a weather shelter.

At the Cascades Recreation Area a 0.8-mile loop trail showcases Falls Creek, which glides along the edges of the trails until it reaches Cascades Falls, a high, pounding waterfall down a cliffside. Falls Creek continues down fifty feet to an upper overlook and another 200 feet to a lower overlook. Water and restrooms are available at the Cascades pullover.

Ashe County is home to the MST for thirty miles, from around E. B. Jeffress Park to Laurel Springs at NC 18. From the MST it is about seven miles to Jefferson. Arts-related assets of the area include barn quilts on the Ashe County Barn Quilt Trail (wooden panels and murals on building walls) and seventeen murals in downtown West Jefferson. The area is also part of Blue Ridge Music Trail and Blue Ridge National Heritage Area. Festivals and annual events in the area include the New

Jim Hallsey, MST
visionary since 1977
and volunteer for
Ashe County, in E. B.
Jeffress Park at the
Jesse Brown cabin.
Photo by Jerry Barker.

River Blues Festival, Art on the Mountain, the Artisan Festival, the Ashe County Fiddler's Convention, the North Carolina Downhill Race at Mount Jefferson State Natural Area, the Annual Canoe Race on the New River, and the Festival of the Frescoes. At St. Mary's Episcopal Church, three frescoes painted by noted muralist Ben Long in 1974 are well worth a visit.

Home to the state's oldest cheese-making plant since 1930, West Jefferson also features the Mountain Bogs National Wildlife Refuge, the first wildlife refuge in western North Carolina. There is also a large cattle-farming industry and lots of pumpkins. In the fall, the county hosts the Corn Maze and Pumpkin Festival. The agricultural highlight for Ashe County is Christmas trees, a $95 million industry for the "Christmas Tree Capital of America." Fraser firs, one of the most popular varieties for the holidays, thrive here due to climate and elevation. The county is one of the top producers in the nation, a huge economic benefit to farmers, with "choose and cut" venues attracting many tourists during November and December. Recreational opportunities in the county include biking, canoeing, kayaking, tubing, trout fishing, and, according to the website Disc Golf Scene, the best disc golf course in North Carolina.

Near Jefferson, New River State Park covers 3,323 acres in the protected New River watershed. The river's South Fork is one of the oldest rivers in the United States, and twenty-two miles are designated as a National Wild and Scenic River, one of only five in North Carolina. Easy paddling, shallow water, mild rapids, and spectacular scenery make the New River accessible and attractive to inexperienced paddlers. The ancient, north-ward-flowing river passes through valleys and bottom lands, including many stretches through remote countryside.

The MST passes through a hillside meadow near the parkway's Mount Jefferson Overlook (EB 50.6; MSP 266.8). When the parkway first opened, the overlook sign pointed out to Negro Mountain, so named for suppos-edly being a hideout for enslaved people fleeing north. Citizens of Ashe County had the name changed to Phoenix Mountain Overlook around 1950 and again to Mount Jefferson in 1960. At EB 56.5 a side trail heads uphill to the Wyatt and Bare Cemetery, shaded by a giant oak tree. This cemetery includes eighty-six graves with headstones featuring names and dates (dating to 1824) and more with fieldstone head and foot markers, which usually identify the graves of enslaved people.

When hiking eastbound you intersect with the Jumpinoff Rock sign at EB 56.9, where the overlook view is 100 feet to the right. Jumpinoff Rock was purchased by the Conservation Trust for North Carolina in 2001 and transferred to the National Park Service in 2005. About a half mile farther on the MST is Jumpinoff Rock Overlook parking (MP 260.3).

The area around EB 59.1 is busy, with the Northwest Trading Post, New River Inn and Cabins, and the community of Glendale Springs, which is 0.5 mile to the left, just off the parkway on NC 16. Glendale Springs has two historic churches, a crafts store, lodging, restaurants, and Glendale Springs Inn and Restaurant, an elegant country inn built over 120 years ago and listed on the National Register of Historic Places.

The first hiking pilgrimage on the MST was organized by Dottie Cooke and Betsey and David Horth for ten members of Holy Trinity Episcopal Church in Greensboro in May 2019. On June 6, 2019, it was reported on the Friends of the MST webpage as the "May Pilgrimage on the Moun-tains-to-Sea Trail." Hiker ages ranged from fifty-four to seventy-seven. The group's favorite places were "Station's Inn Motorcycle Resort and Freeborne's Eatery and Lodge in Laurel Springs" (EB 71.3). They also "had a wonderful time ending our day's hike in the bar, a delicious dinner in the restaurant and good night's sleep in the motel."

More MST History

Lore from the trail includes the story of MST founder Allen de Hart and task force leader Don Bergey discovering stacks of rocks when they were scouting where to blaze the trail. The stones are located a bit south of MP 254 on the parkway. The current route of the trail passes them on the west side of the parkway. Though not very visible during summer, they are quite visible in the winter after the leaves fall. Ashe County MST leader Jim Hallsey, the thirty-second person to thru-hike the MST (and paddle the rivers), wrote,

> Allen and I had the Park Service archeologist visit them while he was surveying the section of the MST prior to construction. The archeologist's opinion was that these stacks of rocks were probably military in purpose. As such, soldiers during the Civil War may have constructed these "pickets" as defensive structures for defending a gap or suspected enemy travel way. He said it was common for commanding officers of infantry soldiers with time on their hands to order them to "build pickets." We speculated that Union soldiers would have been well familiar with such stacking methods from clearing farm fields. The presence of Union forces under [Gen. William Tecumseh] Sherman in the area is known and documented near US 421 in Deep Gap where there are hand-dug defensive breast works. The rock piles remain a mystery and great fodder for the imagination of winter hikers. It's not Stonehenge, but it's interesting.

Back on the Trail

You can visit the Sam Miller Cemetery at EB 60.3 by following the gravel road on the right instead of turning onto the MST. The road leads to the Sheets Cemetery at EB 65.1. Go around the Sheets Cemetery gate and pass the MST turn. Follow the gravel road to its end. You can also bushwhack a shorter route farther down the trail if you look up at the ridge on your left. It is easier to see it in winter. Martin Sheets acquired the cemetery land through the Homestead Act in the 1770s; the land was valued at ten cents an acre and bought by trading corn.

Across the parkway from the trail (MP 252.3; EB 65.9), you'll see Jesse Sheets's log cabin, built in 1818 by his father, Andrew. The cabin shows how one family lived in the mountains from 1815 until the 1930s. Just before reaching NC 18, the high, 546-foot-long parkway bridge on the left, built in 1939, will be replaced in 2024.

In this section, hikers will frequently spot running cedar, also known as ground cedar or clubmoss. When it reproduces each year, the spore-bearing structures are yellow. Photographers of old would collect the yellow spores and use them for primitive flash power.

Laurel Springs to Devils Garden Overlook

At EB 72.1, Miller's Campground, just off the MST, is a wonderful layover for hikers or tourists. John S. Miller (1835–1929) married Biddie Long (1834–85) in 1857, and they had eleven children. After Biddie's death, John married Belle Kerr and they had seven children together. Biddie Long's ancestors had received four land grants in the late 1700s, totaling 40,000 acres. Each of John's eighteen children received a minimum of 200 acres at age eighteen. John and Biddie are buried in the John Sam Miller Cemetery at the top of the hill, up past the tent sites. Visitors are welcome; it is also a great place to watch the sunset. MST hikers may request a discount for tent sites.

Craig Miller, whose great-grandfather was John S. Miller, shared several stories about the northern parkway area. His grandpa Fred sharpened the drill bits for the Works Progress Administration workers cutting the parkway from the sheer cliffs that extend from Alligator Back to the Bluffs. The rock face where the parkway was cut was called the Ice Rocks, and this ice is responsible for the parkway's being closed in winter weather.

Miller heard stories of land in the area selling for fifty cents an acre in the early 1900s. On Grassy Gap Lane there is a large white farmhouse on the left. Johnny Miller (1863–1932) built the house around 1920, and the property passed from him to his son-in-law John Woodruff when the parkway split the property in that area in the 1930s. The Woodruffs donated the farmhouse and land to the Friends of the Blue Ridge Parkway, who pledged to restore it.

At EB 74.3 the parkway maintenance center can be seen down to the right from the MST. The Civilian Conservation Corps (CCC) camp that housed workers who helped build the parkway in the 1930s was on this same site. During FDR's New Deal, CCC workers were paid thirty dollars a week, with twenty-five dollars sent home. Laurel Springs was the only CCC site along North Carolina's northern parkway.

Beginning at EB 74.6 at the Basin Cove Overlook (MP 244.7), the MST follows the Bluff Mountain Trail for 7.5 miles as it traverses the Doughton Park area along the parkway. The relatively level trail boasts a good number of scenic vistas. In this area, the MST runs near the parkway and is accessible from many locations along its route from Basin Cove Overlook to Brinegar Cabin. One fun option is to park at the restrooms in the Doughton Park Parking Area immediately off the parkway at MP 241 (EB 78.7) to walk the meadows. This might be the easiest trail in Doughton Park and the one with the most views. Online review comments include "big views, cow patties, steep climb north of Alligators Back, dogs on leash, very sunny, cold and icy in winter"—it's got everything!

Located between parkway MP 238.5 and 244.7 is the Bluffs Recreation Area, a 6,000-acre park created in 1935 when the parkway was routed through this part of North Carolina as part of the New Deal. Renamed Doughton Park in 1953, it was one of the first parks to be completed and remains the largest recreation area the National Park Service manages on the parkway. In late spring, the park is full of blooming flame azaleas and rhododendrons. In the summer, visitors can enjoy guided nature walks and craft demonstrations. More than thirty miles of hiking trails traverse Doughton Park's pastures and streams, all of them easily accessible from the highly rated campground. Trails range in difficulty, so there's something for everyone, from those looking for easy strolls to those wanting more of a strenuous challenge.

The park is named after North Carolina politician Robert L. "Bob" Doughton, who played a key role in the parkway's creation. It is thought that Doughton sold much of this park land to the parkway in the 1930s. Originally from Laurel Springs, Doughton was a successful farmer and banker before entering politics. He owned over 5,000 acres in his native Alleghany County by 1900. In 1911, Doughton was elected to the US House of Representatives as a Democrat, and he served for forty-two consecutive years, through 1953. During his time in Congress, he oversaw the passage of the Social Security Act in 1935. Doughton died in 1954 at age ninety and is buried beside his wife, Lillie, in the cemetery at Laurel Springs Baptist Church. The Robert Doughton House, off NC 18 two miles from the parkway, was listed on the National Register of Historic Places in 1979 and is now the Doughton Hall Bed and Breakfast.

Task force leader Jeff Brewer told how Friends of the MST mobilized volunteers in the late 1990s to build new trails along the northern parkway. Many Friday–Sunday workdays, some called Big Digs to attract large numbers of workers, tackled trail-building from Devils Garden Overlook to the Bluffs, and then from the Bluffs to Basin Overlook, then from NC 18 to NC 16, until it was all completed. "We used Doughton Park campground as a base camp and always had a tradition of eating at the Bluffs Restaurant for Saturday night dinner. Saturday nights around the campfire were short as we were all so tired and ready for bed and back up early Sunday for another day of trail work. We hosted many college groups from ASU and UNC-CH and had good volunteer support. In 2006 we had an American Hiking Society 'Volunteer Vacation' group that did trail building for a week, with people from across the US." Brewer also served as board president of the newly formed Friends of the MST, so board meetings were often conducted while eating lunch at parkway overlooks.

In 2021, the Bluffs Restaurant at Doughton Park (BluffsRestaurant .org, MP 241) was reborn. It is open seasonally spring through fall (closed Monday and Tuesday), serving three meals daily, with beer and wine available. The Blue Ridge Parkway Foundation spearheaded renovation efforts. The restaurant opened as the Bluffs Coffee Shop and Gas Station in 1949 and closed in 2010. The now-abandoned Woods picnic area was designated for African Americans (from 1942 to the 1960s). The Bluffs was the first dining facility on the parkway. The Bluffs Lodge, with its rustic stonework and magnificent meadow view, was built in 1950 and closed in 2010 due to its age, insufficient finances, and lack of an operator.

Along the parkway in North Carolina, just south of the Virginia border, sits Bluff Mountain. While not as tall as other mountains in the state, it still stands out and is easily recognizable because of its "Alligator Back" formation. This geological feature, commonly seen in other areas of the North Carolina High Country, is made up of schist (rock identified by grainy layers of minerals) and gneiss (similar to schist but formed at higher temperatures). Because of these rock compositions, which peek through the meadows and forests, Bluff Mountain has survived the erosion that has worn down the Appalachians. The views from the summits and overlooks in this area are as grand and mesmerizing as any in the eastern United States. (Bluff Mountain is not to be confused with the Bluff Mountain Preserve, nearby in Warrensville and West Jefferson.)

The Bluff Mountain Trail traverses the Doughton Park Area along the parkway, sharing footpath with the MST. The trail's terrain is relatively level and provides a number of impressive views.

Nearby

The Caudill Cabin looks isolated 800 feet below Wildcat Rocks Overlook at the Bluffs (MP 241; short spur from EB 78.7; there is a memorial marker for Robert Doughton), but in reality the structure was part of the vibrant Basin Cove community of over fifty families. Martin and Janie Caudill raised six children in the cabin and cleared ten to fifteen acres of fertile bottom lands. Their children attended school for four months each year, with fifty students and one teacher. The Caudills moved to Virginia in 1906 and back to Basin Cove in 1915, but to another cabin. The community, with cabins, a church, a school, crops, and livestock, was washed away in the great flood of 1916, except for the Caudill cabin. After the flood, they stayed with their "neighbors," the Brinegars, for three days and later moved back to Virginia. Robert Doughton purchased the Basin Cove area after the great flood and donated it to the National Park Service in 1938. The cabin was restored in 2001. The cabin is accessed from Long Bottom Road in Stone Mountain State Park.

It's hard to say just how much of the MST crosses meadows and open areas. Speculation varies on what caused these open areas and balds. Some suggest that they stem from past agricultural use, fires set by nature or Native Americans, elk and cattle grazing, or erosion from the last ice age. Not only are the vistas enjoyed by hikers, but these open areas also provide habitat for birds and other animals, and are worth preserving for their environmental diversity. Open areas are threatened as shrubs, trees, and invasive plants encroach. Keep in mind that the Blue Ridge Parkway allows cattle grazing, so you'll often find cow patties along the MST and will have to climb a stile or wooden ladder to cross a fence.

Some of the largest open areas along the MST are in the High Country of Segment 5. In the Moses H. Cone Memorial Park, near Blowing Rock, the MST uses its carriage trail system through a mix of wooded and open land. Hikers will find a "pasture with a view" uphill of the Mount Jefferson Overlook, scenic meadows along Blue Ridge Church Road, and many more open areas along the parkway and country roads. Farther east and north about ten miles of meadows and pastures are scattered along Doughton Park, Grassy Gap, Air Bellows Gap, and Devils Garden

Along the Blue Ridge Parkway at the 1886 Brinegar Cabin. *Photo by Jerry Barker.*

Overlook. Many smaller plots of open land are visible as you walk east on the MST.

The MST goes right through the Brinegars' front yard. A marker at the Brinegar Cabin Parking Area (EB 81.9; MP 238.5) reads, "The Brinegars were not famous or rich, but important to their families and neighbors. In 1876 Martin Brinegar purchased the 125-acre farm from Henderson Crouse, Caroline Joines' uncle, for $200. Two years later Martin and Caroline married; he was 21 and she was 16." This is a great cultural heritage stop, with parking, historical markers, and several buildings to explore. In the summer, there are gardening, weaving, and interpretive history talks. The parkway purchased the Brinegars' property in 1935, and Caroline didn't leave the cabin until parkway traffic got too noisy for her.

It's difficult for folks now to understand how challenging things must have been for the Brinegar family. The Brinegars' lives were defined by hard work, self-sufficiency, and a deep faith. Looking at this farmstead today, one wonders what the winters would have been for the Brinegar family (note that the buildings were strategically located to protect them from ridge-top winds). How did they travel? Where was the nearest store? Where was the school or nearest doctor? Going to church was for faith but also for "social media": networking and social life.

Thurmond Chatham Game Land covers 6,529 acres on the eastern side of the parkway (in two parcels) and is administered by North Carolina Wildlife Resources Commission. Its combination with Doughton Park (6,300 acres) and Stone Mountain State Park (14,351 acres) forms an extraordinary amount of contiguous protected land, providing natural habitat for wildlife—it's a black bear sanctuary—as well as great views for hikers and tourists. Thurman Chatham represented North Carolina in the US House, was a philanthropist, and ran Chatham Manufacturing Company (founded by his grandfather), then the world's largest manufacturer of blankets.

What's the Weather Like in North Carolina?

There is a lot of seasonal variation, regional variation, and daily variation. Few days demonstrate the variety quite like August 9, 2020, did. The 5.1-magnitude earthquake that hit Sparta was North Carolina's worst in 102 years. The epicenter was three miles from Devils Garden, where the MST begins descending to Stone Mountain State Park. The same day, a tornado touched down in Bladen County (MST Segments 12–13), and a hurricane caused damage along the North Carolina coast. Scout's motto: Be prepared.

Segment 5 ends at EB 84.9, Devils Garden Overlook (MP 235.7), and eastbound hikers descend into the Piedmont region of North Carolina.

PIEDMONT REGION

308.2 MILES

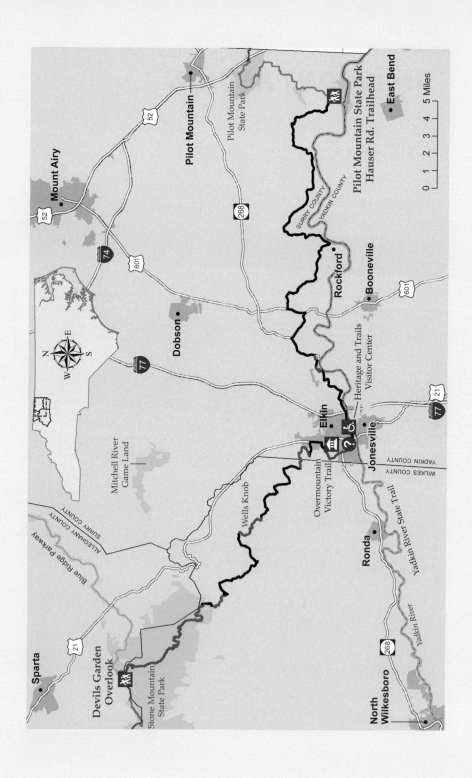

Mount Airy

Pilot Mountain

Pilot Mountain State Park

East Bend

Pilot Mountain State Park
Hauser Rd. Trailhead

0 1 2 3 4 5 Miles

52

52

52

268

74

601

SURRY COUNTY
YADKIN COUNTY

Rockford

Booneville

601

Dobson

77

N
E
W
S

Mitchell River
Game Land

Heritage and Trails
Visitor Center

Elkin

Jonesville

21

77

YADKIN COUNTY
WILKES COUNTY

ALLEGHANY COUNTY
SURRY COUNTY

Blue Ridge Parkway

Wells Knob

Overmountain
Victory Trail

Ronda

Yadkin River State Trail

Sparta

21

Devils Garden
Overlook

Stone Mountain
State Park

North
Wilkesboro

268

Yadkin River

The Elkin Valley

Devils Garden Overlook to Pilot Mountain State Park

69.2 MILES

When you have worn out your shoes, the strength of the
shoe leather has passed into the fiber of your body.

RALPH WALDO EMERSON

It's hard to miss the two peaks that bookend this segment—Stone Mountain and Pilot Mountain—but as you hike this section, you'll love the town of Elkin and the Yadkin River. Two state parks provide amenities for outdoor adventure for the family. The Elkin Valley Trails Association has built much of the MST in this segment and sponsors a weekend North Carolina Trail Days with the motto "All trails lead to Elkin" (elkinvalleytrails.org).

Devils Garden Overlook to Elkin

A hike of this Piedmont area begins going east at Devils Garden Overlook (MP 235.7), elevation 3,428 feet. The MST makes a steep descent into the Elkin Valley, six miles down into Stone Mountain State Park, following Widow's Creek the last mile. By the junction with Stone Mountain Road, elevation 1,310 feet, the trail has dropped over 2,100 feet.

Mahogany Rock Cable Car

Near the Devils Garden Overlook was the Mahogany Rock Cable Car, which used to be one of the longest gondola cables in the country. In the 1960s, the line, owned by Worth Folger, included four cars. Early on,

Mahogany Rock encountered challenges, including clogging the Blue Ridge Parkway with traffic and lacking sufficient parking. It cost fifty cents to ride, but business was hurt by frequent high winds and cold, foggy weather. Folger sold the Mahogany, the nearby housing development, and the 250 acres it sat on, to The Nature Conservancy for "$10 and other considerations," and it was soon passed to the National Park Service. The cable car system and housing development were removed in the late 1970s.

From the overlook, go eastbound 0.4 mile where the MST goes left "on old forest road." If instead you turn right on the "old forest road" and go about a quarter of a mile, you will get to foundations with steel supports for the tramway, a gift shop, and restaurant. The cable cars actually left from Mahogany Rock Mountain, which is the peak to the northeast, then landed at the top of Scott Ridge, on this concrete pad.

Back on the Trail

As you come down from the parkway on the MST, look closely at your feet and sometimes you will see BB-sized garnets. In Stone Mountain Park, just after a 130-degree switchback, there is a steel drum on your left (EB 2.5). Closer examination shows it to be remnants of a moonshine still. Over 160 still sites have been located within the park boundaries. While we don't encourage off-trail hiking, if you do so in Stone Mountain Park, there is a good chance you will run into an old still site.

North Carolina has created popular drinks such as Pepsi Cola in New Bern and Cheerwine in Salisbury, but during Prohibition we also helped popularize moonshine. Moonshine was "distilled in the light of the moon," thus the name, and its history goes back to colonial days. The backwoods and creeks around Stone Mountain were havens for moonshine stills, out of sight of lawmen. Wilkes County dubbed itself the "moonshine capital of the world." The raw ingredients were available, and fast cars delivered the finished product to thirsty towns along the East Coast. Some say that NASCAR got its start in 1948 when these fast drivers wanted to race stock cars at local tracks in North Carolina.

Around EB 2.6–2.8, as you go down the ridge, you can sometimes catch a glimpse of the "Forbidden Falls," over 200 feet high, if the leaves are off the trees. They are called the Forbidden Falls because there are no trails to the top or bottom. You cross the creek that comes from the falls at EB 2.8.

The 600-foot granite monolith, Stone Mountain, viewed from the MST as it crosses Cedar Rock. *Photo by Joe Mickey; used by permission.*

Stone Mountain is a 600-foot granite dome about four miles in circumference, with portions in both Wilkes and Alleghany Counties. The North Carolina Division of Parks and Recreation details the amenities of the park best: "The massive dome at Stone Mountain State Park keeps watch on park visitors enjoying nearly every type of outdoor activity—hiking, picnicking, horseback riding and more. There are more than 18 miles of trails, matched by more than 20 miles of designated trout waters in this park that spreads below the Blue Ridge Parkway. A campground offers 90 sites, and backpacking campsites are nearby. Rock climbing is allowed by permit on the towering granite face of the landmark mountain." The MST covers eleven miles within the 14,353 acres of the state park, which was established in 1969 and designated a National Natural Landmark in 1974. The MST lies between Devils Garden through the park to the entrance on John P. Frank Parkway (EB 13). At EB 4.7 join the Widow Creek Trail.

After you depart the backpack parking lot at EB 5.7, Garden Creek Baptist Church is located on the bank of the East Prong of Roaring River (500 yards to the right on Stone Mountain Road). Constructed in 1897, it is one of the few churches in Wilkes County untouched by major repairs or renovations, and it still holds services on Sundays.

The Hutchinson Historic Homestead cabin with Stone Mountain in the background. *Photo by Jerry Barker.*

You'll likely encounter an old standing chimney and another one not far off the trail—these remnants from the past can't help but grab your attention. A roof deteriorates, logs or framing will eventually rot, but the stones stay behind. Stone chimney and rock foundation remains are frequently evidence of house fires that began in fireplaces and wood stoves, mostly in the times before fire departments or running water.

You can spot important history near here. "My grandfather (with 4 greats in front) sold Solomon Campbell 100 acres on the mountain now called Campbell Mountain, that can be viewed from Wolf Rocks" (short right at EB 8), writes Keith Sidden, a local trail maintainer. "Solomon was a freed slave thanks to the Emancipation Proclamation, and he chose to call this beautiful place home. He raised a family here. His two sons created a newspaper called the Intelligent Banner that was operated from their home." At EB 8.2 merge left with Cedar Rock Trail (marked with red circles.)

Stone Mountain State Park's Hutchinson Homestead (near EB 8.9) features a log cabin, barn, blacksmith shop, corncrib, meat house, and original furnishings. Originally built in 1855, the farm grew to over 400 acres. It was restored in 1998, and today recordings and informational displays provide insights on how the farm ran and the daily lives of early European settlers in the area. During peak tourist season, the homestead is open to visitors on weekends, but make sure to check with the Park Service to confirm.

The alternate 4.5-mile Stone Mountain Loop Trail is worth a side trip from the MST. Go down the gravel road from the Hutchinson Homestead a short distance, and the round-orange-blazed trail begins on the right. The trail climbs wooden steps to the summit, then meanders across the top where there are intriguing rock erosion features, somewhat like a skateboard park. When the loop trail reaches an old chimney, a blue-blazed trail to the left leads to Upper Trailhead Parking and 500 yards farther to the campground. The trail to the right leads to descending stairs past the 200-foot Stone Mountain Falls and soon rejoins the MST. At the white blaze for the MST, turn left to continue eastbound. The MST through Stone Mountain was rerouted in 2020, so pay careful attention to white blazes. At EB 13 turn left on John Frank Parkway and reach the Stone Mountain Country Store at EB 14.2.

The MST follows the Wells Knob Trail for about two miles (EB 22–24.4) up and over a steep, "switchbacky" knob (elevation 1,865 feet, prominence 465 feet; easement granted 2022). About a mile farther, hike 2.1 miles east on Shoaley Branch Road (EB 25–26.6). This quiet, country gravel road is surrounded by pastureland, with a farm and large white barn on the left. Carter Falls Trailhead (EB 29.9) is off Martin Byrd Road. Above Carter Falls are low dam remnants of Carter Falls Power Company. The ruins of a concrete building are what remains of the powerhouse for this early dam on Elkin Creek. The actual dam is located some 1,000 feet upstream of the building. A planned reroute of the MST will take it near this building and the dam.

Carter Falls? It's Elkin's Fault

The Elkin Valley Trails Association May 2020 newsletter posed the question, "What made Carter Falls?" It turns out it is Elkin's fault. To be clearer, the area is part of the Brevard earthquake fault, which runs just north of Elkin, from Alabama through Georgia and along the Blue Ridge escarpment. If you examine a terrain map you will see a straight "line" that extends from Kerr Scott Reservoir almost to Pilot Mountain. The fault is ancient, having formed about 480 to 300 million years ago. It is also considered inactive, but occasionally you might feel a small tremor. The last major earthquake in this area was on August 31, 1861, and registered 5.1 magnitude. The next time you visit Carter Falls, be aware that the earth shaking under your feet may not be the power of the falls. It just might be Elkin's fault.

Megan Stainback and her children enjoying Carter Falls along Elkin Creek (added to NC State Parks in 2017 and maintained by Elkin Valley Trails Association). *Photo by Bob Hillyer; used by permission.*

All the rivers and creeks that come down from the mountains have waterfalls along this line. The largest area waterfall is Carter Falls on Big Elkin Creek in Yadkin County. But there are also falls and cascades on the Roaring River, Grassy Creek, Mitchell River, Fisher River, and Ararat River. A hundred years ago, many mills grew up along these falls to take advantage of the waterpower they supplied.

I highly recommend you make time to see Carter Falls. With a total drop of about sixty feet, it has become a major local attraction. There's even some American history here for you: at the top of the falls on the west side is the grave of William Harris, a bodyguard for George Washington. In 1914, Elkin Power and Light Company built a ten-foot dam at the top of the falls, the seventh dam on Big Elkin Creek. A wooden flume line diverted water over 1,000 feet downstream to a powerhouse that generated electricity for Elkin and the area. Production of electricity stopped in 1967 when the flume line and the dam burst, but remnants of the foundation remain. Forty-three acres including the falls were sold by Dan Park to the state of North Carolina in 2017, and the MST was allowed access in 2018. A 165-foot suspension "Bridge of Dreams" is planned, with a reroute of the MST along the property.

Don't miss "birdhouse row" or a stop at Byrd's Branch Campground for ice cream, snacks, and camping options (EB 30.1). The Byrds are faithful

volunteers with the Elkin Valley Trails Association (EVTA; Elkinvalleytrails
.org). Next, you enter what is locally known as "the Enchanted Forest."
Look for faces in the trees and gnome houses along the trail. Many say
that close to Halloween the forest is eerie and seems haunted (EB 30.2).

What's in a Name?

The Elkin Creek used to be known as the Elkin River. One story is that
in the late 1890s the federal government passed a law that you could not
dam up a "river" without lots of permits, so locals just changed the name
to Elkin Creek. Over time at least nine dams have been built on the Elkin
Creek (meanwhile, the nearby Mitchell River had only three). Another bit
of history attached to the area dates to 1865, when the Union army under
Col. William Palmer was delighted to discover the Elkin Manufacturing
Company along the Elkin Creek. Almost out of rations, there they found
plentiful supplies of bacon, flour, butter, honey, molasses, and tobacco,
and the mill's sixty or so employees gave the soldiers a warm reception.
Union general George Stoneman's orders were to destroy any Confederate
manufacturing facilities, but because of the hospitality, Elkin Manufacturing Company was spared.

One of the dams on the Elkin Creek is the Shoe Factory Dam (EB 35.7).
Originally the dam supplied power for the manufacturing of shoes. Farther up the creek, Alexander Chatham and Thomas Lenior Gwyn opened a
wool mill in 1877. The mill eventually became the Chatham Manufacturing
Company, the largest employer in Elkin for 100 years. In 1936, it began
manufacturing upholstery for cars and in 1940 fabrics for furniture. It
shipped millions of "Chatham Blankets" to soldiers in World War I and
World War II, and in the 1940s and 1950s it was one of the largest blan-
ket manufacturers in the world. By 1988, control of the company went
abroad and, like all US textile manufacturing, its fortunes dwindled. In
2020, several of the Gwyn Gristmill's stone portions, dated from 1866,
were found after being uncovered by floods. They are now on display at
the Shoe Factory Dam rest station.

Back on the Trail

Nearby is the Grassy Creek Vineyard and Winery, 0.4 mile on a trail to
the left (EB 31). Off the Grassy Creek Trail, in 2020, the EVTA opened
the three-quarter-mile Klondike Creek Trail, the first "forest bathing trail"

along the MST. Hikers are encouraged to turn off their cell phones, put away their ear buds, and "Stroll. Listen. Look. Smile. Walk softly, stop often, close your eyes and just breathe." If you continue another quarter mile to the Grassy Creek Vineyard tasting room, you can partake of their fine wines, chocolates, and cheeses. Winemaking around Elkin dates back to the colonial era. It continues today with certification as an American Viticultural Area due to its suitable climate and terrain. At EB 31.6, a 0.4-mile hike on the Skull Camp spur trail will take you to restaurants and one of Elkin's craft breweries.

Elkin opened the new Hurt Bridge in memory of Harold and Kay Hurt in 2020. They lived in the white farmhouse before the bridge was built and were thrilled that the MST traversed their property.

Just after passing a restroom, joining the Elkin and Alleghany Railroad bed, and crossing a 178-foot bridge over Elkin Creek, you will pass the first of two gongs (EB 35 and 35.2). The first gong is dedicated to John Hillyer (who wrote about the MST and was Bob Hillyer's dad), an early supporter of the MST who helped flag and build much of the MST trail in the Asheville area. The second gong is a quarter mile farther on your left. Legend has it that ringing the gongs three times brings you luck. In 1911, Elkin leaders started building the Elkin and Allegheny Railroad from the southern line to the northwest; it was abandoned in 1931. Only eighteen miles of track were laid because the building of US Highway 21 from Elkin to Sparta made the line obsolete.

The Overmountain Victory National Historic Trail recognizes that Patriots traveled through Yadkin County and joined with another contingent of militia from present-day Elkin (EB 36.8) in the Revolutionary War. On October 7, 1780, these Americans fought in the Battle of Kings Mountain, emerging victorious over a group of British loyalists in South Carolina. It was the first major victory for the Patriots after the British invaded Charleston in May 1780, and Thomas Jefferson called it "the turn of the tide of success."

Elkin to Pilot Mountain State Park

The town of Elkin, nestled in the foothills of the Appalachians, in the Yadkin Valley, is a premier outdoor destination (elevation 906 feet). Since 2012, Elkin has groomed over twenty-two miles of off-road trails along the MST from Stone Mountain State Park to downtown Elkin, thanks to hard work by the community and members of the EVTA. Eventually, an updated MST trail will also connect Elkin to Pilot Mountain State Park. English colonists arrived in the area in the mid-eighteenth century, finding Cherokees who had settled there years before. Richard Gwyn crossed the Yadkin River from Jonesville around 1840 to settle on the north side in Elkin. He recognized the town's valuable natural resources—namely, the tree-covered hills and the powerful waters of Elkin Creek—and his family established the Elkin Manufacturing Company not long after their arrival. The Northwestern NC Railroad arrived in 1890 as waterpower drove gristmills, forges, and sawmills.

Elkin businesses look forward to MST hikers walking into their downtown, as Main Street is directly along the MST. There is a big, beautiful hiking mural on one of the buildings downtown. Look for the Daniel Boone Trail marker at North Bridges Street and West Market Street. Elkin is a great place to stay and refuel, but also near an RV primitive campground, winery, cabins, and Airbnb's. The Yadkin River always remains open for outdoor enjoyment and is a perfect excursion for fishing, kayaking, and canoeing on the "Blue Water Trail." How about the Insane Terrain 5K and 10K races? Elkin is also home to a beautiful seven-mile mountain bike trail if that's more your speed.

Elkin is also known for its many wineries, over forty, and has a Wine Hopper Shuttle on weekends from the downtown Heritage Center. There are also two microbreweries and the annual Yadkin Valley Pumpkin Festival. Elkin and the EVTA were energetic and gracious hosts of the fortieth and forty-first annual "Gathering of MST Friends." Trail angels are waiting, so let the EVTA know you are coming. As you head east from Elkin, the MST crosses the Mitchell River, rated the fifth-best trout fishing stream in North Carolina. The EVTA plans a "Spice Way" section (EB 42.4–43.9) with seasonal aromas and parking after Friendship Speedway and Gentry Road: cross the Mitchell River, then cross NC 268.

What's a Sonker?

Some places have their cobblers, crumbles, crisps, or even pies. Elkin has the sonker, a delicious baked good made from fruit and sweetened dough. It's been around since the 1800s, many believe as a way to make fruit last through hard times when produce was in short supply and pantry shelves were bare. Others say it was a way to use overripe fruit—waste not, want not. In Elkin, the sonker is serious business, as seen by the Surry Sonker Trail. Hikers on the MST can visit five sonker-serving spots near the trail:

Skull Camp Smokehouse in Elkin, Southern on Main in Elkin, Rockford General Store in the village of Rockford, Miss Angel's Heavenly Pies in Mount Airy, and Anchored Bakery in Mount Airy. North Carolina is also known for its fruit-filled handheld pies, often made at the end of the day using leftover biscuits and stewed fruit.

Back on the Trail

Near the Thunder Hill Overlook on the parkway, in the northwestern part of the state, the Yadkin River rises. It is the second-largest drainage area in North Carolina—7,221 acres—of the seventeen drainages in the state. The river flows 215 miles, then merges with the Uwharrie River south of Badin to become the Pee Dee River before it enters South Carolina and empties into the Atlantic Ocean in Georgetown. Throughout the region's history, the river has been vital to Native Americans, colonists, and industrialists. There is current evidence of fish weirs in the Elkin area of the river. With increasing development and deforestation, sedimentation and habitat destruction are key water-quality concerns. WaterShedNow.org has been formed in Elkin with a mission to celebrate and preserve the watershed. YadkinRiverkeeper.org is also a valuable source of information.

The Yadkin River MST paddle option covers twenty-eight miles from Elkin to the Pilot Mountain corridor trail. In 1985, the North Carolina General Assembly established the 163-mile Yadkin River State Trail as part of the North Carolina State Trails System. Elkin and Rockford vendors offer equipment rentals and shuttles. Caution: Don't paddle the Yadkin if the flow is too low or too high, or the temperatures too cold.

Rockford Methodist Church was built in 1914 but closed in 1964. It was purchased by the Rockford Preservation Society in 1984. Fresco artist Tony Griffin, who studied in Florence, Italy, was hired to paint a fresco mural in the church, and in 1989 he revealed his work, titled "Come unto Me."

What would you name a town located near a rocky ford? Rockford (EB 54.2), situated along the Yadkin River, was founded in 1790 and incorporated in 1819 as the seat of Surry County. While the river here may look unassuming today, those who forded it in a buggy or horse-drawn wagon centuries ago had to cross with caution. Large rocks and deep holes hidden from view made a straight crossing impossible, even treacherous. Instead, you had to follow a ripple arcing from one side to the other—a natural crossing. A ferry was approved in 1795 to move people and vehicles across the Yadkin River, but it ceased operation in 1900 when a bridge was built by R. F. Bland, a piano salesman. Bland charged people twenty-five cents to cross the bridge from the banks in Rockford to a nearby island. The original bridge was destroyed by floods in the 1930s and replaced by a modern high-rise bridge in 2002.

A number of buildings remain from Rockford's time as the county seat in the nineteenth century, most notably the old county courthouse. Rockford General Store is another popular stop where little has changed since it first opened in 1890, from its uneven wooden floors to candy displayed in glass jars; visitors can also peruse old photographs of the town for a glimpse back in time. In its heyday, Rockford hosted a number of distinguished visitors, including Andrew Jackson, Aaron Burr, and James K. Polk. To capture all this history, the Rockford Preservation Society was established in 1972. With the support of state and federal grants, the society has restored and preserved Rockford's Methodist church, the Dudley Glass store, and the post office building, all of which are open to the public today. Not long after the founding of the Rockford Preservation Society, the Rockford Historic District was listed on the National Register of Historic Places in 1976. Today, the Historic Rockford Inn Bed and Breakfast (established around 1848), on six rolling acres, is a great place to spend a night or two and get a taste of the past.

Not far from Rockford sits the community of Siloam, established in 1818 around Siloam Methodist Church, which gets its name from the biblical Pool of Siloam. The community is bordered to the south by the Yadkin River and to the east by the Ararat River, which flows between Siloam and the community of Shoals. In 1890, the former Southern Railway installed a station in the area, leading to a period of growth. Near the intersection of River Siloam Road and Siloam Road, a number of sites listed on the National Register of Historic Places can be found, including the Samuel Josiah Atkinson House, the C. C. Cundiff House, the Marion House, and the Marion Brothers Store.

The C. C. Cundiff homestead and cemetery (EB 61.2) is located on the right before Shorty's Country Store (EB 62.6) on River Siloam Road. Built around 1865 in a blend of Greek Revival and Victorian styles, the two-story brick home has two sections with a total of six rooms and a covered front porch on the first floor. In addition to the living quarters, the homestead's well and wash house, smokehouse, privy, and family cemetery still stand.

As you approach Shorty's Country Store, you see a giant pile of salt near the railroad tracks on the right. This is Scott and Creel Salt and Feed's stockpile, possibly used by the regional Department of Transportation

(DOT) during winter storms when highways are covered in snow and ice. Shorty's is a traditional, rural general store, known for its flip-flop burger, and a welcomed sight for a hungry and thirsty hiker or tourist.

On Hardy Road is the Reeves Homeplace, a stop on the North Carolina Civil War Trail. An informative display stands next to the white frame structure, which is the 1835 farm office and the only remaining building on the property. Schoolchildren in North Carolina learn about Stoneman's Raid, and North Carolina DOT historical roadside markers dot the landscape. Union general George Stoneman raided North Carolina in March and April 1865. He passed through Jonesville on April 1 and was at the Reeves Homeplace on April 1 and 2. One Union soldier was killed, and two locals ran to the river and managed to escape.

The MST runs along Quaker Church Road and crosses the Ararat River (EB 65.2), reflecting the prominent history of Quakers in this area. The Yadkin River attracted many settlers from Pennsylvania in the mid-1700s via the Great Wagon Road, which modern I-81 somewhat follows through the Shenandoah Valley of Virginia then on to US 220 and 52 into North Carolina. Most pioneer settlers were isolated on their farms, but Quakers settled near each other in communities. Salisbury was established in 1753 where the migration routes crossed—the Great Indian Trading Path and the Great Wagon Road.

Horne Creek Living Farm State Historic Site, in Pinnacle, North Carolina, is adjacent to the Pilot Mountain State Park Corridor Trail parking lot (Hauser Road, EB 69.2 end of Segment 6). It is dedicated to preserving the state's farming practices of the early 1900s. The property includes the well-preserved late-1800s home of Thomas Hauser, as well as a corn crib and a tobacco barn. A modern visitor center, filled with antiques from the period and educational displays, offers tours, classes, special dinners, and apple tree sales. Every October, the farm hosts its annual Cornshuck Frolic, during which early-1900s farm practices are demonstrated in conjunction with a corn harvest festival.

One of the noteworthy features of the site is an apple orchard filled with varieties collected from across the Southeast. Creighton Lee Calhoun Jr., author of *Old Southern Apples*, and his wife Edith Calhoun found and cultivated over 425 varieties of heirloom apple trees over many years, including those in this orchard. In March, apple trees are offered for sale. The history of southern dinner tables includes peas, corn, beans, and, of course, lots of apples.

SEGMENT 7

The Sauratown Mountains

Pilot Mountain State Park to Hanging Rock State Park

35 MILES

All we get on the mountaintop is a good view. The real
change comes through the hard work of the climb.

JIM AMOS

This area is known as the "mountains away from the mountains," with two
dominant peaks bookending this thirty-five-mile segment. In the middle,
the MST joins the Sauratown Trail as it weaves a twenty-one-mile route
primarily on private property, thanks to the generosity of landowners.
Hikers will encounter the last steep, rocky climbs and descents before
they pick up their pace on generally flat terrain heading east to the coast.

Nearby

Winston-Salem is located about twenty miles south of Pilot Mountain.
Before the Revolutionary War, Moravian colonists from Pennsylvania
occupied the Bethania Town Lot, land purchased from Lord Granville in
1753. They clustered the individual home lots in the center of the 2,500
acres and surrounded these with orchards, bottomland, and upland lots.
From 1849 to 1862, a 129-mile plank road went from Bethania to Fayetteville, the longest wood road ever constructed in America.

Bethania, about eight miles from the Shoals area of Pilot Mountain
State Park, was the first planned Moravian settlement in North Carolina.
Incorporated in 1839, it is still inhabited today, as the only continuously
active Moravian village in the southern United States. It is now known
as the Bethania National Historic Landmark district, the largest national

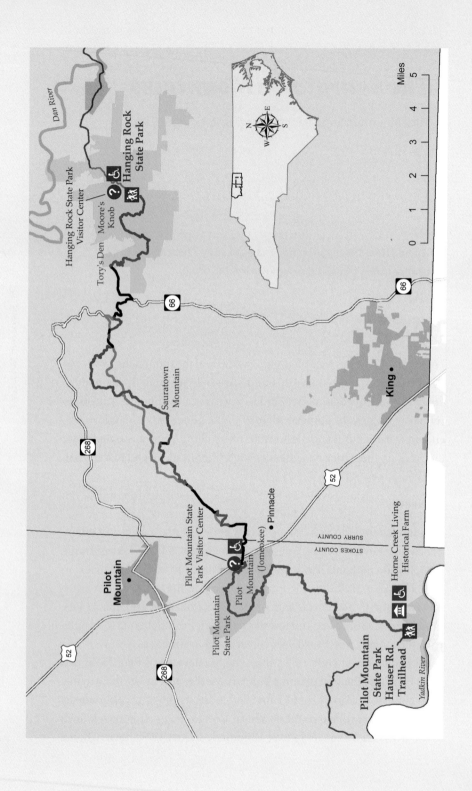

Miles

Dan River

Hanging Rock State Park
Visitor Center

Moore's
Knob

Hanging Rock
State Park

Tory's Den

66

Sauratown
Mountain

268

King

52

Pilot
Mountain

Pilot Mountain State
Park Visitor Center

Pinnacle

Pilot
Mountain
(Jomeokee)

Pilot Mountain
State Park

SURRY COUNTY
STOKES COUNTY

Horne Creek Living
Historical Farm

52

268

Pilot Mountain
State Park
Hauser Rd.
Trailhead

Yadkin River

66

landmark in Forsyth County, at nearly 500 acres. Bethania, completely surrounded by the city of Winston-Salem, is the state's only municipality that is an enclave of another. Nearby is public Historic Bethabara Park, a 1753 Moravian historical site within a wildlife preserve with a reconstructed village and church.

More MST History

A southern, urban route was added to the MST plan in 2008, creating a great loop with Winston-Salem and the Sauratown Mountains. During a series of regional planning meetings between government and stakeholder trail organizations, two routes for the MST became apparent, the current route and another one through Winston-Salem via the city's extensive planned greenway system. A compromise was struck to adopt both as "dual primary routes," forming a loop. Currently, no part of the southern route has been designated as MST.

Back on the Trail

The mountain portion of Pilot Mountain State Park is connected to the Yadkin River section by a 6.4-mile trail corridor (EB 0.0–6.4). The extensive trail network includes miles of hiking trails as well as a bridle trail and canoe trail (accessed via the Yadkin River Trail) with canoe-in sites. Hikers have the option to paddle the MST from Elkin to Pilot Mountain State Park instead of walking the roads.

From the Bean Shoals Canal Trail on the Yadkin River, paddlers can see 1,000 feet of the Bean Shoals Canal Wall, a sixteen-foot-high wall built by the Yadkin River Navigation Company between 1819 and 1823. Today the Yadkin Valley Railroad tracks run along it. One canoe access is located on Shoals Road, and there are two sizable Yadkin islands on the paddling trail.

The Cundiff Cabin is about 2.6 miles up the Pilot Mountain Corridor Trail in an area called Stony Ridge. Built in the mid-1800s, the cabin is named for Billy Cundiff, a former enslaved person. Billy farmed in the area and with his wife raised nine children there. Two of his daughters, Ida and Isabell, sold the cabin and small farm to the state in the early 1970s. The cabin bears a Keep Out sign, which must be heeded. A turkey vulture has been known to hang out in the cabin. There are tentative plans to relocate the cabin to nearby Horne Creek Farm and restore it as an exhibit.

Pilot Mountain State Park offers miles of trails, camping, and spectacular scenery. In 2020, the park recorded 1 million visitors for the first time. The Pilot Mountain quartzite monadnock (elevation 2,421 feet) has served as a navigational landmark for hundreds of years, with Pinnacle Rock towering 1,400 feet above its surroundings. The mountain summit is the most popular part of the park (it is very crowded in the fall). Rock climbing and rappelling are allowed on some of the steep cliffs within the park. Nonclimbers can enjoy sweeping views of the Sauratown Mountains and the Piedmont from cliffs around the summit. Family camping is available in a forty-two-site campground.

A Nonexhaustive History of Pilot Mountain

The Saura Native people, also known as Cheraw, called the peak Jomeokee—meaning "the Great Guide [or Pilot]." Spanish expeditions in 1540 and 1566 made mention of the Native villages. In 1710, the Saura abandoned their villages in the Pilot Mountain region, possibly due to disease or attacks by the Seneca, and may have been incorporated into the Catawba Tribe. The first mention of the Pilot by Europeans came from William Byrd II in his diary of surveying the North Carolina–Virginia border in 1728.

In 1855, the mountain's owner, H. T. Gillam, built an inn and charged "man and horse, per day, $1.50" to climb to the top. In 1929, it cost a car fifty cents to drive to the top of Pilot Mountain, and there were stairs built to the top of the Pinnacle. In 1949, a stone ticket office was built to collect admission for the summit road and a swimming pool was installed. The MST passes alongside the building today (EB 10.8). In the 1950s, steps still led to the top of the Pinnacle. The land was sold to the state in 1968 by Mrs. J. W. Beasley and turned into a state park.

Back on the Trail

The state added over 1,000 acres along the Yadkin River in 1970, and today Pilot Mountain State Park totals 3,872 acres. A new park visitor center opened in 2020 (EB 11.5). On weekends and holidays, a shuttle bus ferries visitors to the summit (fee). The MST continues, but note that detours are common on the private land for the next eighteen miles.

At the annual Audubon Hawk Watch in September, bird enthusiasts gather at the Little Pinnacle overlook to count hawks and other migratory raptors in their annual migration from northern breeding areas to southern wintering grounds, some even all the way to South America. Bird watchers have counted up to 5,700 broad-winged hawks in a single month, sometimes in large groups called kettles, along with ospreys, bald eagles, kestrels, and other hawk varieties. They use thermals to gain lift over the mountains. High schooler Ethan Rehder from Summerville, who joined the Hawk Watch for four years, recalled seeing "some individual and small kettles of broad-winged (small stocky raptors) in addition to red-shouldered hawks, black vultures, turkey vultures, and osprey. Birding appeals to a curiosity of mine. You get to know the birds. I think it is something that I can enjoy anytime, to keep an eye or an ear out for birds. It adds color to my time outdoors."

One hundred years ago, the Pilot Mountain area looked very different than it does today. There were good-size farms at the mountain's base, and it was the regular custom to burn the mountain to nourish the land (or, legend might say, to kill the rattlesnakes). Most of the old structures have long since fallen, their foundations swallowed by the forest. The graves of Confederate soldiers, with headstones, are discreetly located on the property.

The Surry County town of Pilot Mountain, population roughly 1,500, inspired the fictional town of Mount Pilot, a larger town near Mayberry, on *The Andy Griffith Show*. In real life, it is a small town five miles northeast of Pilot Mountain State Park with several good places to eat. Pinnacle, about a mile south of the MST along NC 268, is another small town that's worth a visit.

Nearby

The town of Mount Airy, eight miles north of the Pilot Mountain portion of the MST, offers Mayberry-themed attractions, including the Andy Griffith Playhouse, Andy Griffith Museum, Andy Griffith birthplace, and the Earle Theatre. The nearby granite quarry, which is the world's largest open-faced quarry, provided stone for the World War II Memorial in Washington, DC, and the Wright Brothers Memorial at Kitty Hawk. In the 1940s, old-time mountain music's top artists performed a "merry-go-round" every Saturday from the Earle. The program, which aired on WPAQ-AM, became the second-longest-running live radio show in America.

With Pilot Mountain towering in the distance, Tara Stremic hikes along the Sauratown Trail. *Photo by Jerry Barker.*

More MST History

The Sauratown Trail Association (STA) was formed by volunteers to build and maintain a hiking and equestrian path linking Pilot Mountain and Hanging Rock. The first trail was opened to the public on October 28, 1979. It was created through a series of "handshake agreements" between landowners and the North Carolina Trails Association's Sauratown Trail Committee. The effort was led by R. M. Collins, who went door to door asking landowners for permission to build the trail, and continued under task force leader Steven Mierisch. It was considered a potential route for the MST, but concerns that landowners might object to state government involvement kept it from being formally designated as a part of the MST at the time. However, the Sauratown Trail's blaze, a three-inch white dot, was adopted as the official blaze of the State Trail System and, by extension, the

MST. In 1985, a lack of formal agreements and weak liability protections for landowners led to the trail's closure.

In 1988, the STA was formed again to promote and maintain recreational trails for equestrians and hikers in Stokes and Surry Counties. The STA's initial work was at a former mineral spring resort called Vade Mecum. At the time, the property was managed by North Carolina State University's 4-H program and commonly known as Camp Sertoma. The STA was permitted to build a twenty-mile network of hiking and equestrian trails across the property, and the organization converted an old barn and tobacco barn into an equestrian campground known as the "Horse Motel."

In 1993, the STA lobbied along with other groups to pass "the Landowner Protection Bill." The new law provided legal protections for landowners who permit public trails across their property at no charge. This law ultimately paved the way for the establishment of trails across the state. James Booth was the first landowner to agree to a trail under the new law. A trail cuts across his property from the Horse Motel to Tory's Den at Hanging Rock State Park. The Booth Loop remains a spur of the Sauratown Trail/MST, accessible from EB 29.5. The STA continued to rebuild trails, obtaining written agreements with each of the landowners. The work was slow, as much of the original trail route had changed hands, and some former landowners were no longer interested. By the late 1990s, the STA had assembled a new route connecting the two parks. On National Trails Day, June 1, 2002, the Sauratown Trail and its loops were formally designated a part of the MST.

The Friends of Sauratown Mountains (FSM) was established in 2010 as the local Friends of State Parks chapter for Pilot Mountain and Hanging Rock. As steward of the first trail to connect two state parks, the group helps organize volunteer work in the two parks and raises funds to assist the parks. In 2014, the FSM led the effort to preserve Vade Mecum and Moores Springs.

Back on the Trail

The STA continues to promote horseback riding and hiking in the Sauratowns. Home to over 256,000 horses, North Carolina is the eighth-most horse-populated state in the country. Riding is not permitted on natural surface MST trails except in a few identified places. The group cautions against riding when trails are wet or muddy. The Sauratown MST offers about twenty miles for equestrian use. At EB 30.3 horses can continue on the Ruben Mountain Trail. The Friends' MST guidebook also describes horse-trailer parking and horse trails in Pilot Mountain State Park. The Sauratown MST is closed during hunting season in November and December but provides an alternate road route during these times.

Family gardens were on every property in rural America but gradually disappeared as folks moved to cities. Then during the world wars, families once again cultivated their family "victory gardens," no matter how small, to meet their needs and support the war effort. There are fewer family gardens now, but you do see them along the MST. Larger farms grow crops like lima beans, snaps, corn, okra, peppers, tomatoes, melons, and salad greens for their local farmers markets and roadside stands.

The MST passes by the Volunteer Schoolhouse (EB 16). It was constructed as a two-room building in the early 1900s to teach the first through sixth grades. About forty students were taught in two classes, first through third grades and fourth through sixth grades. The school closed in 1935, and many in the community thought it was torn down, not realizing that the building was relocated to make room for the nearby house. Half the schoolhouse was converted into an adjoining outbuilding while the other half was destroyed. When a new landowner discovered part of the schoolhouse was intact, she set about restoring it. Renovations were completed in 2020, with plans to open the schoolhouse as a museum to educate children once more.

Sauratown Mountain is the midpoint of the Sauratown Trail and the Sauratown Mountain Range. Its name is derived from the Native Saura settlement of Upper Sauratown along the banks of the Dan River. The settlements were abandoned by 1710, as the Saura population was decimated by an epidemic introduced from Europe. Most of the mountain is privately owned; however, in December 2019, Hanging Rock State Park acquired a 166-acre tract off Section 9 of the Sauratown Trail, with the aid of the STA. Due to its prominence above the surrounding foothills, the summit has become a major radio communications site in North Carolina, hosting more transmitting facilities than any other location in the state. The mountain is also home to youth camps—Mountain Top Youth Camp and YMCA Camp Hanes. In the winter, rock climbers flock to the south-facing cliffs. At one time, the mountain was also a popular spot for hang gliding.

The Martin Rock House is half a mile from the MST at EB 23. Continue on Rock House Road about 0.4 mile, then turn right on Col. Jack Martin

Road, where a house stands on the left. Jack Martin moved to Stokes County in 1768; he married Nancy in 1784 and they raised ten children. The Rock House, built in 1785, was two stories, plus an attic and basement, with a large fireplace and three-foot-thick walls. The white stucco house could be seen from a great distance. During the early war years, the Rock House was used as a fort against Native Americans and Tories, with gun ports built into the walls. Col. Martin also fought at Guilford Courthouse. The house burned in 1890 and only walls remain.

In the early 1900s, the area around Hanging Rock was known for several mineral spring resorts. Vade Mecum Springs was started in 1900, when John Sparks purchased 3,000 acres of land. He built hotels on the property in 1901 and 1902. The land went through several owners, private and public, until 2014, when the North Carolina General Assembly gave the properties to the state park system. Hanging Rock developed a master plan for the properties, including restoration of the 100-year-old hotel as a hostel, developing a backcountry campground, and possibly routing the MST through the Vade Mecum property. In 2016, the STA restored a trail connecting Vade Mecum to Tory's Den and named it in honor of R. M. Collins.

A side trip to Tory's Den (EB 29.5) is worth the 0.2-mile walk. During the Revolutionary War, Loyalists hid in the cave, and visitors can read about the site's fascinating history at an informative display in the parking lot. From there, a trail leads to the cave and Tory's Falls, the tallest waterfall in the park, at 240 feet.

The Sauratowns were almost home to a national forest. In 1934, the US Forest Service established the "Sauratown Purchase Unit" in the region, but high land values in the area led it to abandon the plan. Soon afterward the Stokes County Committee for Hanging Rock and the Winston-Salem Foundation acquired 3,096 acres of the area, land they donated to the state to establish Hanging Rock State Park.

Upon entering Hanging Rock State Park, from EB 29.3 the MST steadily ascends. Equestrians turn right on the Ruben Mountain Loop Trail, the last MST portion open to horses. The trail continues to climb to Moore's Knob (elevation 2,574 feet), the highest point in the park and in the Sauratown Mountains. The views are spectacular, and information displays identify the peaks in every direction. As you descend the next mile to Cascade Creek, your knees will get a workout stepping down 684 stone steps; 200 yards farther you reach the campground. Watch for trail twists and turns as you work your way to the lake and stone bathhouse

Moore's Knob, 2,574 feet, highest point in Hanging Rock State Park. *Photo by Jerry Barker.*

(EB 34.6), then continue 200 yards to the visitor center (built in 1993, renovated in 2020). From the visitor center are easy hikes to the Rock Garden Trail (0.1 mile) and Upper Cascades Falls (0.2 mile).

Hanging Rock State Park covers 9,011 acres in Stokes County and is in the National Register of Historic Places. The park now offers a seventy-three-site campground, a picnic area, a lake full of trout that's good for fishing, swimming, and canoeing (rentals are available), and over twenty miles of scenic trails to hike along pristine streams and waterfalls. Pay attention as there are eleven different trail blaze colors and shapes. The MST travels 7.3 miles through the park. There are nine bike trails with a total of fifteen miles of trails.

To recover from the Depression in the 1930s, sixty-six Civilian Conservation Corp (CCC) camps were established in North Carolina, with 13,600 men in forty-seven counties. Reforestation, conservation, and recreation projects aided development of national and state parks and forests statewide. Many facilities at Hanging Rock were constructed by CCC Camp 3422 between 1935 and 1942. A concrete and earthen dam was completed in 1938 to impound a twelve-acre lake. At the entrance to the Group Campsite, there are five historical markers regarding the CCC Heritage Trail (0.1 mile; Segment 8, EB 1.0).

This is the end of MST Segment 7. The signature location in the park is "the" Hanging Rock, a side trip off the MST. From the visitor center parking lot, the 1.2-mile Hanging Rock Trail begins as a paved path before changing to gravel, dirt, and rock. The 603-foot climb to the top generally takes about an hour. Hanging Rock's quartzite offers hikers a nice place to rest and take in the magnificent views of the park down below.

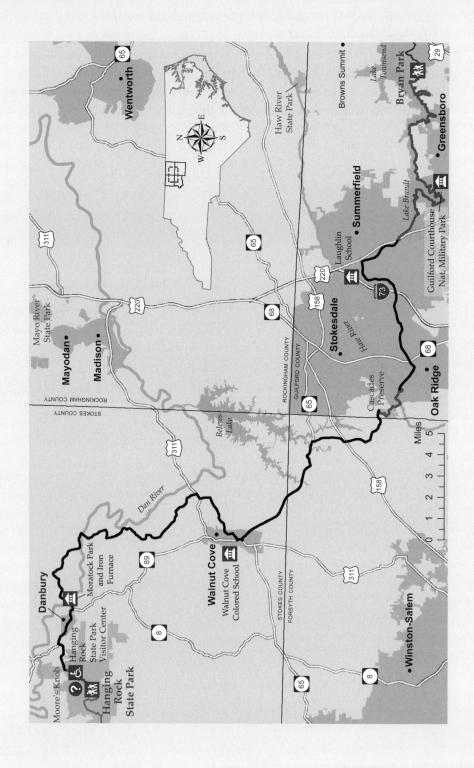

Rivers, Railroads, and Lakes

Hanging Rock State Park to Greensboro's Bryan Park

64.7 MILES

*These adventures . . . are of my passage from the old me to
the new. The conditions of these passages require me to take
every step. Without them I am less. With them I am more.*

MARK UDALL

Let me introduce you to a changing trail (and alert you that EB mileage may change). A future MST reroute will bring hikers over the ridgeline that contains Hanging Rock peak and along a portion of Mill Creek into the town of Danbury. This new section of trail will use North Carolina State Park's recently added 875-acre Three Sisters-Mill Creek tract and a 179-acre tract purchased in 2021. Other reroutes are being considered near the Dan River, Belews Lake and near Oak Ridge; other trail links will happen north of Greensboro. The recent addition of the Cascades near Oak Ridge adds a beautiful reroute from the road to a cool cascading creek.

Hanging Rock State Park to Oak Ridge

The start of Segment 8 may change, so follow MST blazes. Currently hikers depart the Hanging Rock Visitor Center on the MST, and Indian Creek Trail (orange square markers) will pass through a nice picnic area with shelters and restrooms (located downhill on the right side). Along Indian Creek, Hidden Falls appears on the right after 0.5 mile, and Window Falls is another 150 yards down 112 rock steps. At EB 1.0 a side trail leads a quarter mile to Group Camp/CCC Heritage Trail. Here was a bustling Civilian Conservation Corps (CCC) Camp, home to hundreds of young men from 1935 to 1942, who were paid $1 a day. These men built the park's roads and most of its facilities, including the bathhouse, picnic shelters, lake, and trails.

Continue following the beautiful creek, and at EB 1.7 you reach Hanging Rock Park Road, turning right along the road on the MST. Across the road, Indian Creek Trail continues, and an old log barn is within fifty yards. It is two miles down Indian Creek to the Dan River Canoe Access on Flinchum Road, crossing several streams without bridges along the route. The Riverbluffs Trail is a delightful, flat 1.3-mile loop along the Dan River.

Nearby

Paddling a portion of the Dan River State Trail is a potential alternate from EB 1.7 to EB 13.2, with historical remains along the way. Launch from the Dan River Access, part of Hanging Rock State Park, on Flinchum Road (left off NC89 before the river). River mileages going downstream mark these sites: 3.7 miles to Sandy Run River (on the left, where iron ore from Rogers Ore Bank was floated to Moratock Furnace, now a down-river canoe access point); 4.9 miles to rapids and the old dam site; 5.4 miles to Moratock Iron Furnace and canoe access (on the left); 6.3 miles to Riverson's Fish Trap; 7.9 miles to the fish dam at the foot of Old Mill Shoal; 9.2 miles to Fulcher's Ford and Pilzer Steel Bridge (built in 1918); 9.8 miles to Thompson's Fish Trap; 10.9 miles to Davis's Upper Ford, a branch of Great Wagon Road crossing; 11.5 miles to Davis Bluff (aka Mount Horrible); 12.7 miles to a ford for a branch of Great Wagon Road; 14.3 miles to "broken dam" (caution: some rebar is under water); and 30 yards downstream from the broken dam, exit the river on the right at Hemlock Golf Course access (MST trail EB 13.2).

Back on the Trail

In Danbury (EB 3.7), a National Historic District, stands the classic 1904 Stokes County Courthouse (EB 4.1). Right next door is Moody's Tavern where Union general Stoneman, commanding 4,500 men, had his headquarters April 9–10, 1865. Historical information is displayed out front. There is a history museum downtown. The town was formed in 1849 and renamed Danbury in 1852 due to its nearness to the Dan River.

Moratock Park at EB 5.3 preserves a Civil War–era iron furnace used to make bar iron, built in 1843. Most of the original foundry works were destroyed by Union cavalry under Stoneman's command. This is a rustic facility with picturesque views of the Dan River.

Priddy's General Store opened in 1888 on Pitzer Road in Danbury. N. D. and Lula Priddy purchased the store in 1929, now managed by third-generation Jane Priddy Charleville. Their Facebook page says, "Priddy's is a journey you'll never forget" where "time stands still." Walk their squeaky pine floors to find sourwood honey, Nehi peach soda, pink flamingos, or just about anything you want. Lisa "Conundrum" Speas, who completed the MST in 2019, spoke of the joy of places like Priddy's, saying, "I stopped into several rural general stores and elected to enjoy homemade apple pies, peach sonkers, and moon pies." Country stores were essential to communities until the automobile allowed easier travel. Everyday life needs were met in a single place—whether you needed to buy kerosene, vote, or even have some light dental work done.

At EB 15.7–18.8, the MST passes by the archeological remains of Upper Sauratown's historic village, located near the Dan River in Stokes County. Walnut Cove (EB 21.4), incorporated in 1889, is in Stokes County. In the mid-eighteenth century, before becoming Walnut Cove, the town was known as Town Fork. Town Fork grew into a large plantation and then a railroad town. The remnants of the train depot still stand on Depot Street. The 1821 Colonel Covington House, the oldest in Stokes County, is located on over five acres and features garden stonework believed to be original to the house.

Duke Energy constructed Belews Lake (pronounced "blues"; EB 27.3) in 1973 to collect cooling water for its coal-burning power plant, Belews Creek Steam Station. The 3,864-acre lake includes eighty-eight miles of shoreline and is not far from the township of Belews Creek. Preliminary trail and conservation survey work conducted by Friends of the MST will be reviewed and discussed with Duke Energy and the Piedmont Land Conservancy to see what public recreation future is possible at Belews Lake.

Along Segment 8, on Kernersville Road, a memorial plaque erected by descendants of Thomas Linville offers travelers historical information on Linville and his family's legacy in the state, including the naming of the western North Carolina town of Linville Falls. A parking lot for Cascades Preserve (7359 Goodwill Church Road, EB 32.7), constructed by Guilford County and the town of Oak Ridge, and dedicated in 2016, is the start of 3.4 miles of beautiful wooded MST trail. Just 100 yards into the woods on the right are remnants of an old chimney. Highlights along this section include the cascades created as the creek descends over layers of exposed metamorphic gneiss and igneous granite typical of a narrow geological region called the Milton Terrane. The path crosses a tributary to East Belews Creek, and its Keyauwee Loop is named for the Native American people who originally inhabited this land. The community leaders and trail volunteers have worked tirelessly to connect the 130-acre Cascades section via well-groomed sidewalks to the Headwaters Trail, showcasing the very small beginnings of the Haw River. Shortly before you conclude this quiet wooded trail, a loop trail on the left takes you around a beaver pond. At EB 35.8, hikers reach the Headwaters parking lot along Linville Road and continue to the right into the town of Oak Ridge.

Nearby

The Old Mill of Guilford is located a mile south of the MST at Oak Ridge along NC 68. The origins of the mill date back to 1767, when Daniel Dillon constructed a small tub mill on Beaver Creek for early colonists to grind their corn and wheat crops. During the Revolutionary War, on February 10, 1781, British general Charles Cornwallis led his troops past the mill on the trail of Patriot general Nathaniel "Nat" Greene and his men camped out at Guilford Courthouse. If legend is to be believed, Cornwallis's troops seized the mill, ground grain, and fed the soldiers who later fought in the Battle of Guilford Courthouse on March 15, 1781.

After the war, in 1808, Joel Sanders bought the mill and house on the property for $900. A little over a decade later, in 1819, the mill was moved 500 feet downstream, and the millpond was increased to ten acres. The gristmill is still in use today, making it one of the oldest operating in the United States.

Oak Ridge to Greensboro's Bryan Park

At EB 37.5, in the town of Oak Ridge, is Oak Ridge Military Academy, a college preparatory military school. The town was name after the school, which was founded in 1852 and built in 1897. On the road between Oak Ridge and Summerfield is a memorial to James Gillies, known as the "bugler boy." He was a fourteen-year-old boy serving under Light Horse Harry Lee, killed by Banastre "Bloody" Tarleton and his British dragoons on February 12, 1781, after he gave up his fresh horse for an American soldier to escape during a skirmish before the Battle of Guilford Courthouse.

The bugler boy's story is etched in memorials at Guilford Courthouse National Military Park and on Summerfield Road (EB 43.7) in front of Summerfield Elementary School (and depicted on the town seal and the town logo).

In Summerfield, Saunders Inn opened in 1822 and was a stopping point on the wagon road from Georgia to Pennsylvania (now NC 150). Efforts to save the inn were unsuccessful, and it was demolished in 2020. Sydney Porter, grandfather of short story writer O. Henry (born William Sydney Porter), taught in a one-room log schoolhouse at Bruce's Crossroads, now Summerfield. Andrew Jackson also lived in Summerfield for one year before he became the seventh US president.

As you leave Summerfield (elevation 909 feet), you take a tunnel under four-lane 220, then cross a bridge over Lake Brandt. For nineteen miles (EB 45.9–64.3) the trail generally follows the shoreline of Greensboro watershed lakes, namely municipal reservoirs Lake Brandt and Lake Townsend. Lake Brandt (816 acres) was constructed in 1925 and Lake Townsend (1,542 acres) in 1969, and both are used for kayaking, sailing, rowing, standup paddleboarding, fishing, and hiking. There are an additional 5,277 acres for watershed and over 7,000 acres for park land, the lands that hikers' feet touch as they navigate through Greensboro.

From EB 45.9 to EB 51 the MST mostly follows the old railroad bed of the Atlantic and Yadkin Railroad, now named the A&Y Greenway, Greensboro's only "rail-trail." The A&Y was a short line railroad that operated from 1899 to 1950, running from Mount Airy southeast to Sanford, Fayetteville, and Wilmington. The MST passes by Bur-Mil Park, established in 1989 when Guilford County bought the old Burlington Industries recreation facility. Sitting on 250 acres next to Lake Brandt, the park offers a variety of outdoor recreational opportunities, including hiking and biking trails, tennis courts, a golf course, an event hall, a nature classroom, and a swimming pool. Spot common and migratory birds as you travel over the 140-foot H. Michael Weaver Bridge, through the watershed and along thirty miles of lakeshore trails.

Along the trails from Laurel Bluff Trail to Lake Townsend (EB 54.1–64.3) are patches of invasive plants that occur throughout the Piedmont region. To protect native plants, we must be ever vigilant to reduce invasive and damaging plants common to the trail. At one point there is a large field of bamboo, then a field of kudzu, even forming an arch to walk through. Kudzu grows fast and blankets other plants, thus its nickname "the vine that ate the South." Another common invasive plant is the autumn olive,

Shaded boardwalk along an MST stretch of the almost fifty miles of Greensboro watershed lakes trails and greenways. *Photo by Jerry Barker.*

a shrub that can reach twenty feet high and spread thirty feet wide. The leaves of the autumn olive are elliptical in shape and are easily identified by their shimmering silver scales.

The 3.6-mile Nat Greene Trail is named for Nathanael Greene (1742–86), a major general of the Continental army in the American Revolutionary War. Greene was demoted to brigadier general when George Washington took control of the individual armies, but he soon rose to second-in-command under Washington and became his close friend. Greene is best known for his integral role in the southern theater during the war, when he drove the British out of the Carolinas and Georgia. Greene was defeated at the Battle of Guilford Courthouse, but the British were so weakened by their victory that Cornwallis—who lost over a quarter of his soldiers—decided to not pursue Greene and instead marched to Wilmington to resupply, then continued into Virginia. Cornwallis surrendered at his next battle, Yorktown. After the Revolution, Greene contributed to restoring civil government and order to a South wracked by years of war. His nickname was "The Savior of the South." Oh, he also is the namesake of Greensboro.

The Nat Greene Trail is sponsored by the Piedmont Hiking and Outing Club and is on the southeast side of Lake Brandt. The Battle of Guilford Courthouse was fought in part on the eastern edge of the Horsepen Creek watershed, and Horsepen Creek is a tributary of Reedy Fork, which flows into Lake Brandt. The trail begins at Old Battleground Road and connects with the MST at EB 51.6, following the MST for 2.5 miles to the Lake Brandt Marina (EB 54). You can also ride or stride the 14.5-mile Bicentennial Greenway that connects many trails in northern Greensboro, including Bur-Mill Park and the military park.

For those seeking mountain biking trails, the Wild Turkey Trail (4.2 miles) parallels the Nat Greene Trail. Also at Lake Brandt is the Owls Roost Trail (4 miles), once rated the best urban trail in the country and still a local favorite. Check out the one-way mile called the Shady Side Trail. Not on the MST but nearby are the Bald Eagle Trail (4.6 miles), Copperhead Trail (5 miles), Reedy Fork Trail (3.8 miles), Blue Heron Trail (3.5 miles), and King Fisher Trail (2.4 miles). Since these trails are used by bike enthusiasts (helmets required for fifteen and under) as well as hikers, please practice caution and courtesy. Other MST biking areas include the Blue Ridge Parkway, Elkin's bike trail, greenways in Hillsborough, Raleigh, Burgaw, and Jacksonville, and Coastal Crescent and Outer Banks roadways.

Nearby

Guilford Courthouse National Military Park commemorates the Revolutionary War Battle of Guilford Courthouse, fought on March 15, 1781. It was a watershed moment in the southern theater of the war, turning the tide that ultimately led to American victory over the British. The park is conveniently located "just off the trail," a mile south of the Nat Greene Trail parking area on Old Battleground Road. Another great spot for children, about a mile east of the military park, is the Greensboro Science Center, a science museum, zoo, aquarium, and treetop adventure park, all in one.

South of the MST is Greensboro, the county seat of Guilford County and the third-most populous city in North Carolina, with over 300,000 residents. The city hosts the annual North Carolina Folk Festival and many other cultural and athletic events. Yum Yum Better Ice Cream is an old-school restaurant, operating since 1906. Ask for a Carolina dog "all-the-way." Nearby Hops Burger Bar was awarded #1 Most Delectable Burger Joint in America by TripAdvisor in 2015.

In addition to food, Greensboro offers MST travelers history. North Carolina's first state college for women, the State Normal and Industrial School, was chartered by the General Assembly in 1891. Its name has since changed a number of times, from Woman's College in the early twentieth century to the University of North Carolina at Greensboro since men first enrolled alongside women in 1963. In 1893, around the same time that the Woman's College opened, the General Assembly also chartered the Agricultural and Mechanical College for the Colored Race. Known today as North Carolina Agricultural and Technical (A&T) University, it is the largest historically Black college or university in the country and has the largest number of African American graduates in engineering and agriculture.

A Quick Detour into Civil Rights History near the MST

The International Civil Rights Center and Museum, a top 100 site on the US Civil Rights Trail, is located in Greensboro's downtown, just five miles south of the MST, in an old Woolworth's. It was at this Woolworth's "whites only" lunch counter, on February 1, 1960, that four freshmen from North Carolina A&T decided to stand up to Jim Crow by sitting down and refusing to get up until they were served. From that moment forward, sit-ins spread across the country as a way to challenge segregation laws. Their courage catalyzed the creation of the Student Nonviolent Coordinating Committee, a pivotal civil rights group. Today, visitors to the museum can immerse themselves in this history through the permanent exhibit, "The Battlegrounds," and other educational displays, artifacts, and video reenactments.

When the first installment of *The Negro Motorist Green Book* came out in 1936, during the Jim Crow era of legal segregation, it provided African American travelers with a list of "safe" places to stop, including hotels, restaurants, movie theaters, and barbershops. There were 327 sites listed in North Carolina. As of 2019, sixty-six of these places were still standing, and four are still in operation near the MST: Speight's Auto Service and Friendly Barbershop, both in Durham; Magnolia House in Greensboro; and Dove's Auto Service in Kinston. The North Carolina African American Heritage Commission created a traveling exhibit, which you can also see online, of North Carolina's *Green Book* history: "Oasis Spaces: African American Travel in North Carolina, 1936–1966."

Back on the Trail

The Osprey Trail (EB 58.7–60.9) and the Townsend Trail (EB 60.9–63.9) finish up Segment 8 walks around Piedmont lakes. Wet spots, especially following rains, nourish a variety of mushrooms, dragonflies, and damselflies. A kaleidoscope of butterflies is a large gathering, and when swallowtail butterflies are thick around a puddle of water it is called "puddling." Strange as it sounds, butterflies rely on their feet to smell and taste food.

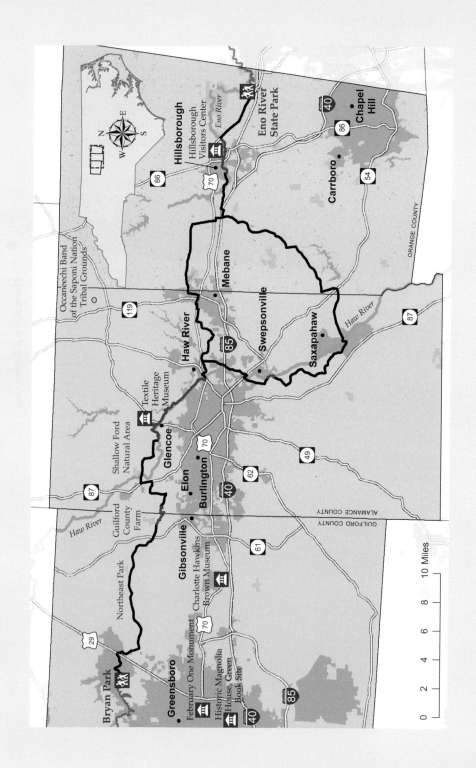

Revolution and Textiles

Greensboro's Bryan Park to Eno River State Park
at Pleasant Green Road

60.7 MILES

People don't take trips, trips take people.

JOHN STEINBECK

The next sixty miles of the MST are rich with the history of the Revolutionary War, the state's textile mills, and Indigenous peoples. It is a segment
that follows two key rivers in North Carolina—the Haw and Eno—and
includes travel on natural surface trail, roadside, and greenway. The towns
of Glencoe and Hillsborough are exciting to visit, along with a number of
parks and preserves. This segment hosted several Friends of the MST's
annual gatherings at the mill in Saxapahaw until moving to Elon College
from 2014 to 2016.

Greensboro's Bryan Park to Haw River

After ten miles of road walking, the MST at EB 10 along Huffine Mill
Road offers easy access to Guilford County's 374-acre Northeast Park.
Go down on High Rock Road 0.1 mile and you'll find parking, water,
and restrooms. There are trails for hiking, biking, and horseback riding,
and a paddle access on Reedy Fork Creek (ten miles to Shallow Ford on
the Haw River).

At EB 14.4, you begin on Howerton Road, which leads to the 720-acre
Guilford County Farm, "The Community's Gathering Place" (formerly
the Gibsonville Prison Farm, EB 15.7–18). The prison began in 1924 with
white inmates and later became Black-only in 1935 when the prisoners'

Off Howerton Road,
an MST hiker strides
beside a fence row on
the Breakaway Trail at
Guilford County Farm.
Photo by Jerry Barker.

dorm was built using rocks from the farm grounds. It was North Carolina's only county-run prison farm. Prisoners worked ten-hour days, five and a half days a week, feeding themselves with crops they grew and products from cattle, pigs, and chickens. Greenhouses were built in 1995. In 2015, officials closed the prison, and now the farm is a site of agricultural history, cultural history, and conservation. Local farmers lease 600 acres for crops and cattle. Trail names include the Breakaway, the Chain Gang Connector, and the Prison Run Pass. The farm is a birdwatcher's paradise.

Graham Zimmerman, who in August 2020 was 530 miles into his eastbound MST march, said he

turned off the road east of Greensboro to follow the trail as it meandered through Guilford County Farm. It was early when I spotted a man standing in the corner of one the farm's meadows. He had a pair of binoculars hanging from his shoulders and a telescopic lens attached to a camera atop the tripod. I was curious. The man's name was Sean and he was on a personal quest to photograph 365 of North Carolina's 469 species of native birds—one for each day of the year. That morning Sean was after the Lincoln's Sparrow, a small and shy bird that stays hidden in the cover of meadows just like the one where we stood. He was planning to be out there all day, and there was no other place he'd rather be. I thought the same thing as we said our goodbyes and I continued my journey.

Nearby Black History

The Haw River watershed was home to many stops along the Underground Railroad, likely because of the large numbers of Quaker settlers in Guilford, Alamance, and northwest Chatham Counties. Many Quakers were abolitionists who helped enslaved people get to freedom by acting as agents on the Underground Railroad. Guilford College in Greensboro grew out of the 1837 Quaker New Garden community, and a tulip poplar tree stands on the campus today, paying homage to Quakers and freedmen who aided enslaved African Americans.

East of Greensboro, the private Palmer Memorial Institute opened in 1902 to educate rural African American students. It operated for more than sixty years. The school was founded by Charlotte Hawkins Brown, who led the school for half a century. In 1900, North Carolina was home to over 2,000 private schools for African Americans, but they rarely offered more than an elementary school education. Under Brown's leadership, Palmer Memorial Institute was eventually able to offer college preparatory education up through junior and senior high school, with a curriculum that included classes in art, music, drama, literature, Romance languages, and math. It was also the only school at the time to teach African American history.

In 1937, Brown phased out all but the college preparatory classes at the school, eliminating the elementary and junior college programs. Alongside her work at the Palmer Memorial Institute, she successfully pushed Guilford County to establish its first public high school for rural African American students. Palmer Memorial Institute closed altogether in 1971, ten years after Brown's death. Today it is a state historic site honoring the contributions of African Americans and women, the first state-supported site to do so. It is just five miles south of the MST.

Back on the Trail

Greg and Germaine Yahn section-hiked the MST, often together, Greg completing the trail in 2014 and Germaine in 2015. They also were leaders in building and maintaining the MST in the Upper Haw River area.

When hiking the MST they especially loved camping in the Mount Pisgah Campground, then having breakfast at Pisgah Inn (Segment 2). They were the first to hike the alternate River Valley Route from Deep Creek to Waterrock Knob (known as Segment 1B but no longer a route). They love the trails in their area for the quiet of nature and the sounds of the river.

Ossipee is a town in Alamance County near Shallow Ford, incorporated in 2002. The villages of Altamahaw and Ossippee were founded in 1868 after the Civil War. In 1878, James N. Williamson and his sons established the Ossipee Cotton Mill, complete with a company store and mill houses. In the 1930s, the mill started working with silk instead of cotton and was later bought by Glen Raven Mills. The original mill houses still stand today.

The MST follows the Haw River for 11.5 miles near NC 87 at Shallow Ford to 335 at Watkin Bridge in the town of Haw River. The Haw is a 110-mile tributary of the Cape Fear River. *Down along the Haw*, by Anne Melyn Cassebaum, is a fascinating look at its history. The book follows the Haw from its source and tells of its rich geographic, ecological, and cultural history. Cassebaum interviewed many whose lives have been touched by the river, including mill owners and workers, environmentalists, and farmers, providing an informative glimpse of life along the waterway and the ways humans interact and depend on its unique ecology. As she writes,

> The Haw draws hikers' gaze to its running waters and it may cool their feet. For the Peoples, living by it for thousands of years, the Haw's clear waters were for drinking, cooking, bathing, and eating—fish were in abundant supply. For travelling? Maybe for short hauls but the drop of the river made it too rocky for much transport. Settlers arrived by riding down the Great Wagon Road. They settled by the Haw and its streams for the same reasons Native peoples had, plus one. They saw power in the Haw's rocky rapids, so the mills and their dams came and grew, and the river changed. In the 1950s eleven mills and ten municipalities were dumping their waste directly into the river. Foam, dye, and stink were what people found in the Haw then; no one would have routed a trail by it. Thanks to reforms driven by those who still saw a river and not a sewer line, we got the Clean Water Act of 1972, and the Haw rebounded to the river we fish, paddle and play in today—much healthier but still needing our protection.

Alamance County started focusing on the Haw River Trail (www .thehaw.org) as a collaborative effort between Elon College, the county, and several municipalities. The original focus was conservation, but they decided that building a trail—both paddle and walking—fit the communities' interest more. Brian Baker, hired as the first Haw River Trail coordinator, lined up all the paddle accesses and acquired easements and land to build a lot of hiking trails. After Baker was promoted to director of Alamance Parks, Guil Johnson became trail coordinator. The organization hosts several fun fundraising events including YeeHaw! River Paddle and the Haw River Triathlon.

The MST passes the entrance to Shallow Ford Natural Area at 1955 Gerringer Mill Road in Elon (EB 22.4). The natural area's name harkens back to the days before bridges when the river was largely impassible, except by ferry or shallow points, or fords, dotted conveniently with rocks. Fords were few and far between, and the most popular natural crossing in Alamance County was known as "The Shallow Ford." The county park includes 197 acres, four trails, and a wildflower meadow (accessed via a 0.7-mile loop). Between the parking lot and paddle access, on the left, is machinery used in the L. M. Gerringer Mill (a small tub mill built in 1884). The rocks you see just upstream of the paddle access steps were part of the dam, likely a crib dam. Right next to the bank, you can still see two wooden rails running parallel to the bank indicating the location of the vertical turbine. Within twenty yards of the parking lot is a stone cooler box that was used to store drinks and milk in the stream for the Gerringer Store. One of the park trails passes the early 1800s Tickle/Gerringer homestead ruins. The Battle of Shallow Ford was fought on October 14, 1780, when 600 British Loyalists were ambushed by 300 Patriot militia at the Haw River ford, with the Patriots prevailing.

The Sissipahaw people (also known as the Saxapahaw) were part of the eastern Siouan people and lived along the Haw River. Archeological research by scholars at UNC–Chapel Hill provides a glimpse into the daily lives of the Native peoples, including the Sissipahaw, at sites on the Haw and its tributaries in Alamance County. They lived in small, interconnected villages along the ridges above the lower portion of the Haw River, where they built houses and storage buildings from logs, bark, and saplings. They made the most of the river and its surroundings through hunting, fishing, and farming. The Sissipahaw and other Native groups on the Haw and Eno Rivers likely spoke an eastern Siouan dialect, similar to many of their neighbors in North Carolina's Piedmont. The Sissipahaw thrived in the area for generations before the arrival of European settlers. But by the 1600s, their communities had dwindled and their populations significantly diminished, likely due to the introduction of European diseases and people leaving the villages to pursue trading contacts elsewhere. English explorer John Lawson wrote about encountering the Sissipahaw on his travels in 1701, but few remained by the time European colonists began to permanently settle in the area. Those who did live to see that day joined other Native groups, particularly the Occaneechi Band of the Saponi Nation, who spoke a similar language. Today their descendants live in northeast Alamance County.

At EB 25.6 you pass the Indian Valley Paddle Access to the Haw River and can enjoy the next eight miles on natural surface trail. Great Bend Park at Glencoe (EB 26.8) features thirty wooded acres along the Haw River. Parking, picnicking, fishing, hiking, and paddle access points are available. The park is also a part of the Haw River Trail/MST. The Haw River Trail was formed in 2006 when ten governmental agencies agreed to conserve land along the waterway.

In 1979, the Glencoe Mill Village was listed on the National Register of Historic Places, and in 1999 the Burlington City Council made it a local historic district. At the heart of the village was the Glencoe Mill textile company, which produced plaid flannels called Glencoe or Alamance plaid. Built in 1882, Glencoe was the last hydroelectric-powered mill built on the Haw. When production ceased in 1954, a number of small businesses operated out of the original building, but the larger mill complex was mostly abandoned.

The Glencoe dam routed Haw River water into the mill race, which provided waterpower for the mill. In the mid-1800s, the state supported the construction of hydroelectric-powered textile mills on Piedmont rivers, many of which were built in the same areas where older gristmills had stood. These new factories created jobs and generated money, using cotton grown in North Carolina. In the 1890s laborers worked eleven hours a day, six days a week; men were paid two dollars a day and women one dollar a day. Workers could rent a room for twenty-five to fifty cents a month. Kerosene provided light until electric lights were invented in the 1940s. Often African American women cared for workers' homes and children during their long shifts at the factories. Mill houses were built near the mill because few workers could afford a car. The towns had water towers to put out fires in the mills, which were common due to cotton dust and heat.

In 1997, the entire mill village and mill complex were donated to Preservation North Carolina (PNC), which managed the protection and

The historic Glencoe Dam on the Haw River was built around 1950 to replace the original 1880s stone and timbers dam.
Photo by Bill Meador; used by permission.

revival of the entire property. Built between 1880 and 1882, the dwellings had fallen into extremely poor condition when the project began. Houses in the village, placed under protective covenants by PNC, were offered for sale to the public starting in 2004. The village of Glencoe officially opened to the public in March 2004, and today it has been largely restored by private residents and organizations. The quaint neighborhood consists of mill structures, historical markers, and forty-one delightfully colored frame houses where mill employees and their families lived. The original two-chair barbershop, where the barber lived, is now available for nightly rental. The Victorian house of the 1882 mill owner stands facing NC 62. The mill building itself is now owned by a developer who specializes in revitalizing old mills, and adaptive uses are being sought for it. Look for North Carolina's largest shuttle sculpture in Glencoe.

The Textile Heritage Museum, located in Glencoe on the right, is North Carolina's only museum solely dedicated to one of the state's most historically important industries. Admission is free, and hours of operation can be found at textileheritagemuseum.org. The museum is housed inside the old company store and management offices; at 6,000 square feet, it offers hundreds of artifacts from more than fifty textile mills across North

Carolina. Burlington Industries (Burlington Mills), Cone Mills, Copland Mills, Holt Hosiery Mills, and Glen Raven Mills are some of the textile giants featured here. Within the captivating exhibit gallery are military uniforms and equipment manufactured in America's textile mills, as well as weaving looms, spinning wheels, and sock-making machinery. In addition to textile, there were six other types of mills: grist, foundry, forge, saw, paper, and oil (linseed oil from flaxseed). Colonists harnessed water energy to grind, saw, forge, or spin raw materials into usable goods.

The Haw River Paddle Trail (www.thehaw.org), mainly in Alamance County, has six access points north of I-40. One of the showcase paddles is the five miles from Glencoe Paddle Access (EB 27.9) to Red Slide Park (EB 33.2), a stretch of river that was a natural crossing on the Indian Trading Path and first populated by Europeans 300 years ago. In 1999 George and Jerrie Nall purchased two acres along the Haw, and in 2007 they donated the tract in memory of their son for use as the Glencoe Paddle Access. Two and a half miles from Glencoe Paddle Access, the river is split by the mile-long Goat Island, the longest on the Haw. As you paddle by, look for an abandoned school bus, an eighteen-wheeler, goats, and "Chris Chris," the seven-foot ape-like monster said to live here. The mill race for the Hopedale Cotton Mill begins shortly after going under NC 62 at Glencoe, and the MST is on top of the raceway about one mile downstream. The mill opened in 1869, originally under the name of the Carolina Mill, after the Holt brothers (James, W. E., and L. Banks), owners of the Granite Mill in Haw River, bought the land on which it stands, next to High Falls. It operated for almost a century before closing in the 1960s. A little farther on at EB 29.6, the MST skirts around the 140-acre Stoney Creek Marina, the oldest and smallest of four marinas operated by the City of Burlington. Prior to 1886 Burlington was known as Company Shops; when Burlington Industries was founded in 1923, it became known as "the hosiery center of the South."

Herman Johnson, owner of Burlington Mechanical Contractors, built a sixty-foot, $65,000 bridge over Boyd's Creek in 2021, on land he owns. He has granted the MST an easement. Funding came from Impact Alamance, Alamance Parks, and the town of Haw River. Johnson's ties to the Haw go back to playing on the riverbanks in the 1950s. In June 1962, Johnson, Billy Watkins, and Roy and Jerry Maness tied together three truck tire tubes, roped a plywood board on top, affixed a two-horsepower outboard motor, and headed down the stinky, polluted Haw River. Despite flipping the raft, losing their food, and soaking their sleeping bags, they made it down the Cape Fear to bays past Wilmington. In May 1974, with a better raft, Johnson repeated the trip. The US 70 bridge over the Haw is called the "three governors bridge" for Thomas Michael Holt, Kerr Scott, and Robert Scott, all from Alamance County. After you cross the US 70 bridge, on the right you might see other metal structures made by Herman Johnson, including the seventeen-foot man. In addition to his artwork, Johnson has made a great contribution to the community by donating the land for Red Slide Park in 2009, one of the most historic places in Alamance County, where the Indian Trading Path crossed the river at "Piney Ford." Red Slide Park is in the town of Haw River, elevation 564 feet, population 2,500. In 1745, Adam Trollinger and his family left Pennsylvania and settled here, building a gristmill on the Haw. Later, in 1844, Benjamin Trollinger built Granite Cotton Mill, which was bought by the Holt family in 1858 and became known for its Alamance plaids. Another mill, later known as Tabardry Mill, was built across from Granite Cotton Mill. By the late 1800s, as more mills were built, small company villages of mill houses, like Terrapin Slide and Red Hill, were popping up in the area. In Haw River a loud gong called people to the river to unload barges. Food trash was put in slop buckets to feed the pigs, but other trash made its way to the river.

Moses and Caesar Cone bought Granite Cotton Mill in the 1930s; by the early 1980s the mill produced more corduroy than any other plant in the world, then it moved on to denim, before finally closing in 1983.

Haw River to Eno River State Park at Pleasant Green Road

At this time, the MST has two routes between the town of Haw River and Hillsborough. The "current route" that heads in a largely eastward direction through Mebane and Efland is shorter and the one currently used by most thru-hikers. The alternate route heads south toward Saxapahaw and then northeast through southwest Orange County past the Cane Creek Reservoir to Hillsborough.

On the current route, as you depart Red Slide Park (EB 33.4), turn left across the John Robert Watkins Memorial Bridge, and the Haw River Town Museum is at 201 East Main Street. Located in the town's old fire hall, built 145 years ago, the museum tells the history of the town through photographs, artifacts, and memorabilia. At 509 West Main Street (0.2 mile to the right exiting Red Slide Park) is a Civil War Trails historical marker on the Southern Diaspora and Nathaniel Polk DeShong, a French

Protestant (Huguenot) immigrant. In 1862 he enlisted in the Sixth NC State Troops and served as an ambulance driver at Antietam and Gettysburg, returning to Haw River in 1865. During the postwar depression, his family moved to Texas.

Ten miles to the north, on Dailey Store Road, are the tribal grounds of the Occaneechi Band of the Saponi Nation, land they migrated to in the 1790s and where their tribal office and homeland preservation project is now located. Just 2.5 miles north of EB 33.8, on NC 49, is the town of Green Level, which was known in the 1930s as Ruby Dew, a Black American tobacco farming community.

Carla Gardner completed her MST section-hike in 2017. She encourages more people to hike the MST to "understand the diverse economies and lifestyles of the people of North Carolina." Among her favorite memories, she recalls that "at Oak Ridge (Segment 8), the director of Parks and Rec let us park in his driveway for the night and spent the evening talking to us while sitting at a City Park picnic table. In Haw River, the town manager gave us the town keys (keys to use the bathroom) and directions to Dickie Do's BBQ place for lunch."

Mebane has a lovely downtown built around the railroad. Textiles weren't the only product manufactured in this area. White Furniture Company was founded in Mebane in 1881 when mass furniture production began across the state. In 1913 it became the first company in the South to use electricity; by 1939, North Carolina led the United States in manufacturing wood furniture.

The future planned and current alternate route for the MST here follows the Haw River from the town of Haw River to Swepsonville, to Saxapahaw, and then north through land around the Cane Creek Reservoir toward Occoneechee Mountain and Hillsborough. Fourteen miles is in the planning stage under the slogan "Blaze Orange County." Swepsonville's first mill was constructed around 1760. George Swepson began Falls Neuse Manufacturing Company in 1868, which became Virginia Cotton Mills in 1893; it closed in 1970, and the building was destroyed by fire in 1989. The Swepsonville River Park area is thirty acres, protecting over a mile of western riverfront.

The Saxapahaw Cotton Factory, constructed in the 1840s by John Newlin using enslaved labor, closed in 1944. Newlin's neighbor entrusted the people she enslaved to him, with the understanding that he would release them from bondage. In 1850, he traveled with forty-two formerly enslaved people and families to Ohio and officially set them free.

Attendees of the Friends of the MST annual meeting held in Saxapa-haw in 2012 and 2013 enjoyed the Saxapahaw General Store, the Rivermill (former home of Dixie Yarns Cotton Mill), Eddy Pub, and views of the Haw River. Saxapahaw Island Park, which opened in 2018 and spans thirty acres, features a ten-foot-high wooden fish slide measuring forty-five feet from head to fin. Alamance Parks maintains and operates Saxapahaw Lake Paddle Access and Saxapahaw Mill Race Paddle Access. The Haw River Canoe and Kayak Company is located in a building that was a hardware store until the 1970s. About 1.6 miles downriver from Saxapahaw, across a nice reclaimed bridge from Old Salem, along pastures of Reverence Farm, is where the alternate MST route will turn toward Hillsborough.

There are many dams and remnants along waterways and the MST. They have provided power for grinding corn, cutting lumber, powering textile mills, generating electricity, helping with flood control, and provid-ing reservoirs for drinking water. There are 1,634 dams in North Carolina, about 85 percent on private property, in places like ponds, lakes, camps, communities, towns, and power plants. There are 165 dams on the Haw River, seven on the main channel.

As you near the town of Hillsborough, you can visit the Kings Highway Park (EB 51.7) "just off the trail." This eighteen-acre natural area on Ben Johnson Road opened in 2007 and is owned and managed by the town. Thanks to the work of volunteers, the park boasts trails, bridges, and a kiosk. Its name is based on the presence of remnants of a river ford and road that connected Wilmington to Salisbury and likely was once the Na-tive American trading path (also known as the Indian Trading Path, Great Trading Path, or Hillsborough Road) that became a link in the pioneer route from what is now Washington, DC, to Atlanta. It was also part of a "street" in Hillsborough, currently known as King Street.

A great resource on old roads and trading paths is Tom Magnuson of the Trading Path Association (http://tradingpath.org/). He empha-sizes walking the riverbanks, searching for fords, scanning old maps, and looking for home ruins and graves near roads to learn more about where Native peoples and colonists traveled on foot, by horseback, or by wagon.

John Lawson, naturalist, explorer, and surveyor for the Lords Propri-etors, did much to introduce Europeans to the North American conti-nent. One of the first to promote colonizing the Carolina territories, he founded both Bath (in 1705, where he had a home) and New Bern (in 1710). Between 1700 and 1701, Lawson traversed 550 miles of the interior of the Carolinas, publishing his findings in *A New Voyage to Carolina* in

1709. In December 1700, he and several Virginia traders and their Native guides journeyed through the little-known backcountry of Carolina, near communities of present-day Hillsborough and Raleigh—maybe over terrain of the future MST. Lawson died at the hands of the Tuscarora Indians in 1711 while exploring the Neuse River. Not long after, the Tuscarora War began (1711–15).

Currently an eastbound MST hiker could continue on Eno Mountain Road (past the MST left-hand blaze at EB 52.9) for about 500 yards, then turn right onto a connecting trail for 100 yards to join the Occoneechee Mountain trails to the summit.

Occoneechee Mountain State Natural Area offers three miles of trail along the Eno River through forest and thickets of mountain laurel and rhododendron. The bluffs of Occoneechee Mountain rise 350 feet above the river, reaching 867 feet, the highest point between Hillsborough and the Atlantic Ocean. The park's picnic area sits on a grassy area shaded by majestic oak trees. Rangers regularly provide educational programs and tours highlighting the Piedmont monadnock and its unique flora and fauna.

Occoneechee Mountain is an estimated 600 million years old. The area was home to the Occaneechi Band of the Saponi Nation and is considered sacred to their people. A quarry operated from 1850 to 1908, producing material for house foundations and rock walls. John Thomas Cates purchased 137 acres of the mountain in 1880, most south of present-day I-85. By 1950, there was a ranger tower on the summit and, along the Eno Mountain Road, the Cates Brothers Store. The Eno Cotton Mill, established in 1889, built thirty-five houses for mill workers in the village and in 1956 sold them for twenty-five dollars per room. Most homes were moved to West Hillsborough, but some foundations remain. In 1993, Margaret Nygard and George Pyne set out to preserve Occoneechee, with land gifts from Allen and Pauline Lloyd, Cone Mills, and the Town of Hillsborough. North Carolina State Parks purchased 122 acres in 1997, and now the natural area contains 250 acres and is managed by Eno River State Park.

The Hillsborough Riverwalk is a 3.1-mile paved, accessible greenway along the Eno River in West Hillsborough's Gold Park that switches to natural surface trails east of town. Connecting several Hillsborough neighborhoods, the Riverwalk is popular among walkers, joggers, and cyclists. The trail is mostly flat and hosts beautiful views from the banks of the Eno River. Enjoy the Bee Pollinator Garden east of Gold Park. Up Eno Street and Nash Street to the left, look for the Margaret Lane Cemetery, also known as Old Slave Cemetery, at the corner of West Margaret Lane. The MST follows a portion of the greenway downtown, one of the few urban sections of the MST. Here hikers can access restrooms, restaurants, and shopping. Look out for Peggy's Kissing Bench along the way.

Orange County was established in 1752, stretching sixty miles south from the Virginia border to the Earl of Granville line, bordered by Granville, Johnston, and Bladen Counties to the east and Rowan County to the west. In 1771, nine counties were formed from Orange County. Hillsborough (elevation 600 feet; originally called Orange Courthouse in 1754 when it became the county seat, and renamed Hillsborough in 1766) was established where the Great Indian Trading Path crossed the Eno River. It is known for its history, architecture, arts, and culture. First laid out by William Churton on 400 acres from the Honorable John Earl Granville, it was a major town in the region for many years. It was here that on April 12, 1776, the Halifax Resolves were signed, the first official action calling for independence from Great Britain. The 1788 Constitutional Convention met here in old St. Matthew's Church to demand that a Bill of Rights be added to the US Constitution. The current courthouse was built in 1846; the town clock first appeared in the late 1760s, was restored several times, and is still ticking. UNC–Chapel Hill, the nation's oldest state university, was established twelve miles to the south in 1784.

In the downtown historic district today, you'll find the visitor center. It is housed in the old headquarters of Confederate general Joseph E. Johnston, who officially surrendered his armies to Union general William T. Sherman at Bennett Place, marking the beginning of the end of the Civil War. While downtown you'll also find the Orange County courthouse, built in 1844, as well as the Burwell School Historic Site, where you can learn about and be inspired by the history of Elizabeth Keckly, a former enslaved woman who became a successful seamstress and one of the town's most nationally recognized residents. In 2020, the Colonial Inn on King Street, built in 1838 expressly as a hotel for travelers to the county seat, was fully restored. Mount Zion AME Church was built in 1882 on an acre plot bought for ten dollars and given to the church. Barbecue lovers look forward to the annual Hog Day each May, and the streets of downtown fill with music and art each Friday night. Hillsborough has much to offer tourists (especially those interested in history), inspires and attracts artists and writers, and makes a great place to live for those lucky enough to call it home.

The Eno River starts in Orange County, travels thirty-three miles east, and joins the Flat River to become the Neuse River as it flows through Falls Lake. It moves quickly and is mostly shallow, except for a few deep parts like Sennett Hole. It was named after the Eno Indians who lived along the river before the arrival of Europeans. The Native people left by 1733 according to a map by Edward Mosley that first showed the Eno River, and European settlers first came to the area in the mid-1700s, establishing farms and building gristmills. The last of these mills stopped operating by 1940, but many of their remains can still be seen today.

Nearby

John Blackfeather Jeffries, a tribal elder and former tribal chief of the Occaneechi, oversaw the rebuilding of a replica Occaneechi Native American village in 2020. He first built a full replica village in Hillsborough in 1997, almost single-handedly, cutting 396 cedar poles for the palisade wall, four of them with a stone axe, and more for the handmade huts. The site fell into disrepair, so in 2020, the Alliance for Historic Hillsborough, town staff, and community members worked to re-create this village. Jeffries, an Eagle Scout and former marine, had the tenacity and dedication to lead this project.

John (as he preferred to be called) could often be found sitting on a bench beside the MST across from the replica village—"at home" just like sitting on his front porch—talking to anyone who stopped to ask about the village. "If you travel the roads around here—86, 70, I-85—they all follow Trading Paths," he says, "and the Native people lived right here along the Eno, in structures just like these." Just past the replica village, the MST crosses a segment of a trading path, then skirts a twenty-acre area in the Eno River Bend, considered the site of Indigenous settlements. This site is managed by the Archaeological Conservancy.

In his years of research, John discovered that thousands of years ago his people, the Occaneechi Indian Tribe, left the Ohio River Valley, crossed the Blue Ridge Mountains, and settled in present-day Clarksville, Virginia. In 1676, during Bacon's Rebellion, the tribe was forced out and retreated to what is now Hillsborough. Though they found refuge for a short time living in the rich lands along the Eno and Haw Rivers, near the Great Indian Trading Path, their oasis was quickly quashed. Native Skakori, Shocco, Eno, and Occaneechi peoples made contact with German explorer John Lederer in 1670. In 1701, English explorer John Lawson arrived. As

John Blackfeather Jeffries at the replica Occaneechi tribal village along the Eno River in Hillsborough. *Photo by Jerry Barker.*

increasing numbers of Europeans settled in the area, Jeffries's ancestors migrated back toward Virginia and sought protection from the Virginia government in 1712. Their requests for refuge were repeatedly denied, and by the late 1770s, the tribe gave up on Virginia and returned to North Carolina, settling in Alamance County. Jeffries cites more struggles during the 1800s and 1900s, but he does celebrate one major achievement, when the Occaneechi Band of the Saponi Nation obtained state recognition in 2002. There are 140,000 Native Americans in North Carolina, the most of any state east of the Mississippi and eighth-most nationally.

Back on the Trail

River Park in Hillsborough offers wide-open grassy areas in downtown with the MST running right through it and along the Eno River. There is often a farmer's market, and visitors can attend outdoor concerts and movie screenings during warmer months. At EB 54.6, the first bridge after the replica village crosses a remnant of Fish Dam Road. A nearby sign describes this as a Native footpath from the seventeenth and eighteenth centuries, when Hillsborough was the colonial capital of North Carolina. It grew wider as colonial wagon traffic used it, but by the 1920s it fell into disuse as paved roads became the norm. This is the first of nine remnants of Fish Dam Road that the MST crosses in the next thirty miles.

From Elizabeth Brady Road (EB 55.1) to US 70 (EB 56.2), hikers will find the Historic Occoneechee Speedway Trail and the James M. Johnston Nature Preserve, whose combined 206 acres were added to the Eno River State Park in 2023. Classical American Homes Preservation Trust, which first bought the Speedway's forty-four acres in 1997 and restored the grandstands and the mile-long oval track with help from the Historic Speedway Group, contributed to the transfer of those properties to North Carolina State Parks. The trust also owns the nearby Ayr Mount Historic Site, which includes the 1815 Ayr Mount house (the first major house in the Piedmont built of brick) and grounds on St. Mary's Road. William and Margret Kirkland, owners of the home and estate, enslaved twenty individuals, who worked at the home and William's store and tannery in town. Black Craftspeople Digital Archive was established in 2019 by the trust to collect and share the stories of Black craftspeople in the slave-holding South (https://blackcraftspeople.org).

Located just east of Hillsborough, Occoneechee Speedway sits on what was called the "Occaneechi farm" in the late nineteenth century. In September 1947, Bill France found a half-mile track for horse racing on the land and turned it into a 0.9-mile dirt track for stock car racing. This was two months before NASCAR was organized. Occoneechee Speedway held its inaugural season in 1949, making it one of the first two NASCAR tracks to open. Races ranged in length from 99 to 200 miles, and the track hosted racing legends such as Fireball Roberts, Lee and Richard Petty, Ned Jarrett, David Pearson, Buck Baker, and Junior Johnson. Richard Petty won the last race at the Speedway on September 15, 1968 (150 miles, '68 Plymouth, speed 87.68 mph, purse $6,900), the year it closed. Local high school football teams played games on the infield in front of the grandstands in the 1950s and 1960s, and now the track makes for a pleasant walk.

Native History on the MST

You can see and feel Native American history along the MST. The Occaneechi Band of the Saponi Nation in Alamance and Orange Counties, with over 1,100 members, is a state-recognized tribal nation. The MST also traverses tribal lands of the Eastern Band of Cherokee Indians (the only North Carolina tribe with federal recognition), located in three mountain counties; the Coharie Tribe in Sampson and Harnett Counties; and the Waccamaw Siouan Tribe in Bladen and Columbus Counties. With Hillsborough being the earliest town on the North Carolina frontier, Native peoples were displaced as settlers moved in. While the Cherokee's Trail of Tears is the most recognized historical event, Native Americans still battle for civil rights and are proud of their linguistic and cultural uniqueness. Native Americans didn't receive the right to vote until 1924. In 2021, Deb Haaland became the first Native American US cabinet secretary as secretary of the interior (the department that administers the Bureau of Indian Affairs), and Charles Sams III became the first Indigenous director of the National Park Service in the agency's 105-year history.

Tutelo-speaking peoples translate "Mountains to Sea" as "Oheki yetai," thus, the name of our trail is the Oheki Yetai Trail. This translation comes courtesy of Corey Roberts, a linguistics graduate student of Occaneechi heritage, and Alexa Lawrence, a member of the Saponi community working with Roberts on language revitalization for Tutelo-Saponi (Yesànechi), the language of some of their shared Indigenous ancestors.

As the MST goes east from the speedway and the Johnson Nature Preserve, it concludes Segment 9 with 4.5 miles of US 70 highway walking to Pleasant Green Road (EB 56.2–60.7). US 70 was first paved in 1923. Tentative plans have the trail going under US 70 and connecting with the Eno River State Park Cox Mountain Trail for several miles to Pleasant Green Road, providing access to more side trails in the park, primitive camping, restrooms, shelter, and parking.

Segment 9 ends at the Pleasant Green Road access to Eno River State Park, where you can see a portion of a low dam that was removed in 2006 (built in 1915, 122 feet long, 12 feet high). The MST continues east under Pleasant Green Road. A short side trip at the upper end of the parking lot crosses a discharge area from the Southern Power Plant (built in 1915 and demolished in 1960), with views of the current Duke Energy substation on the left. Along the trail are remnants of the former operation, and it's about 100 yards to the dam on Stony Creek and the Eno Steam Station spray pond. Be sure to obey No Trespassing signs. Turbulent Stony Creek discharges into the Eno River.

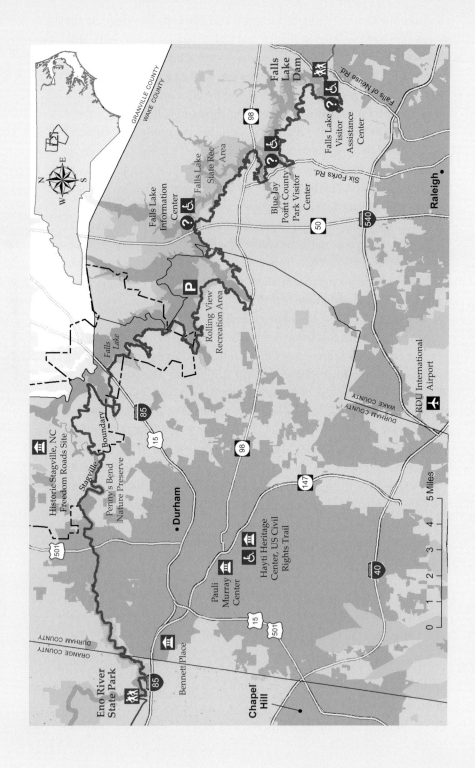

Eno River and Falls Lake

Eno River State Park at Pleasant Green Road
to Falls Lake Dam near Raleigh

78.6 MILES

Conservation at its core is a celebration of diversity:
diversity of plants, diversity of animals, diversity of
landscapes, and diversity of cultures and people.

ENO RIVER ASSOCIATION

This segment meanders near shorelines of the Eno River and Falls Lake. Though near the heavily populated Triangle—Raleigh, Durham, and Chapel Hill—the MST is mostly on natural-surface trail due to large parcels of adjoining public land. The first eighteen miles parallel the Eno River; the trail then winds in and out of coves along Falls Lake for the remainder.

Eno River State Park at Pleasant Green Road
to Penny's Bend Nature Preserve

At the Pleasant Green trailhead for the MST, there are ruins from the Southern Power Station (currently a Duke Energy substation) on the west side and maybe an earlier mill. Across Pleasant Green Road from the state park access parking and trailhead was an 1800s home site, now marked only with a chimney rock pile, some fence post and wire, and a nearby spring. The *Eno River Journal* published two special issues, titled "Ribbons of Color along the Eno River," that share the underheard stories of the people of color whose history played out on the banks, forests, and communities of the Eno. Durham resident Beverly Scarlett can trace her family back to Bunsheba, an enslaved person purchased in 1817 at sixteen months of age by John Scarlett, whose father Steven Scarlett came to the Eno River from England in 1759.

Bunsheba's son and Beverly's great-grandfather, Levi Christmas Scarlett, was born into slavery around Christmas Day in 1855. Two sisters, Mariah and Delilah, were his enslavers. When he was ten years old, almost three years after the Emancipation Proclamation was signed, the sisters promised that if he would care for them until their death, they would grant him their land. True to their word, Mariah Scarlett's will deeded him 149 acres along the Eno River on both sides of Pleasant Green Road. In 1874, Levi married Laura Pratt. Their children included Beverly's grandfather William "Bud Chris" Scarlett, whose own family would include Beverly's father, John A. Scarlett. By tracing her lineage several generations, Beverly Scarlett is able to tell her ancestors' stories.

About twenty yards east of Pleasant Green Road bridge, there are remnants of an earlier truss bridge across the Eno that was removed in 1958. About 0.2 mile farther east, at the first creek drainage, follow the creek up about seventy-five yards to the remains of the Scarlett family BBQ grill, built in the 1920s, and a spring built by Levi Christmas Scarlett. Please be respectful of historic property.

Nearby

Bennett Place State Historic Site is located on Bennett Memorial Road in Durham, about a mile from the MST at Pleasant Green Road/US 70 Business. After Gen. Robert E. Lee surrendered to Gen. Ulysses S. Grant on April 9, 1865, at Appomattox Court House in Virginia, Gen. William Sherman and Gen. Joseph Johnston met at James and Nancy Bennett's farm near Durham Station to decide the terms of surrender for some 89,000 Confederate soldiers. The terms were finalized on April 26, which formally surrendered all Confederate soldiers fighting in Florida, Georgia, and the Carolinas, making this settlement the largest surrender of the Civil War. Included on the North Carolina Civil War Trails, the site offers a variety of experiences. The original house burned in 1921. The buildings were reconstructed in 1962 on 3.5 acres of land for the historic site.

Durham became a town when its post office was established in 1853. It became the "Bull City" when Blackwell Tobacco Company named a product "Bull" Durham Tobacco in the late 1800s. Durham has a rich

African American history. In 1898, North Carolina Mutual Life Insurance Company was founded; until its liquidation in 2022, it was the nation's largest and oldest African American–owned life insurance company. Mechanics and Farmers (M&F) Bank, founded in 1907, continues to operate as the second-oldest minority-owned bank in America. North Carolina Central University, a historically Black university, was established in 1910. The area became famous across the country as "Black Wall Street." Its last original structure (built in 1891), the Hayti Heritage Center, is now a cultural arts and education venue dedicated to preserving and furthering the area's heritage and culture as well as documenting the African American experience.

Back on the Trail

Eno River State Park (ERSP) sits on 4,319 acres in Durham and Orange Counties and is the third-most visited state park in North Carolina, welcoming over 1 million visitors in 2021. It abuts the Durham city park West Point on the Eno, and together the two parks protect over fourteen miles of the Eno River and its surrounding lands. The park offers nearly thirty miles of trails. This MST segment starts in the state park at the Pleasant Green Road trailhead.

The Eno Quarry (EB 1.4–1.6) was once a sixty-foot-deep stone pit mined by the North Carolina Department of Transportation between 1960 and 1964 to construct I-85. It was then abandoned by the state and filled with water. The resulting four-acre pond, added to the ERSP in 2002, is today a popular summer hangout, with twenty-five-foot depths at the banks. Locals call it a "swimming hole with a history." It can also be accessed from the park's Cabe Lands access on Howe Street. The MST leaves the quarry as it crosses Rhodes Creek and in 200 yards crosses the second remnant of Fish Dam Road. Just 130 yards farther, at four wooden steps, is the third intersection.

The Cabe Lands Trail (1.4-mile loop, red blazes) is in the ERSP in Orange County and connects with the MST (EB 2.1 and 2.5). The "Cabe" of Cabe Lands refers to Barnaby Cabe, who owned the land before the American Revolution. In 1780, John Cabe owned 304 acres along the Eno. He built a successful mill (1779–1832) and, by the time he died, owned 4,000 acres, known as the Cabe Lands. As Durham grew into an industrial and tobacco center and people migrated to more urban areas, business from the Eno River mill and farm communities declined. The train stop, Durham Station, and the Eno communities could not compete economically. The Eno River Valley was like a wilderness by the 1950s.

"Just off the trail" in the Cabe Lands are ruins to explore (parking available at Cabe Lands trailhead on Howe Street). As you turn right by the river at EB 2.2, immediately to the right is the beginning of the Cabe Mill headrace, which, if dry, you can walk in for about 1,000 feet to the mill. At EB 2.3, just after crossing two small bridges over the tailrace, turn right, and as you begin ascending, remnants of the old Cabe Mill stone foundation walls, once the mill's basement, are visible on the right; the foundation is about twenty-five square feet. In the Eno River Valley, at least thirty-two mills operated between the mid-1700s and early 1900s.

After crossing the second bridge, the MST goes straight uphill, and within 100 yards on the left you see a mound of remains of the old homestead (look for daffodils in the spring on the flat ridge top). After passing the Cabe Lands Trail to the right, continue straight to EB 2.5 to an unmarked trail (that also goes to Cabe Lands parking); it is 200 yards to the 1806 Cabe-McCown family cemetery on the left. There are over fifty graves but only twelve headstones. The oldest marked grave is of Rachel Cabe Sims (1792–1865).

Hiking the Laurel Bluffs Trail/MST between the Cabe Lands area and the park's pump station, you will encounter the chimney of Sam Sparger's hunting lodge (EB 3.3) south of Bobbitt Hole. Sparger was a man about town in Durham, with a 1924 Nash automobile and membership in two country clubs. He bought forty-eight acres on the Eno River from the Cabe family and lived there until his death in 1951. His widow, Florence Wyatt, head nurse of Watts Hospital, continued to live there far from town. Sam Sparger wrote about his love of the Eno River in his will, concluding, "It is an area which has great appeal to the lover of nature and has potential value as a park." As you walk under Cole Mill Road, you enter Durham County.

An undated historical record, shared by the Eno River Association, says about the area, "Four colonial roads are shown within the lines of this great tract: the old Fayetteville Road, the old Hillsboro Road, the old Oxford Road which crossed the Eno River at Cabe's ford, and the Fish Dam Road." Fish Dam Road initially connected two Native villages, near the rivers where they erected fish weirs. It was incorporated into present-day roads connecting Hillsborough to East Durham, such as US 70 and Cheek Road (the MST crosses at EB 32.2). Over time, the settler community of Fish Dam developed, and it even boasted a post office at one point.

The thirty-five-foot steel I-beam bridge with wood decking over Nancy Rhodes Creek (EB 5.9) was washed out by flooding in 2018. With a grant from the Durham Open Space and Trails Commission, volunteers used a winch to pull the 1,200-pound beams out of the creek, straightened them, built two large new foundations, and reinstalled the bridge about two feet higher. Nancy Rhodes Creek and the dam remains are prominent in the history of the Durham Pump Station (EB 6.1) and worth exploring. The basic history can be explored on signboards at the Pump Station designed in 2013 by Youth Conservation Corp member Jonathan Hill. Look for the old spillway for the lake behind the Nancy Rhodes Creek Dam. The pump station was in use from 1887 to 1927. Explore for ruins of the steam plant, filter house, boilers, pump house, and the Old Durham Dam.

Between EB 7.1 and EB 8.5, the MST passes several points of interest, including Fish Dam Island, Gebel Rock (check out this nice rock outcrop high above the river), Panther Cliffs, the ruins of Guess Mill Dam, and the remains of a home site. You can walk in an old mill sluice, step on a millstone, and study the remnants of a former gristmill. Seeing this history, it's easy to envision a lively Eno River with bustling homes and mills. At EB 8.7 the MST goes under Guess Road. Just on the other side is the headquarters of the Eno River Association that helps protect nearly 7,600 acres in the Eno basin. The blue-blaze Eagle Trail starts by the Eno River Association headquarters and runs parallel to the MST higher on the bluff for 0.5 mile before joining it to run concurrently by the river until reaching North Roxboro Road.

Eagle Scout projects have built two stone arch bridges. Task force leader Fred Dietrich said, "My inspiration for this was when walking a narrow trail in Switzerland years ago and [I] crossed a stone arch bridge over a narrow gorge. The date on the bridge was 1700. I am hopeful they will be much lower maintenance (than our wooden bridges)."

At EB 9.6 is Sennett Hole, a huge swimming hole formed in the river where large boulders (Mafic dike) block a lot of the water flow. This is a deep hole, with spots over ten feet deep. The Sennett mill raceway can be seen across the river along the upper portion of Sennett Hole, but nothing remains of the mill. This is generally the area where Caroline Terrane transitions to Triassic Basin geology. Just past Sennett Hole, on the left, are a chimney and the brick ruins of a residence. Beyond that begins what was a level farm field (now covered in mature trees) with evidence of trenches used for both irrigation and drainage (EB 9.9). About 120 yards back in the northwest corner, you can discover a water box that provided drinking water to those working the field as well as irrigation. You'll have to search for it, as the water box is not clearly marked.

Margaret Nygard's Legacy

You should know the influence and impact of Margaret Nygard, who helped save the Eno River and establish a state park. On August 16, 1966, a group led by activist Nygard, who was originally from England and passed away in 1995, voiced opposition to a Durham plan that would dam the nearby Eno River. Nygard, a local English teacher and social worker, and other concerned citizens, formed the Association for the Preservation of the Eno River Valley (now known as the Eno River Association) in 1965. The association worked with local governments and the state to save the area's natural resources and, by 2020, helped protect 7,480 acres of watershed. The idea for a state park was born, and a local farm made an initial donation of ninety acres. In 1973, the state, with help from The Nature Conservancy, opened Eno River State Park with more than 1,000 acres. By 2020, the park was over 4,300 acres.

Without the work of "the indomitable, articulate, and deceptively soft-spoken" Nygard, the Eno River we know and love today might have looked very different. She worked tirelessly to save the river, using not only political action but also hikes, paddle trips, educational materials like slide shows and maps, mill histories, and wildlife catalogs to endear the waterway to both the public and policymakers. Seventy-five people attended the first hike sponsored by the association, while 450 attended the second. Public support grew, and association membership swelled. The rest is history.

The home of Margaret Nygard is close to the MST, near the Cole Mill Road Bridge (EB 4.8). From the trail you can see the water pump house for the home. The house was associated with the mill, and a second house where the mill keeper lived, now run down but visible from the trail, is just upriver of the mill site.

Back on the Trail

The City of Durham established West Point on the Eno in 1973 as a natural and historic park along two miles of the Eno River, six miles north of downtown on US 501. Once home to the Shocco and Eno tribes, and later attracting European settlers (mostly farmers and millers) in the 1750s, little of its 404 wooded acres, waterways, and wildlife have changed in the last three centuries. At EB 10.3, the bridge to the right crossing the Eno leads to West Point on the Eno (the longest pedestrian bridge in Eno River State Park). Nearby is the renowned Museum of Life and Science, 3.5 miles south off US 501, founded in 1946 on eighty-four acres (admission for a fee).

One of the few remaining open agricultural fields can be seen on the left and now serves as an amphitheater (EB 10.1). Crooked Creek also comes in from the left (EB 10.2), just before reaching the West Point dam, and offers an exciting rock-hop crossing of the MST. The Eno River becomes a flat river from here to Falls Lake and even fluctuates due to the Falls Lake water level since the top elevation of the West Point dam (300 feet) is almost the same as the Falls Dam spillway (289.2 feet), sixty-seven trail miles to the east.

West Point Mill (1778–1942) was the oldest, longest-operating, and most prosperous of the mills that once existed along the Eno River. Its success was largely due to its location and topography, as it was easily accessed from all directions and made for an easy crossing. In its time, West Point Mill supported a thriving community of about 300 families, providing a sawmill as well as a general store, a blacksmith shop, a cotton gin, and a still. The mill was the western terminus of the mail route between Raleigh and Roxboro, hence the name West Point for the mill, the community's post office, and the community itself. The mill closed in 1942 and was neglected for the next three decades before collapsing in 1973. Eventually the mill was reconstructed on its original foundation, in part with materials from the original framing as well as materials from nearby gristmills, using old photographs as a guide. Today it is back in operation, powered by the waters of the Eno to grind corn and wheat, and stoneground meal and flour can be purchased in the mill's store. The McCown–Mangum house, built in 1840, is also open for tours on the property.

Festival for the Eno, now called EnoFest, was established in 1980, and is North Carolina's largest and longest-running event on Fourth of July weekend. The three-day festival features live music, a crafts market, local foods, local artists, local vendors, and environmental education. EnoFest promotes the natural beauty, culture, and history of the Eno River, and uses the thousands of dollars in proceeds to protect, purchase, and preserve the river and lands along it. Organizers and volunteers are proud that they divert 98 percent of festival waste from landfills through their Trash Free program.

The MST follows near a sewer easement after leaving West Point on the Eno. River Forest Park is on the left, then on the right side of the river there are remains of a quarry and open fields at Old Farm Park. From approximately EB 11.4 to EB 36.6—over 24 miles—the MST travels on land that was part of the Brennehan-Cameron Plantation, remnants of which now make up the Stagville Plantation State Historic Site.

Penny's Bend Nature Preserve, at the corner of Old Oxford and Snow Hill Roads, consists of eighty-four acres on a horseshoe bend in the Eno River. The US Army Corps of Engineers owns the natural area, and the North Carolina Botanical Garden manages it. The bend that gives the preserve its name is known as a diabase sill, which was formed hundreds of millions of years ago by the intrusion of very hard volcanic rock into the softer sedimentary rock. Over time, the Eno's eastward flow eroded the softer rock, exposing smooth, dark boulders and diverting the river south, which created Penny's Bend and the unique geology of this area. The diabase rock at the bend creates soils that are less acidic than those found in other areas of the Piedmont. Because of these soils—Iredell in the uplands and Wilkes sandy loam at the base of the slopes—visitors to Penny's Bend will find plants not typically seen in this part of the country, like blue wild indigo and hoary puccoon. The MST follows the George Pyne Trail through the preserve, and there is an alternate route, Cash's Point Trail, away from the river.

In 1836, Cameron's Mill was constructed by Duncan Cameron using rocks from the area, and the remains are still visible (EB 15.1). In 1890, his son Paul C. Cameron was the owner of three plantations in the area: Stagville, Fairntosh, and Snow Hill. Snow Hill goes even further back in history. Established in 1763 by William Johnston, it was one of the earliest plantations in what would become northern Durham County, including land that is now Penny's Bend.

Penny's Bend Nature Preserve to Falls Lake Dam

Stagville State Historic Site, approximately 165 acres, is located about five miles from the MST where it crosses Old Oxford Highway and north of Red Mill Road. The site incorporates Horton Grove Nature Preserve, which contains 708 acres of land, including twenty-five acres of grassland and eight miles of hiking trails. Stagville is home to the remnants of one of the largest pre–Civil War plantations in the South and the largest in North Carolina. Among the remaining structures stands the Great Barn,

The Holman, Umstead, and Cameron/Justice cabins for enslaved at Stagville
State Historic Site, a few miles north of the MST in Durham County.
Photo by Jerry Barker.

once considered the largest building in North Carolina. Built in 1860, it
is three stories high and 133 feet long. There are also four quarters for
enslaved people built in 1851 for four families, tobacco barns, the Bennehan family house (1787–99), and a graveyard. The site comprises the
plantations that belonged to the Bennehan–Cameron family from 1776
to 1865; in 1860, they owned a total of almost 30,000 acres of land and
enslaved approximately 900 people.

Willie Horton, a white subsistence farmer, built a small, well-con-
structed plank house before the Revolutionary War (predating the switch
to enslaved labor on the plantation), which still stands. Trails at Horton
Grove are named after Black families—Holman, Peaks, Hart, Justice,
Latta, Walker, Jordan, and Sowell—whose ancestors were enslaved
and forced to work on the land. Fairntosh farm, also part of Stagville
Plantation, eventually became one of the largest plantations east of the
Mississippi. About twenty-four miles of the MST, from west of Penny's
Bend to Little Rogers Road, were once part of the Stagville-Fairntosh
plantations.

How can enslaved people from the past have their identity restored
and regain their voice? Efforts are being made by the Enslaved Persons
Project—a collaborative endeavor between UNC Greensboro Libraries,
the North Carolina Division of Archives and Records, the Wake County
Register of Deeds, and Shaw University—to create a database about

formerly enslaved people identified in bills of sale. Because enslaved people were excluded from typical historical records, these are some of the only records available that will allow their names to be recognized and remembered.

After leaving Penny's Bend and crossing Old Oxford Road, about 500 yards east of the road, go left along the railroad tracks 150 yards to an abandoned 1909 Norfolk and Western trestle crossing the river (for safety, please do not cross the trestle). Another hidden gem is Willie Duke's Bluff, a scenic sixty-foot bluff named for a preacher in the mid-1800s (EB 15.9). It has abundant wildflowers in the spring, especially at the base of the bluff along the Eno.

The Little River, a tributary of the Eno, empties into the Eno on the north side at about EB 16.4. The Little River is 12.8 miles long, and its aquatic habitat is noted for state significance. As our eastward hike leaves the Eno and begins following the waters of the Neuse, we are just past the halfway point of our journey to the sea.

At EB 18.1, there is signage for hiker camping to the right. The Ward family owns the property and has graciously made the shelter and camp-sites available to hikers doing the entire MST. As one nears Red Mill Road, a huge solar farm appears on the right. The area from Red Mill Road (EB 19.3) to Cheek Road (EB 32.2) is low-lying upper Falls Lake land and can be wet or flooded following heavy rain or when the water level is high at Falls Lake (elevation over 256 mean sea level feet). Along the trail one sees evidence of farm activity, including fields, tree farms, a trash dump, and old tires, as well as evidence of Corps of Engineers construction work. The Fogleman family moved to Durham County after the Civil War and worked for the Stagville-Fairntosh plantations, running their mills and farms. A family story says Red Mill Road was named for Mr. Fogleman, who had red hair.

Near EB 22.4, railroad tracks to a Southern Railroad spur end at Ham-lin Road, which is railroad private property with no public access. On the right at EB 22.6 are two old barns, one with a cupola on top to permit light and air to flow in the hayloft. The trail is lined with remnants of old trucks and trash dumps. At EB 23.3 a functioning rail line runs on the other side of Ellerbee Creek. Ellerbee Creek, a tributary of the Neuse River, travels through North Durham for more than twenty miles. Another abandoned railroad trestle is at EB 23.7. You'll find more evidence of active and inactive railroad tracks and trestles near the MST. Fogleman's Landfill is the big hill to the right after crossing Ellerbee Creek (EB 24.3–24.8).

Jeff Brewer served as president of Friends of the Mountains-to-Sea Trail from 1997 to 2009. He was the sixth MST completer and a devoted Falls Lake volunteer leader. *Photo by Meredith Henry; used by permission.*

The trail crosses the Newcombs Lake dam (elevation 443 feet), property of Durham County. At the intersection of Tom Clark Road and Redwood Road (EB 24.9), you are walking along the south shore of Falls Lake and on a remnant of Fish Dam Road.

The Flat and Eno Rivers merge to form the expansive Neuse River, just north of where the MST crosses Red Mill Road at EB 19.2. The waters of nineteen North Carolina counties (containing 17 percent of the state's population) drain into the Neuse River Basin, which spans some 6,200 square miles. People have lived along the Neuse for approximately 14,000 years, the earliest of them including the Tuscarora, Coree, Neusiok, and Secotan Native peoples. The river's name likely came from the Neusiok language and means "peace" or "peaceful."

The Eno River Task Force maintains fifteen miles of MST from Pleasant Green Road to Penny's Bend/Old Oxford Road. The Falls Lake Trail/ MST begins at Old Oxford Road and runs over sixty-two miles to Falls Dam. These miles were completed in 2012 and are maintained by the Falls Lake Task Force of over fifty volunteers. This segment of trail is subdivided into twenty-three sections for identification and maintenance purposes, with trailheads facilitating mostly two-and-a-half-to-four-mile hikes. Jeff Brewer described thirty-seven miles of trail construction from

Penny's Bend to Highway 50 as "taking seven years to get a written MOA [memorandum of understanding], then only five years to build the trail (January 2007 to November 2011). It was officially dedicated on May 19, 2012, with a cookout and ceremony at Rolling View Recreation Area." The Triangle Greenways Council constructed the Falls Lake Trail twenty-seven miles from NC 50 to Falls Dam in the 1980s, and it was designated as part of the MST in 1987.

Falls Lake reservoir covers 12,410 acres, extends twenty-eight miles, and conserves a total of 38,000 acres. The dam was authorized, and construction began in 1978 and was completed in 1981. The lake's normal conservation pool is at an elevation of 251.5 feet mean sea level and contains 42.8 billion gallons of water. The reservoir offers water supply to surrounding areas, reduces potential damage from flooding, improves water quality, protects and enhances fish and wildlife populations, and provides a number of recreational opportunities. Falls Lake State Recreation Area, with over 300 campsites in several locations around the lake, was one of seven state parks with over 1 million visitors in 2020. The MST has parking and trails in the Rolling View and Shinleaf State Recreation Areas.

At EB 26.1, the MST goes under I-85. When I-85 was constructed, a farm was split into two and the one-lane tunnel constructed to allow the landowners access to all their property. The MST passes the end of the runway of Lake Ridge Aero Park at the dead end of East Geer Street (EB 26.4). This private airfield, first known as Ferris Field, dates to 1945 and is mostly used for crop dusting and glider operations. Hickory Hills Boat Ramp (EB 27.2) is the gathering place for the annual Race across Durham marathon organized by Joe McClernon and Bull City Running to benefit the Life Skills Foundation. They also host a ten-mile run from West Point on the Eno, with both races finishing at the Eno Quarry; find more information at www.raceacrossdurham.com.

In 2020 and 2021, the COVID-19 pandemic brought new hikers to the MST, but it also brought more trail time for folks like Joe. He composed a letter to the Friends describing what the trail meant to him, summarizing with this introspective conclusion: "During the pandemic, I've come to realize that the MST is about more than connecting dots across a map of North Carolina. The MST is about connecting us to each other, connecting us to our past, connecting us to home, and connecting us to nature. That's the MST mission as I see it—to bring about a sense of connectedness in everyone who sets foot on the MST, whether they travel one mile or 1,175."

At Redwood Road, a 2.6-mile blue blaze alternate trail allows you to explore the Panther Creek tributary. An abandoned rail line follows it. An old North Carolina railroad map shows that the Durham and Northern became operational in 1889 as part of the Seaboard Air Line system, running from Durham to Henderson and beyond. As you turn left onto the Redwood Road causeway that currently carries the trail over the Panther Creek embayment, on the right of Redwood Road and on the west side of Panther Creek, you'll find the railroad bed intact, with 1.1 miles incorporated into the Panther Creek Loop Trail built by a Falls Lake crew in 2017–20. The loop trail crosses two trestles, then crosses over Panther Creek, returns to Redwood Road, and then continues across the highway on MST white blaze trail (EB 28).

Walking down this former roadbed, you can see a barn foundation on the right, then another on the left, and as the trail veers right (EB 28.2) you can spot a two-story chimney on the left. This is a remnant of the Redwood Hotel, a two-story tavern with a large porch that faced the Neuse River and offered food, drink, lodging, and a corral for horses to Fish Dam Road travelers and passengers from a nearby train stop. The decaying remains of this building were removed in the 1970s as Falls Lake was built. As the MST continues east, remains of two tenant houses are visible on the right. At EB 28.8 the MST crosses a discernable gully, the seventh remnant of Fish Dam Road.

At Hereford Road (EB 31.2), 120 yards to the right are the 1880s Joseph Holloway House and Morgan-Holloway Cemetery (with six headstones; Morgan graves have no markers). The Hereford Road causeway was removed in 2023, causing a relocation of the MST up the 2.1-mile Rocky Branch Loop and through deep woods, crossing two streams. Hikers also pass four nostalgic, rusting automobiles, three tentatively identified as a 1951 four-door Chevy Deluxe, a 1953 two-door Chevy Belair, and a 1954 two-door Ford Skyliner (original manufacturer's suggested retail prices between $1,620 and $2,241). These and other historic artifacts along the MST should be left as found for others to enjoy. Hikers again cross Hereford Road and remnants eight and nine of Fish Dam Road before reaching Cheek Road (EB 32.2). At EB 35.8 a short blue blaze trail leads to the rock and a beautiful lake view.

The trail enters a beautiful area as hikers walk on the abandoned Jimmy Rogers Road roadbed that crosses Little Lick Creek (EB 36.5). This is one of many roads closed when Falls Lake was built. This is also the eastern point where the MST has been on former Stagville Plantation

Thanks to the volunteers across the state who construct, repair, and blaze trails and bridges. This group prepares to construct a short reroute at Falls Lake. *Photo by Jerry Barker.*

property. Along the long boardwalk are wetlands, with cypress trees lining the old creek banks (now underwater). In May 2012 a 110-foot steel pedestrian bridge was dedicated, funded by $205,000 from federal Recreational Trails Program (administered by North Carolina State Parks) and Durham County's Open Space matching grant programs, and Great Outdoor Provisions Company, the "capstone to the 60-mile Falls Lake Trail." This area is a great place to observe the fluctuations of Falls Lake levels: sometimes it is totally dry and other times the water laps just below the highest bridge decking. On July 15, 2023, this bridge was named the de Hart Bridge to honor MST visionary Allen de Hart.

At 877 Santee Road (0.6 mile from the MST) is the unmaintained Union Chapel Baptist Church cemetery that contains the relocated graves from family cemeteries from the Durham County area now covered by Falls Lake. When Falls Lake was created, 675 graves from thirteen family cemeteries were reinterred at this site and a site for Wake County near Falls Dam.

About a mile east of the big footbridge, look for an old farm dump that has been partially bulldozed over, but on the left about twenty feet off the trail, look for four old automobiles about half covered (maybe a 1961 Chevy truck). In that same area a giant pine tree rises on the right; on the left runs the old roadbed of John Rogers Road, currently named Santee Road and Shaw Road (with several caution signs near the lake); and on the right are remains of a Meadow Gold milk delivery truck, active in the area until the 1980s. About a mile west of Rolling View, on the right about where you enter state park land, are horse pastures that belong to Triton Stables.

Near EB 40.7 where you reach Baptist Road and enter Rolling View State Recreation Area (part of the Falls Lake State Recreation Area with 115 campsites, swimming, and kayak rentals) are several historic sites. About thirty yards before reaching the road there is a large oak tree on the left, and ten yards past it into the woods are eight foundation stones from a building. On the blue-blaze MST parking trail that crosses Baptist Road is the fenced Rigsbee Family Cemetery. It includes fifteen graves, four of which are marked; two are World War II veterans, among them Lou Rigsbee, who died in May 1945 while serving as a marine. The Colclough Family Cemetery is also in the recreation area, about 300 yards off the MST, with three marked graves—Alexander, 1830–87; Martha, 1836–1910; and Perlie, 1883–92. Be respectful as these are private cemeteries.

At EB 41.3, a huge oak, estimated to be around 150 to 200 years old, stands on the bank of a farm pond. About thirty yards west of the oak, fifty yards into the woods to the left, a forty-foot cliff rises above a creek. The cliff has a long watery "sliding rock" feature, with remnants of a small dam of cemented rocks. At EB 41.5, on the left, about thirty yards off the trail, are remains of a small cinderblock farm dam and fence, what's left of wire, sheet metal, and boards. Over the next half mile on the left you'll see a low rock foundation, various cans and tires, an old home chimney, the remains of a 1955 Mercury Montclair, the ruins of a cinderblock building with large trash pile of glass jars, and other cinderblock foundations. Always be cautious when exploring old home sites with possible glass, holes, and exposed nails. At EB 41.7 you cross the old roadbed of Boyce Mill Road, which was abandoned when the road was severed and flooded by the lake.

Some MST History

At EB 41.6, you cross a forty-foot fiberglass bridge, built with over $34,000 in grants from the Triangle Community Foundation and Durham County.

Arthur Kelley coordinated construction, which started in 2017 with bridge pieces carried to the site by a large gathering of volunteers and the concrete floated in as close as possible by a Corps of Engineers boat and then carried to the site. Called a "Tinkertoy for grown-ups," the bridge trusses were assembled on the bank on additional workdays, then picked up in July 2018 and carried across the creek by an army of volunteers in "The Big Lift." That same day, the trusses were bolted together and the bridge took shape.

Back on the Trail

The MST reaches NC 98, continues left across Lick Creek, and reenters the trail through Wildlife Resources land. From gravel Boyce Mill Road (EB 46.3), continuing east, look for an old cabin on the right, about twenty yards in the woods. In the spring, buttercups bloom all around this cabin, but be alert to many glass jars around the site. At EB 46.9, cross scenic Laurel Creek and notice the fractured rocks indicative of the Jonesboro fault and Triassic Basin eastern edge.

On the left after entering a recently clear-cut area (EB 47.7) is the Pele G. Rogers Cemetery, also known as the Lick Creek Cemetery. It contains thirty-four unmarked graves and periwinkle ground cover. The last burial was in 1818. Such cemeteries have been called "the forgotten parts of the landscape." This one was likely for enslaved people, since Pele Rogers (1807–66) enslaved twelve people in 1860 and owned large tracts of land on the south side of the Neuse River. He also likely operated Rogers Store at the corner of Boyce Mill and Old Creedmoor Roads, with a post office, blacksmith, and cotton gin. Records indicate that these graves were reinterred prior to construction of Falls Lake. At EB 47.9 are remains of the Lick Creek Farmstead, an area labeled as a cultural and historic resource, with two tobacco barns (two flues, pole hangers; one barn has shed roofs where tobacco was strung); a 1920s-era barn that housed livestock, implements, and overhead hay storage; remnants of a house chimney; and a rusting two-bottom plow—an International Harvester Little Genius, made from 1928 to 1960.

Turn right to walk past the second barn and continue another twenty yards to a potato cellar or root cellar, and another fifteen feet to chimney ruins. Before refrigeration in the 1930s, people preserved fruits, vegetables, nuts, seeds, and legumes to get through the winter by dehydrating, salting, pickling, canning, or storing them in the dark, cool, secure ground.

A hiker approaches a 1950s-era tobacco barn on an abandoned farmstead east of Laurel Creek. *Photo by Bill Meador; used by permission.*

To the left of the MST lie remains of a 170-foot-long cinderblock building—possibly for chickens or pigs. Farmers needed prolific chickens, suitable for life outdoors, that could produce abundant eggs and also have tasty meat. This area is known as Four Corners, where stories have been told of four Black families who owned property surrounding this farm and used some of the farmstead buildings in common.

A Piedmont-region creek that looks more like a cascading mountain stream is at EB 49.5. Shortly past the view of Rolling View Marina, 200 yards to the right up an old roadbed is a decaying farmhouse and barn on the right. In this area the trail leaves Durham County and enters Wake County.

Nearby

Wake County (established in 1771) is the state's most populous, while Raleigh, located south of the Falls Lake Trail/MST, is known as the "City of Oaks" because of its high concentration of red oak varieties. Raleigh is home to a number of impressive museums, parks, historic attractions, and colleges and universities, leading some to call it the "Smithsonian of the South." Freedom Park in downtown Raleigh, which was dedicated in 2023, features a forty-foot-tall Beacon of Freedom and honors the experiences of Black communities in North Carolina.

After you cross NC 50/Creedmoor Road (EB 51.9) going east, about 220 yards on the left is a side trail, which takes you on a 500-yard route to the Falls Lake State Recreation Area Office and Information Center. The next paved road to the left also leaves the MST, passes an old tobacco barn, and ends at the Information Center, with facilities and an excellent Falls Lake history display. This state park unit covers 5,035 acres in Durham and Wake Counties on the banks of Falls Lake. Seven access areas dot the shore of the reservoir.

East of NC 50 at EB 52.6, soon after exiting state park land, near where you enter a cut-over field, on the right is the foundation of a barn. At EB 53.2 you turn left onto a roadbed; twenty yards on the left is foundation of a small building, and nearby is the foundation ruins of a barn for flue-cured tobacco. At EB 53.4, on the right, is the Evans cemetery, fifty feet by thirty feet, with fifteen unidentified graves marked with fieldstone head- and footstones. The area is identified by four concrete boundary markers placed by US Army engineers in 1972 for the Falls Lake project. Possibly this belonged to Eugene T. Evans (1921–79), a Black laborer who owned ninety-one acres along the Neuse River. Rock piles made as farmers cleared land for planting are visible at many places along the lake and should not be confused with graves.

A three-mile hike out of Shinleaf Recreation Area takes you along a big fishhook-shaped peninsula known as Wyatt's Bend. At its end, you are rewarded with a view across the lake at Zigler Rock on the B. W. Wells Rock Cliff Farm, part of a national historic district near Wake Forest. To the east of NC 98 about 200 yards, you walk on the roadbed for "old NC 98," also called the Durham–Wake Forest Road. The MST heads right, but to the left the old roadbed goes into the lake.

Blue Jay Point County Park encompasses 236 acres off of Falls Lake and provides environmental education in natural surroundings. It opened in 1992 and was named after the peninsula—or point—it forms on Falls Lake, and for the many blue jays that lived there when the area was farmed by tenant farmers. Facilities include play areas, an overnight lodge, trails, an environmental education center, open play fields, and a Go Ape Treetop Adventure course (for a fee; www.goape.com). The park also hosts one to two large public events each year that are free to attend. Everyone likes to snap a picture at the MST directional sign. When the MST crosses Blue

A group enjoys a 2019 MST Birthday Hike photo-op at the Blue Jay Point County Park MST directional sign. *Photo by Andrew Jeffries; used by permission.*

Jay Point Trail, a 100-yard detour to the left takes you to the best lake view in the park at Island at Blue Jay Point.

There are two cemeteries in the park that date back to the early nineteenth century. The smaller of the two consists of two graves belonging to William and Amy Tate. William purchased the land where the park now sits in 1788. What was once the Allen property includes the Harris Cemetery, which interred enslaved laborers from nearby farms in the 1830s and later became the churchyard cemetery for the original Pleasant Union Christian Church. Members of the church included emancipated people from the area. A historical survey identified thirty-seven sunken gravesites with only rock markers and four corner markers. Note that these are not public cemeteries.

Native Americans in the area used soft rock soapstone to make bowls, cooking slabs, and smoking pipes 3,000 years ago. Soapstone has a soapy, soft feel and is typically gray, bluish, or green. It is metamorphic rock composed of talc, and a mix of mica, carbonate, and other minerals. Nonporous, nonabsorbent, and heat resistant, it is found throughout Segment 10.

The Yorkshire Center, at the end of Bayleaf Church Road, is an office for Falls Lake Recreation Area, with the MST on state park land from EB 65.9 to EB 66.7. Before Falls Lake was formed, Bayleaf Church Road was Six Forks Road, which continued by bridge across the Neuse River to NC 98. James Keith purchased twenty-one acres in 1961 and operated the Yorkshire House from 1973 until the property was purchased for Falls Lake. In 1975 the buffet cost $2.25 on weekdays and $2.75 on weekends. Abundant mountain laurel grows on both sides of the creek that marks the boundary between state park and Wildlife Resources Commission land (EB 67–68). The blooms can be breathtakingly abundant in late April and early May. This is one of the last large stands of laurel heading eastward.

At 68.1 you'll find the skeleton of an old car, scorched during a pre-scribed burn. At the well-defined road just before the car, go left and follow the old roadbed about 100 yards uphill to the remains of a home site, with two well-preserved chimneys and building debris. On the right are con-crete foundation walls, building debris, and a strange ten-foot-diameter in-ground silo (or something of unknown purpose; be cautious).

At EB 72.3 Possum Track Road dead-ends, like many other roads that were changed due to the construction of Falls Lake. About 100 yards before reaching the road, a heavily used side trail to the left leads 100 yards to the lakeshore, with a great view across to the Falls Lake Dam. This is the dam you can walk across at EB 79. At EB 73.6, you cross an old roadbed, and 200 yards to the left you'll see an old homesite with a standing chimney.

Some Conservation to Consider

The North Carolina Natural Heritage Program (NHP) protects over 720,000 acres of fauna and flora and evaluates the ecological impacts of development, in what is termed "science-guided conservation." As you hike the MST, you may pass through areas with protected or sensitive flowers and plants, usually not identified with signs. When trail is built or rerouted on state or federal land, an on-site assessment is done to ensure that sensitive plants are not endangered.

State game lands are scattered across North Carolina, 232,000 acres of multiuse land open to all for outdoor adventures. These are managed by the North Carolina Wildlife Resources Commission (created in 1947 and now managing a total of 2 million acres). The MST crosses four North Carolina game lands. In Segment 10, the stretch from Old Oxford

Road in Durham County to Falls Lake Dam in Wake County is mostly on Butner Falls of Neuse Game Land—about 40,670 acres in size. Hunting and fishing are allowed to maintain cultural traditions and resources, help families develop a connection to nature, and promote conservation. These lands are great places to walk and hike, to protect endangered species, to host wildflowers and pollinators, and hunting keeps deer populations in check. Hunting and fishing license fees help fund conservation efforts. Wear blaze orange during hunting seasons.

Why active forest management, thinning, and prescribed fires? The North Carolina Division of Forest Resources and the state Wildlife Resources Commission must fight wildfires but also must set prescribed burns to improve forest conditions. Wildfires in the wrong place or at the wrong time can harm life, property, and natural resources. Selective thinning of less desirable species opens the tree canopy, allowing wildflowers to thrive and habitat to flourish. The Wildlife Resources Commission also harvests timber to generate income. While hiking throughout the state, be observant in locations where forest fires, prescribed fire, or timber harvesting might be an imminent danger or might have damaged the trail or directional signage.

Back on the Trail

MST trail races at Falls Lake started in 2012, when Bull City Running Company sponsored the MST 12M Challenge and the MST 50K Challenge. The twelve miles begin at Bayleaf Church Road and end at Falls Lake Dam; the fifty kilometers lead from Blue Jay Point County Park to the dam and back. The narrow course includes roots, rocks, quick turns, logs, and sometimes water, but hundreds register anyway. Few people know that the first group run from the dam to Blue Jay Point was held on October 1, 1994—before most of the bridges were built—with Chad Rehder, Mark Ingle, Debra Parker Mitchell, Mark Wagoner, and Jerry Barker. On October 21, 2020, Nathan Toben recorded a fastest known time on 77.3 miles on the MST from Pleasant Green Road to Falls Dam in twelve hours, twenty-three minutes, and twenty-four seconds. The MST reaches Raven Ridge Road, turns left across the Honeycutt Creek causeway, then left back into the woods. Directly across Raven Ridge Road from the MST kiosk is a sign for the Honeycutt Creek Greenway, part of the Raleigh Greenway System. This 3.8-mile trail to Strickland Road provides orange vests during bow-hunting season.

About 0.4 mile east of Raven Ridge look for a cove with fringetree, also called "old man's beard," along a creek bed with exposed bedrock. This area is in the "fall zone" where the Piedmont region changes to the Coastal Plain. Annie Louise Wilkerson, MD Nature Preserve, named after an accomplished local physician, is a 157-acre parcel of land along Falls Lake, Raleigh's first designated nature preserve, and adjacent to the MST (EB 75.9). It was a 2006 gift to the city from Wilkerson, who asked in her will that the "nature preserve park" be used for nature and wildlife education. It is 0.4 mile from the MST to the preserve center and facilities.

Falls Dam is an earthen structure with a top elevation of 291.5 feet, a length of 1,915 feet, and a height of 92.5 feet above the streambed. The normal water level is 251.5 feet above sea level. Beside Falls Dam Drive near the Falls Dam, which is not on the MST, is the Ray-McReath Cemetery, with eight graves, some with illegible headstones. The oldest grave is that of H. S. McReath (1836–96). In her book *The Battle for Falls Lake*, Janet Steddum tells the story of the small Falls community that inhabited the land before the lake was formed. When the lake was created, over 200 families lost their homes and farms, which they were forced to sell to the government. Their communities were left at the bottom of the lake in the name of progress.

In 2020, MST visionary Howard Lee shared his observations as a senior hiker:

> In 2014, at 80 years old, I considered hiking the entire trail, but logic prevailed and the idea died. However, a friend suggested I should at least hike as many miles as possible. By age 87 I had hiked over 135 miles of the MST (including all of the MST along the Eno River, Falls Lake, the Neuse River Greenway, and other day hikes). This hiking experience has provided many memorable experiences. The first is, having enjoyed the company of many hiking partners. I learned so much about the many ways nature impacts my life. While on the trail the sounds and the quiet of the forest allow for self-reflection and I realize how fortunate I am to enjoy this special opportunity to connect with nature. I hope that when those of us who are hiking the MST today are unable to continue, others will come and experience the joy of this great opportunity.

COASTAL PLAIN AND OUTER BANKS REGION

524.6 MILES

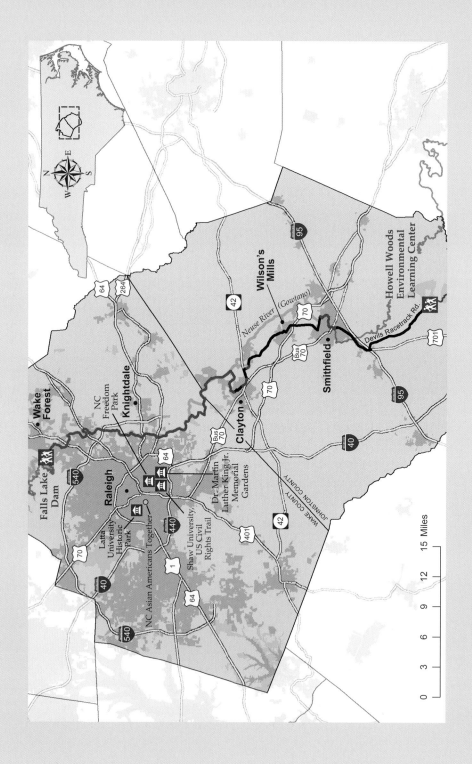

Falls Lake Dam

Wake Forest

NC Freedom Park

Knightdale

64

264

64

Raleigh

540

70

40

540

Latta University Historic Park

Shaw University, US Civil Rights Trail

NC Asian Americans Together

1

64

401

440

Dr. Martin Luther King Jr. Memorial Gardens

Bus 70

Clayton

70

42

401

WAKE COUNTY

JOHNSTON COUNTY

42

Neuse River *(Gowtano)*

Wilson's Mills

Bus 70

Smithfield

40

95

Howell Woods Environmental Learning Center

Devils Racetrack Rd.

701

95

42

0   3   6   9   12   15 Miles

Neuse River Greenways and the Let'Lones

Falls Lake Dam to Howell Woods
Environmental Learning Center

65.9 MILES

*Die with your boots on, with a hundred interesting unfinished
activities for which there is just not time. On such a prescription,
one may live long and happy, often on borrowed time.*

JAY B. NASH

Who doesn't love a wide, paved, scenic place to walk, enjoyable for the
whole family and disabled people? In urban Wake County and neighbor-
ing Johnston County, the citizens are fortunate to have thirty-five miles
of greenway along the Neuse River connecting Raleigh to Clayton. This
segment is mostly flat and transitions from greenway to roadside walking
from Clayton to Smithfield, two accommodating trail-town communities.

Falls Lake Dam to Clayton

Most of the area around the Falls of the Neuse community changed
dramatically when Falls Dam was constructed. "Falls of the Neuse"
rocks are the bedrock foundation for the Falls Dam. Near the Falls Dam
Tailrace, left across the Neuse River bridge, is the 1855 location of the
papermaking Falls of Neuse Manufacturing Company—the only place
east of Charlotte where paper was made in North Carolina. Late in the
Civil War as General Sherman drew near, the mill's machinery was
dismantled and hidden, and Sherman's army overlooked it. After the

war, the mill made paper until 1896. It operated for many years under different names before closing in 1959 as the Erwin Cotton Mill. In 1984 the buildings were converted to River Mill Condominiums, looking much the way they did in 1855.

North of the Falls Dam Tailrace on Old Falls of Neuse Road, about 0.4 mile on the left is the Falls Community Cemetery, which contains remains of Wake County graves reinterred when Falls Lake was built. About 2.5 miles north is Forest Ridge Park, a 587-acre Raleigh park adjoining Falls Lake that includes a welcome center with amenities including two shelters, mountain biking, fishing, multiuse trails, disc golf, and a playground.

The Neuse River Greenway in Wake County (EB 0.0–27.9), Clayton River Walk in Johnston County (EB 27.9–33.2), and Sam's Branch Greenway (EB 33.2–34.4) make for a scenic, relatively flat, wide, paved greenway for hikers, joggers, and bikers. The numerous trailheads, connecting trails, and boat launches facilitate a variety of hikes or paddles. The City of Raleigh Parks and Recreation runs the Neuse River Greenway, where visitors can enjoy scenic river views, wandering boardwalks over wetlands, history, educational signs and markers, and agriculture. Some years fields of sunflowers are planted in Raleigh and the seeds are made into biodiesel fuel for city equipment. Check online for more information.

The greenway from Falls Dam to the WRAL Soccer Center (EB 0–6.6), the first portion to open in 2011, is extremely active with hikers, joggers, bikers, strollers, and dogs, especially on weekends. Abbotts Creek Trail (EB 2.9) is 2.9 miles and connects Simms Branch Trail with the greenway. It is a wide, flat, paved trail carving through a shady forest between the Falls River subdivision and Abbotts Creek. At EB 4.8, a junction with the Smith Creek Greenway connects with the town of Wake Forest. The town funded the $1.4 million pedestrian bridge over the Neuse River, which at 558 feet is the largest pedestrian bridge in North Carolina (it is not part of Capital Area Greenway). At EB 6.6, there is a connection to the WRAL Soccer Center, which has twenty-five fields, including a 3,200-seat lighted stadium.

The Capital Area Greenway System, established in 1974, is one of most comprehensive systems in the state, with twenty-eight trails totaling over 100 miles, covering 3,700 acres. Connecting to the MST are Abbotts Creek Trail, Crabtree Creek starting at Anderson Point Park at EB 17.4, Walnut Creek Greenway at EB 19.4, and the Neuse River Greenway to the Johnston County line.

A December snow blankets Abbots Creek Trail, three miles east of
Falls Lake Dam along the Neuse River Greenway.
Photo by Bill Meador; used by permission.

Just across the river in northeastern Wake County sits Horseshoe Farm
Nature Preserve, with a bounty of natural and cultural resources. Its 146
acres, mostly pastures and woodland areas, span a peninsula surrounded
by the Neuse River, whose waters carved its shape over time. The fields
upland from the river have been farmed and pastured for generations.
The state designated the forests along the river's banks as a significant
natural heritage area because they are home to unique bottomland hardwood forests, wetlands, and natural river levees. A farmhouse and a horse
pasture stood on the land before the city purchased it in 1994. A paved
connector trail leads to the Neuse River section of the greenway (EB 8.1)
from the preserve's restroom building.

At EB 15.1, there is the site of the former Milburnie Dam. Col. John
Hinton purchased large swaths of land along the Neuse River in the mid-
1700s. In the late 1700s, dams were constructed along the river to use its
power, and these dams formed a long, narrow lake upstream. The most
recent dam was built around 1900, from pine, stone, and concrete, and
it slowed and narrowed the Neuse up to six miles upriver. This blocked
the migration of fish and impacted the natural ecology of the river. Years
of negotiation and thoughtful planning led to a plan for restoration of the
original stream ecosystem. The dam was demolished in 2017—a safety
hazard removed, the six-mile Neuse River impoundment behind the
dam drained, fish migration restored, and Milburnie Falls re-created. Of

Cedric Turner-Kopa and Howard Lee enjoying a sunny day on the Sam's Branch and Clayton Greenways. *Photo by Jerry Barker.*

interest is the Mullein plant near the observation platform, known as rag paper or the toilet paper plant because of its soft leaves.

Anderson Point Park (EB 17.3–17.9), established in 1988 on ninety-eight acres, was named for the place where Crabtree Creek flows into the Neuse, known as the Point. The park provides a number of recreational opportunities, including diverse habitats and wildlife, walking trails, canoe sites, shelters, restrooms, and parking. It is one of the few remaining Piedmont prairies ("early successional habitats") in existence, and its grasslands are home to a rich biodiversity of meadow birds, insects, amphibians, and other flora and fauna. These rare biomes were largely destroyed over the last 200 years as prairies were plowed for agriculture or developed for expanding suburban populations. Every Christmas and spring, the Audubon Society hosts a bird count in the park to survey the species present. To date over 130 species have been recorded in this Piedmont prairie. In addition to the fauna, the park has ten acres dedicated to a variety of wildflowers and native warm season grasses. It is also a "pollinator pitstop" on the Butterfly Highway. Built in the early 1900s, the Anderson Family Homestead cottage is used primarily as a rental and program space. At Anderson Point Park one can connect with the Capital Area Greenway's Crabtree Creek Trail.

The East Coast Greenway, a 3,000-mile route from Maine to Florida designed mainly for biking, intersects the MST at EB 19.3 at the Walnut Creek Trail and follows the Neuse Greenway to Legends Park in Clayton (EB 34.4) and beyond. In 2021 it became a part of North Carolina State Parks.

At about EB 18.4, you'll see Panther Rock Rapids. A marker for Stone's Mill is at EB 19.5. In 1816, an inland navigation survey was done on the Neuse River to determine how trade might be improved to help this part of the state. Results suggested removing logs and sandbanks from the river and building three locks between Judge Stone's Mill and Smithfield, at a cost of $35,000. East of Auburn Knightdale Road (EB 22.1), you will pass fifty yards of mountain laurel on both sides of the greenway, with blooms in April and May, and in another 100 yards, you'll pass the largest boulders you'll probably see from here to the coast.

At the corner of Auburn Knightdale Road and Battle Bridge Road (0.8 mile south of MST parking) is a marker by the Wake County Historical Society (1979): "General James Robertson (1742–1814) 'Father of Tennessee' led a delegation from Wake County across the North Carolina mountains in 1771 and founded Watauga, the first independent self-government in North America." Robertson moved to North Carolina in 1750 to a 320-acre plantation south of the Neuse River, along land now used by the City of Raleigh for resource recovery (EB 24–26). He traveled with Daniel and Squire Boone to what is now Tennessee, and among his many military duties he served as a government commissioner with the Cherokee.

At EB 26.5 is the Mial Plantation Road greenway parking lot, featuring a "monarch waystation" that provides milkweed, nectar sources, and shelter for monarch butterflies. The Tippett's Chapel Free Will Baptist Church cemetery is 200 yards to the left up Mial Plantation Road, with ninety-five marked graves (the oldest dating back to 1835) and fourteen graves marked with rough stones. The church was founded in 1899, meeting in the shade of a large oak tree, then in 1900 purchased an acre of land for five dollars and started construction on a new church. In 1930, the congregation built a new church about a mile away.

Mial Plantation

Near Shotwell, North Carolina, Mial Plantation Road (SR 2509) crosses the MST in the Walnut Hill Historic District. Within the district are a number of structures, including forty small homes and agricultural buildings related to the Walnut Hill Plantation, the Mial-Williamson farm, and the Joseph Blake family farm. In 1761, Mallichi Hinton acquired the land from Lord Granville in England in one of the state's first land grants. Hinton sold 430 acres to Thomas Mail Sr. in 1775. By the post–Civil War period, the 2,700-acre area had become one of Wake County's largest agricultural operations. In 1860, the Mials enslaved thirty-three people, and as many as 130 lived and worked on the area plantation and farms, tending crops and animals, building fences, cooking, weaving, and taking care of children. After Emancipation, most Black families stayed as tenants or sharecroppers. About three miles north on Mial Plantation Road, you'll find Lakeside Retreats @ Walnut Hill, with a yurt and tent sites on a seven-acre lake.

At the Bailey and Sarah Williamson Preserve, it is easy to get lost in the 405 acres of natural and cultural beauty. The preserve was once a farm, whose rich soils produced crops including cotton and eventually tobacco before it ceased operation in 1967. In 2013, after the land had been in the Williamson family's hands for over 225 years, the daughters gave the property to the Triangle Land Conservancy. Today, the preserve provides education on the region's history and connects visitors with nature. The preserve can be reached off the Neuse River Greenway/Clayton River Walk (EB 27.7 in Johnston County, via the Neuse River Connector Trail) or preserve parking at 4429 Mial Plantation Road (three miles north of the MST). Seven miles of multiuse trail currently exist, and more will be developed.

Back on the Trail

Covered Bridge Road (EB 31) has a long history that is well documented on an educational sign near the MST. Local Boy Scout Thomas Wright from Troop 421 in Clayton designed four great educational signs for the Clayton Greenway as part of his Eagle Scout Project. The Sam Branch Greenway tunnels under North O'Neil Street / Covered Bridge Road to connect to downtown Clayton (EB 35.5).

Johnston County was heavily populated by Tuscarora Indians until they were defeated and dispersed in the Tuscarora War (1711–13). Johnston County has more farms than any other county in North Carolina. A long-term, countywide plan proposes to build approximately fourteen miles of trail and connect the Clayton section to the Buffalo Creek Greenway / MST in Smithfield.

Johnston County Schools display student art along the Clayton Greenway. *Photo by Jerry Barker.*

Hop off the trail in Clayton or Smithfield if you need a bite to eat or a place to stay for the night. Both Johnston County sections bring trail users into the heart of these downtown areas, which boast locally owned cafés, restaurants, taverns, and shops.

Some Safety Information!

Every day 1,800 thunderstorms erupt around the world, but the only one that matters to you is the one nearby while you're hiking the MST. We're no match for a big cumulonimbus storm cloud that weighs 4,400 tons (about the same as thirty-seven blue whales). Lightning is worst in June, July, and August in North Carolina. Be prepared. Seek shelter indoors if possible. Have your phone charged to monitor weather forecasts, and don't walk in the rain. Safety is twenty minutes after the last clap of thunder. Stay away from power lines and watch for falling limbs. Lightning position on the trail is seated on your pack or pad (not touching any metal), feet and knees together, before the storm gets close.

Summer in central and eastern North Carolina from late spring through early fall can have tropical, humid, hot weather with temperatures exceeding 95°F and heat indexes of over 110, which is not great weather for hiking. However, prevention is the key: avoid the outdoors on afternoons (know the temperature and humidity; asphalt is hotter than wooded trail); wear a wide-brim hat and loose-fitting, light-colored, sweat-wicking, UPF-protective shirts; seek shade whenever possible; remove shoes and socks during breaks and elevate your feet; stop before it's too late; and immediately seek first aid or medical attention if you experience symptoms of heat exhaustion.

Remember to drink water. While the desert camel can drink fifty-two gallons of water in three minutes and then go weeks with none, you aren't a camel.

Back on the Trail

Bootleg alcohol was made from the 1930s to the 1960s in Sampson and Johnston Counties. Moonshiners grew the corn but had to buy the sugar, which revenuers traced to find stills, leading to fast cars making deliveries. Moonshine was shipped in quart Mason jars and frequently just left on a tree stump. One major player in the moonshine game was Percy Flowers of Johnston County, born in 1903. In adulthood, Flowers owned and farmed almost 5,000 acres, where he grew corn and tobacco, like most farmers in the area in the twentieth century. Eventually he decided to start making illegal liquor, using his corn for the spirits and his tobacco barns to conceal the distilling. By 1958, he was known as the "King of the Moonshiners" and was seen by some as a sort of local Robin Hood.

At EB 49.8 you reach Smithfield, a small town (population around 13,000) and the Johnston County seat, started near John Smith's ferry on the Neuse River. It is home to the Ava Gardner Museum (0.1 mile off the MST), the Johnston County Heritage Center, Bright Leaf hot dogs, and, since 1986, the Ham and Yam Festival. Every June since 2010 the Johnston County Visitors Bureau has promoted the Route 301 Endless Yard Sale. The 1830 Hastings House served as Gen. Joseph Johnston's headquarters during the Civil War as he fought General Sherman at the Battle of Bentonville. The Neuse River Paddle Route officially begins in Smithfield, though some paddlers begin at the Falls Lake Dam or in Clayton. It is 31.8 river miles from the Falls Lake Dam to Clayton (NC 42 launch) and another 14.2 river miles from Clayton to Smithfield.

The Buffalo Creek Greenway, also known as the Smithfield Neuse Riverwalk, begins at EB 50.3 and continues to EB 53.1. In Smithfield, at the junction of Bridge and Front Streets, look for the "Rise Above" sculpture that celebrates contributions of African Americans from colonial times to the present. Cross under West Market Street and note the old stone bridge pilings with a plaque describing the covered bridge built before the Civil War and used until 1907.

As you cross over I-95 and US 701, the MST follows Devil's Racetrack Road (EB 57.7 for 8.2 miles) to Howell Woods Environmental Learning Center. The road was used by Sherman's troops on their march from Goldsboro to Raleigh. It may have been named for the gambling and drinking houses once plentiful along its route. According to legend, two mean brothers, George and Jeb, who lived along the wilderness road, swore they raced the Devil's horse one cold night and lost.

Howell Woods Environmental Learning Center (the end of Segment 11) is a 2,800-acre preserve owned by Johnston Community College. The office and parking is 0.1 mile into the property. The North Carolina Natural Heritage Program has designated it "the most significant terrestrial natural area in the county." At the entrance, check out the sign for NC Civil War Trails and the Hannah's Creek Bridge educational panel.

The vast floodplain wilderness along the Neuse River is known as the "let'lones" by the locals because of the tangles of roots and vegetation that make it a challenge to navigate and unsuitable to farm. The area is also called the Mashes, the Neuse Lowgrounds, and the Neuse Islands. The area was also an ideal location for illicit distilling: "let'lones" came from an admonishment for would-be intruders to "leave it alone" to avoid being shot by moonshiners.

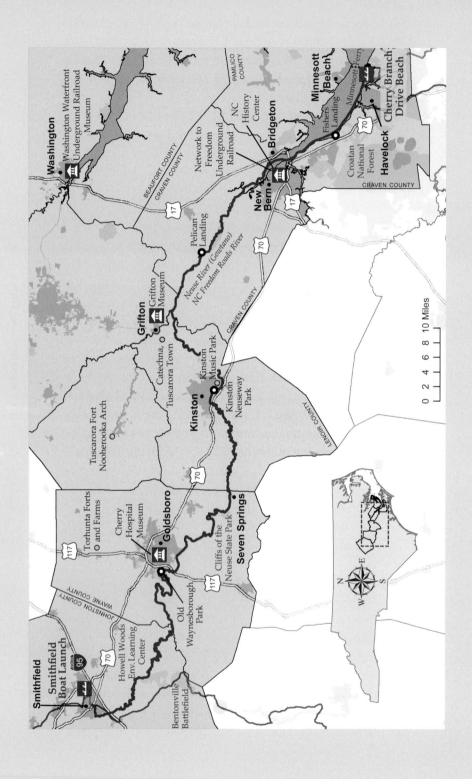

Neuse River Paddle Route

Smithfield to the Neusiok Trail

169.3 MILES

Open water is a highway to adventure, best traveled by canoe or kayak.

UNKNOWN

Instead of hiking the MST through the coastal plains, you can take the alternate paddling trail on the Neuse River from Smithfield to the northern end of the Neusiok Trail near Havelock, where you reconnect with the hiking route. The Neuse River measures 227 miles from Falls Lake Dam in Raleigh (river mile 0.0) to the Pamlico Sound. The MST paddle route runs 169 miles from Smithfield (river mile 46.8) to Pinecliff Recreation Area (river mile 216), where hikers can pick up the Neusiok Trail and continue east to the coast. (The Neuse continues another eleven miles to reach Pamlico Sound, where it spreads to six miles wide.) There are nineteen river access locations but other points where one can get on or off the river. If you don't want ups and downs, come to this segment with a descent of about 148 feet, and no ascent, on the eastbound downstream paddle.

The Neuse River, named by English explorers Barlowe and Amadas in 1584 (the Tuscarora called it Gowtano, meaning "pine in water"), runs 275 miles from its origin in Durham to Hobucken. The Neuse is not a designated wild and scenic river, but it does have wild and scenic portions. It is a pleasant paddle under the right conditions: when the river is not too high or low; avoid buggy seasons; steer clear of strainers (limbs and trees that water flows through); and keep safety in mind regarding wind, waves, and boat traffic when the river widens at miles 175–216. Sound Rivers offers excellent suggestions for camping; launches; food, supplies,

181

water, and restrooms; outfitters and logistics; cautions; what to take; and links to maps and other resources on the MST website. Most of the river is in rural, isolated territory.

Lisa "Conundrum" Speas shared the following recollection of her 2018 Neuse paddle:

> Instead of hiking blacktop, I elected to kayak the Neuse River from Raleigh to Oriental—over 200 miles. I went with Hope Floats NC, a kayaking group of family and friends who have been kayaking the Neuse for the past nine years to raise donations for the American Cancer Society (ACS). The trip occurs annually in April for eight days—it is highly organized and requires paddling an average of 25 miles/day. My time with Hope Floats NC was the highlight of my MST trek, meeting 20 new friends, spending 24/7 with them, and raising over $40,000 for the ACS. While this segment of the MST may not be the choice for everyone, I highly recommend that MST hikers who enjoy paddling . . . consider joining Hope Floats NC to complete this segment of the coastal region, or even select a few legs of the paddle route.

Jason Nieuwsma completed the MST in 2017 taking the Coastal Crescent route. In 2021, he completed the 170-mile Neuse paddle route (plus forty-five miles from Falls Dam to Smithfield) and is thought to be the first to complete all MST route options, both land and water. "That thin little line across our state connects so much," he said. "For me, it's been a way to adventure with friends and family, to see things and places I would never have thought to visit otherwise."

Back on the Trail

Launch at the Smithfield Boat Launch at river mile 46.8, near Smithfield Town Commons, downtown at NC 210/West Market Street, where the hiking route diverges from the river route. The paddle route is commonly split into legs—identified by river miles—that make for a day's travel and include a place to camp.

Howell Woods (river mile 65; Rudolph Howell and Son Environmental Learning Center) is a unique natural resource designed to provide educational experiences while fostering environmental stewardship. Rudolph Howell donated the property to Johnston Community College in 1993 in the hope that it would be used as an outdoor classroom. It is located on

Devil's Racetrack Road in the Four Oaks and Bentonville communities of Johnston County. At river mile 85.7 paddlers are cautioned to not take the sluice intake gate on river right: it is blocked by trees and should be considered dangerous. This is property of the retired Duke Energy H. F. Lee power plant. Stay far to river left through this section to avoid strong currents.

Old Waynesborough Park (river mile 99.2; free), on the outskirts of Goldsboro, sits on land that was once the town of Waynesborough. The town had a stagecoach stop and was the first seat of Wayne County from 1787 to 1847. Today the park includes nine historic buildings from all over the county, including homes, a school, a law office, and a Quaker meetinghouse, that dates from the 1860s to the 1920s. One of the buildings is the old Wiggins home, a one-room structure with no electricity or indoor plumbing that was moved to the park in 1994. In addition to the village, the park offers four miles of walking paths on more than 150 acres along the Neuse and Little Rivers. Paddlers are permitted to camp along the Neuse; facilities are only available during the day.

Nearby

Goldsboro has deep military and agricultural roots. It is also known for legendary BBQ, which put the city on the North Carolina Barbeque Society Historic Trail; Mt. Olive Pickle Company; the free-of-charge Wings over Wayne Air Show; and tubing the Neuse. Goldsboro has 8.7 miles of MST designated on the Neuse River corridor route. About six miles to Dudley is Grady's Barbeque, one of only a few Black-owned BBQ diners in North Carolina, sought after for its old-school southern pit-cooked, whole-hog smokehouse BBQ. See Adrian Miller's book *Black Smoke* for more information on Black BBQ chefs in the South.

The Neuse River region was home to the Tuscarora farming area of Torhunta until the early 1700s. Today the region continues the tradition with many large, productive farms. North Carolina is fourth in nationwide cucumber production, harvesting about 149 million pounds annually. Cucurbit plants, grown on vines, love the loamy, sandy soil found in the eastern part of the state. Between 6,000 and 7,000 acres of North Carolina farmland grow cucumbers, especially for pickles, made at the nearby Mt. Olive Pickle Company. North Carolina is also the fourth-largest strawberry-producing state. They are grown as plants or for berries, and often as a farmer's second crop.

Back on the River

Cliffs of the Neuse State Park (river mile 120.8; established in 1945) is located just west, or upstream, of Seven Springs. On its 892 acres, you can fish, boat, camp, swim, hike four miles of trails, and picnic under shelter. The park is named for the 600 feet of cliffs on the south side of the river that reach up to ninety feet.

Seven Springs (river mile 123.2) is a small riverside town in Wayne County, with about forty to fifty households. There are a number of natural springs in the area, and two resort hotels were built around the springs to attract bathers. The town is steeped in history, with a Civil War battle site and cemetery. Union soldiers occupied the hill atop Highway 55, looking down on Seven Springs, during the Battle of Whitehall in 1862. In 1874, on that same hill, Seven Springs United Methodist Church, known as the "Church on the Hill," was built. The church fell into disrepair but was renovated in the 1940s, and people still worship there today. Camping is permitted beside the Neuse River, and there are two restaurants in town that open on alternate days. On the nearby fertile fields, hundreds of acres of cantaloupes and watermelons are grown.

On December 15–16, 1862, Union troops attacked Confederate troops and the CSS *Neuse* (an ironclad gunboat that was still under construction) with cannon fire in what became known as the Battle of Whitehall. Late on December 15 the Union cavalry reached Whitehall shortly after Confederate troops crossed over the Neuse River Bridge and then burned it before setting up defensive positions. After several hours of futile conflict, the Union cavalry burned the village and returned to their camp. The battle continued the next day until sunset when the Union forces withdrew.

During the Civil War the Confederate army began creating ships covered in iron plating to better resist cannon and gunfire. In 1865, near Seven Springs, the Confederates burned one of the last ironclad warships they had started building, the *Ram Neuse*, or the CSS *Neuse*, to prevent its capture by Union troops. Because of low water levels, the ship never passed downriver or saw combat. The ship remained lost for nearly a century, but it was rediscovered when water levels in the Neuse dropped dramatically in 1963. The ship now resides at the CSS *Neuse* State Historic Site and Governor Richard Caswell Memorial, administered as a single forty-six-acre tract along US 70 in Kinston.

Kinston's Neuseway Nature Park and Campground (river mile 148.2) sits on fifty-five acres on the Neuse River. The campsites, with and without

On their fifth day paddling the Neuse River, Eliza Vistica and Jerry Barker prepare to take a break at Pelican Landing, just upriver from New Bern. *Photo by Johnny Massey; used by permission.*

hook-ups, are within steps of hiking trails and fishing opportunities. The park is open year-round, twenty-four hours a day, and offers river access, hot showers, picnic tables, and a dump station. The Nature Center is worth a peek. It's an easy walk into town for restaurants.

Kinston hosts the BBQ Festival on the Neuse in May, with food competitions, arts and crafts, a wine and beer garden, and more. In October the town hosts the ENC Food, Brew 'n' Que Fest. Northeast of Kinston was the site of a large Tuscarora community known as Catechna. A replica Catechna village is on the banks of Contentnea Creek at Grifton.

Pelican Landing Fishing Camp (river mile 176.9) in Vanceboro is a Neuse River boat landing off River Road about fifteen miles west of New Bern. It is also just down river from the community of Tick Bite, on the

Contentnea Creek in Lenoir County. For those who want to avoid paddling on the widest part of the Neuse near New Bern and beyond, Pelican Landing is a good takeout point.

Near Vanceboro, in 1998 an 880-pound black bear was shot, one of the heaviest ever taken in North America. Some of the largest black bears in America roam through eastern North Carolina. In the fall they feast on peanuts, soybeans, and wheat fields. It is not uncommon to hear of 700-pound bears in the coastal swamplands. They prowl across 60 percent of North Carolina, sometimes even through metropolitan areas.

New Bern (river mile 194; elevation ten feet) is the home of the Friends of MST past president Bill Sadler, who reminds us that the first thing to know about New Bern is that it's *New* Bern, with the accent on the first syllable, not like New *York*. Bill helps organize Bike MS: Historic New Bern Ride, which regularly draws over 2,000 riders and volunteers for the largest multiple sclerosis fundraiser in the southeastern United States.

When paddling down the Neuse River into New Bern, a paddler would likely take out at Union Point Park (river mile 197.5) located at the confluence of the Neuse and Trent Rivers, just a couple of blocks from downtown New Bern and just across the bridge from James City. New Bern is the birthplace of Pepsi-Cola, and two blocks from the river is the Pepsi Store where in 1893 Caleb Bradham invented his famous drink at his drug store soda fountain. Next door are stores that sell gear for hikers and paddlers—Four C's and Surf, and Wind and Fire Outfitters. Downtown has over fifteen restaurants, bars, and shops. The Galley Store on East Front Street is the closest place to the Neuse River where groceries can be purchased.

Tryon Palace Historic Site (1770), also known as Governor's Palace and the state's first capitol, is a popular tourist spot nearby. Located three blocks from the river, it also includes the North Carolina History Center. New Bern historic highlights include the Fireman's Museum, the oldest fire department in the state and two blocks from the Neuse River on Broad Street; Battlefield Park, a thirty-acre site of the 1862 Civil War Battle of New Bern; Pollock Street; an African American Walking Tour; and the Greenwood Cemetery, with over 500 graves.

Across the Trent River is James City, developed in 1862 by Union forces (who occupied New Bern) as a resettlement camp for newly freed enslaved people. It grew to 800 homes, but by 1867 residents were forced to work as sharecroppers or leave. In 1892 courts ruled against Black land ownership in the town. Near James City is the gravesite of Richard Dobbs Spaight, signer of the US Constitution.

Fishers Landing Recreation Site (river mile 205.7) is located on the Neuse River about eight miles south of New Bern, in Craven County, with drinking water and vault toilets (river right). The destination attracts anglers, birdwatchers, and all varieties of nature enthusiasts. Located on a small corner of the Croatan National Forest, it is popular with MST paddlers for its sandy beach and launching area on the edge of the Neuse River. In April, hickory shad swarm the Neuse to spawn.

Pine Cliff Recreation Area (river mile 215.2) ends the Neuse River Paddle Route and begins the twenty-one-mile-long Neusiok Trail, the longest hiking trail in eastern North Carolina (MST Segment 17). The area is great for a picnic or a scenic hike through parts of the Croatan National Forest. If Pine Cliff is not open, Cherry Branch Drive Beach is an alternate endpoint (river mile 216.1).

The Neuse River, the longest river contained within North Carolina, is 275 miles from its beginning in the Piedmont to its emptying into Pamlico Sound. Six miles wide at its mouth, it is the widest river in the United States and the country's second-largest estuary. Nearly one-sixth of North Carolina's residents depend on water from the Neuse River Basin.

Many people and organizations are working to restore and maintain a healthy Neuse River. Sound Rivers is a nonprofit organization that guards the health of the Neuse Basin. It employs upper and lower Neuse Riverkeepers to monitor farm pollution, chemical runoff, industrial waste, waste from hog and poultry farms, and drinking water quality. Threats include urban sprawl, logging, pollution, and factory farming. The fifteen riverkeeper organizations in North Carolina work to protect rivers as part of an integrated environment. In 2022 the river restoration group American Rivers designated the Neuse as River of the Year.

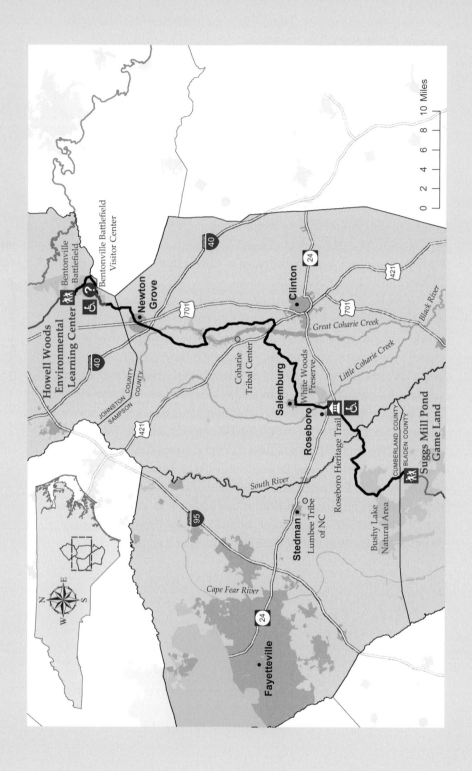

Agricultural Heartland

Howell Woods Environmental Learning
Center to Suggs Mill Pond Game Land

66 MILES

*We move through this world on paths laid down
long before we are born.*

ROBERT MOOR

This segment is named Agricultural Heartland for a reason—well, many reasons. It is sixty-four miles of tobacco, corn, cotton, sweet potatoes, soybeans, forestry, hogs, turkeys, and cattle. Sampson County is first in North Carolina crops and second in livestock and poultry. To make it more exciting, throw in a battlefield, great waterways, game lands, preserves, and several trailside towns.

In 2015, Friends of the MST released a guide for the 270-mile "Coastal Crescent route," and in 2017 the North Carolina General Assembly added the Coastal Crescent Trail as an official MST route. This route encompasses areas of historic importance and ecological interest in Johnston, Sampson, Cumberland, Bladen, Pender, and Onslow Counties, leading hikers through the Cape Fear Arch and Onslow Bight. River sediment from the Piedmont and mountains built up the very gently sloping land of the eastern third of North Carolina. The area is home to rare species and includes longleaf pine, savannas, Carolina bays, pocosins, and barrier islands.

Tobacco's history in the Piedmont and eastern regions started when settlers moved from Virginia to North Carolina in the 1660s, struggling to grow any crop besides tobacco in the dry, sandy soil. The colonists saw an opportunity in the overseas demand for tobacco and invested in growing what they knew would make money. History shows that success: record tobacco crops were recorded in 1950. If there had been a mountains-to-sea trail back then, you would have walked beside many tobacco fields, maybe even puffing on a cigarette. Flue-cured and bright leaf tobacco grew into the major cash crop for eastern Tar Heel farmers, and Wilson was the "world's largest tobacco market." At its peak, over 10,000 small farms produced burley tobacco in approximately twenty counties in the mountains. Tobacco was traditionally one of the most important industries in the state and a backbone of North Carolina's agricultural heritage. North Carolina is known for the American Tobacco Campus in Durham, the town of Tobaccoville, the Tobacco Farm Life Museum in Kenley, the Tobacco Road references in sports, and brands named Winston and Salem. As the state transitioned from an agricultural to a manufacturing, technology, and service-based economy, tobacco was no longer king. However, in 2022, North Carolina still produced some 249 million pounds of tobacco, leading the nation.

At EB 3.2, the MST passes Scout Road, where it is 1.5 miles to Camp Tuscarora, an 1,100-acre Boy Scouts of America camp on the banks of Mill Creek. Word-of-mouth history says there was a Tuscarora village on the other side of Mill Creek. The MST turns right on Harper House Road, which was known as the Goldsboro Road in the 1800s. At the intersection with Devils Racetrack Road sits C. W. Flowers Store, a traditional country store built in 1940 where the community hangs out and buys gas, tires, and convenience store items.

The Battle of Bentonville is called "the Confederacy's last stand in North Carolina" and was the largest Civil War battle in the state. The Union army had 60,000 men and suffered 1,527 casualties, while the Confederates had 21,900 men and 2,606 casualties. Today the battlefield is a state historic site in Johnston County with the MST crossing it from EB 2.2 to EB 9. The grounds and visitor center charge no admission fee and are open Tuesday through Saturday, 9 a.m. to 5 p.m.

John Harper purchased 200 acres in the area around 1800. In 1855, his son John and daughter-in-law Amy built the existing two-story house to raise their nine children, on about 800 acres used mainly for naval stores. They lived in the house until 1897. During and after the three-day 1865 battle, the Harper family remained upstairs, while 600 soldiers were treated by Union medical personnel on the ground floor. Twenty of the Confederate dead are buried in the Harper cemetery on the grounds. The Harpers had three enslaved people acting as domestic help and gardening:

The Harper House at Bentonville Battlefield State Historic Site served as a hospital during the largest Civil War battle in North Carolina. *Photo courtesy of Johnston County Visitors Bureau.*

Lucy, her son Alexander "Harper," and his wife Clarsey. They, along with enslaved people on the Cole Plantation and Morris farm, were freed by General Sherman, enforcing the terms of the Emancipation Proclamation.

The Battle of Bentonville, March 19–21, 1865, marked Gen. Joseph E. Johnston's only significant attempt to defeat the Union army of Gen. William T. Sherman as it marched through the Carolinas. Lee surrendered to Grant three weeks later and Bentonville was forgotten. Johnston surrendered to Sherman on April 26 at Bennett Place in Durham.

The battlefield has extensive groundcover and there was little construction on its 6,000 acres until 1957, so it was relatively untouched when the state purchased the first fifty-one acres of it that year in the interest of preservation. In 1996, it became a national historic landmark. Additional preservation is ongoing by the American Battlefield Protection Program, protecting over 1,800 acres, including 3.3 miles of earthworks trenches. Today private citizens still own most of the battlefield. Eight battleground historical markers along the MST and eighteen roadside pull-offs and markers help illuminate this history. MST volunteers led efforts in 2023 to construct a mile of new trail near previously inaccessible earthworks of the Bull Pen battle area. An annual reenactment of the battle features demonstrations, food trucks, and more.

Charles Milligan and Henry Westmoreland completed the MST in three hikes in 2017–19. "Bentonville Battlefield State Historic Site moved me to tears," said Henry. "We stayed at Howell Woods that evening after hiking through the site. I had to return the next morning to walk reverently through the cemetery and pay my respects at the mass grave before continuing our hike. It was worth the later start that day."

Food Festivals near the MST

Time your hiking right and you can dip into a wonderland of good taste. Food festivals are legion in North Carolina, from apples, pecans, muscadine grapes, watermelon, and potatoes, to livermush, collards, and seafood. The world's largest producer of muscadine wines, and the state's oldest and largest winemaker, is Duplin Winery. Along the MST you'll find the Carolina Cheese Fest in Asheville (Segment 3), the Ham and Yam Festival in Smithfield (Segment 11), the Shrimp Festival in Sneads Ferry (Segment 15), and others. If you want to consume great North Carolina food, check out the Western North Carolina Cheese Trail, the Asheville Ale Trail, and the Surry Wine Trail in Yadkin Valley.

Hankering for some 'que? The North Carolina Barbeque Society has marked twenty-one historic barbecue pits across the state, including towns near the MST like Little Switzerland, Winston-Salem, Greensboro, Burlington, and Goldsboro. Ever since swine were introduced by colonists in the 1600s, we've had coastal, spit-roasted pig for pig pickin' and western-sliced or chopped pork with tomato-based sauce. As you hike, stop and smell the roses . . . and taste the good food across the Tar Heel State.

Back on the Trail

With a total area of 947 square miles, Sampson County is the second-largest in North Carolina. It includes about fifty-two miles of MST, and when you hike through the county, you will see a lot of fields growing crops like peanuts, tobacco, corn, soybeans, cotton, sorghum, millet, and cattle, as well as timber. And abundant grain and soybean crops attract poultry and swine operations. Every day of the week there are more hogs in Sampson and Duplin Counties than any other place in America.

According to 2018 US Department of Agriculture statistics, North Carolina ranks first in sweet potato production in America, with 40 percent of the nation's crop. Sampson County is the largest producer in North Carolina. Most years, the state's growers harvest about 2 billion pounds, with the majority from Sampson, Johnston, Nash, Wilson, and Edgecombe Counties.

Hiking this segment of the MST, you'll walk by many farm fields. Many major crops and larger farms are in the coastal region. Statewide, cornfields cover over 830,000 acres, producing 99 million bushels of corn, with a value of $727 million. Soybeans cover more acres, 1.7 million, than any crop in the state, producing 65 million bushels and over $950 million in value to farmers. North Carolina is second in the nation for poultry and eggs, hogs and pigs, and turkeys; third for barley, oats, and young chicken broilers; fifth for peanuts; and eighth for cotton.

Small churches dot the roadside and leave their mark in the names of roads. Between EB 13.9 and EB 37.5 are North Church Street, South Church Street, Church Road, Seven Mile Church Road, Browns Church Road, and White Oak Church Road. At EB 13.4, 500 feet to the left on Irwin Road is Our Lady of Guadalupe Catholic Church, built in 1874 as St. Mark's Church, on land donated by John Monk, MD. After the Civil War, during Reconstruction, many churches banned newly freed African Americans from worshipping in their buildings, even though they had attended under enslavement. Monk opposed this segregation, and St. Mark's Church (today Our Lady of Guadalupe) opened its doors to all who wished to attend, including Latino immigrants well after Reconstruction.

Nearby

Clinton is 2.5 miles southeast of the MST, but if you are in the area you'll enjoy the annual Clinton Square Fair with a Barbecue Cook-Off (October), festivals, and a weekly farmers' market. St. Paul's Episcopal Church (established in 1832, rebuilt in 1902) supports the Episcopal Farmworker's Ministry, responding to the needs of migrant and seasonal farmworkers and their families. The North Carolina Farmworker Health Program in the Office of Rural Health focuses on improved health and living conditions for the estimated 100,000 farmworkers who have traditionally been underserved, while laboring in some of the most dangerous agricultural occupations. Founded in 1997, the Sampson County History Museum has grown into a "village" of eleven buildings, representing over 250 years of Sampson County history.

Back on the Trail

Just off the MST, the town of Salemburg, established in 1905, is home of the North Carolina Justice Academy, which trains over 42,000 criminal justice officers a year. Named the first model community in the United States in 1914 by the Rockefeller Foundation, Salemburg holds many small-town charms. Salemburg Grill offers classic American food in a historic building, and Royal Trustworthy Hardware is the longest continually operating business in Sampson County.

Just north of Salemburg, off NC 242 on Horse Pasture Road, is the Nut House, where Elbie Powers is owner and Head Nut. His farm, with 900 pecan trees, is the largest pecan processing facility in North Carolina. Pecans thrive in river bottom floodplains, and North Carolina's annual production is 4.5 million pounds (the United States supplies 80 percent of the world's pecans). Nut trees were important to colonists, since nuts were high-energy, easily preserved food. The Cape Fear pecan was created in North Carolina in 1941 and is popular due to its early maturation, excellent thin-shelled quality, and resistance to strong winds.

Roseboro was incorporated in 1891 after the Cape Fear and Yadkin Valley Railroad came through the area, connecting Fayetteville and Wilmington (historic depot at EB 47.1). The old kiln on the right is the 1910 Brick Cone Burn Box, fired by slab lumber that was too short or too thin to run through the first planer mill in Sampson County. In 2022 the MST installed a new pathway in downtown Roseboro on part of the former railroad bed. In 2023 a ribbon-cutting opened the Roseboro Heritage Trail, unveiling engraved brick pavers honoring community residents and donors and presenting a booklet prepared by Ruby Fisher Potter to recognize the contributions of Black residents. A place for "the fellas to hang out" is Buddy Melvin's Treehouse, featured on WRAL's *Tarheel Traveler*. It includes sixteen whimsical rooms around a living water oak (0.5 mile off the MST).

Roseboro calls itself a wonderful place to "take root and bloom," a quaint town with all the essential comforts, and hikers are welcomed. Jason Murrell, a November–December 2018 thru-hiker, agrees: "One particularly fond memory I have happened as a strong winter storm was coming in as I approached Roseboro. I knew the mayor and her husband, Alice and Greg Butler, were trail angels who love the MST. I gave them a call to see if they could help get me out of the storm. They were so gracious, it was amazing—they fed me, let me wash clothes, and even helped so I could get my resupply. I ended up staying three days waiting out the storm. Definitely one of the best experiences I've ever had on a hike." Roseboro's elevation is 125 feet, so from here it's all downhill to the coast.

The Coharie Tribe is centered in Sampson and Harnett Counties. They are descendants of the aboriginal Neusiok Indians, who settled in their present location between 1729 and 1746. The tribe has been recognized by North Carolina since 1971. *Coharie* is a Tuscarora word for "driftwood." The Coharie Tribal Center is located about three miles northwest of the MST (EB 32.2) along US 421, in the Eastern Carolina Indian School building the tribe was given in 1943 (the first Coharie school with twelve grades). "Carol's Room" serves as a museum and welcomes the public. In 2021 a preserved 650-year-old dugout canoe was repatriated to the museum. The tribe offers Coharie River tours and a pow-wow in the fall, and is known for beautiful quilting and deep faith. Pamela Brewington Cashwell, a Coharie and Lumbee, became the first Native American woman to lead a North Carolina cabinet department in 2021.

Named for the Coharie tribe, the Great Coharie Creek and Little Coharie Creek merge to form the Black River east of Garland. A number of bridges cross the creeks, which are popular for paddling. The South River, also a tributary of the Black River, is great for canoeing or kayaking.

The Little Coharie runs along the southeast border of the 2,100-acre Pondberry Bay Plant Conservation Preserve, dedicated in 2002. A Sampson County resident reports that one of her ancestors bought Pondberry Bay in 1829 from former governor Gabriel Holmes for $500. Located between Roseboro and Salemburg, Pondberry/White Woods is managed to preserve and enhance the habitats of rare and endangered native flora and fauna. A permit is required to visit these sites. The first natural surface trail open for public use in Sampson County is set to be established when a new section of the MST opens at the Pondberry Bay Preserve. After many years of negotiation and planning, the Plant Conservation Program, Sampson County Parks and Recreation, and Friends of the MST are on track to create a five-mile loop trail through the preserve. The trail will showcase incredible ecosystems, especially longleaf pine savanna, as well as areas of ongoing ecological restoration, and will include parking.

Spring green abounds
along Gip Road in
Cumberland County.
*Photo by Stan Seals;
used by permission.*

Forestry is big business in North Carolina, with over 18 million acres of timberland, 15 billion timberland trees, and 144,000 employees in forestry and timber. The forest economy supports communities in every county of North Carolina, enhancing environmental diversity, improving forest health, protecting wildlife habitat, and providing recreational opportunities. The industries are diverse, including mills that produce lumber, plywood or oriented strand board, wood pellets, and pulp and paper. In 2020, Sampson County had one of six wood pellet manufacturing plants in North Carolina, with a capacity of up to 150,000 tons per year. North Carolina produces and exports more wood pellets than any other state.

Charles W. Chesnutt was a Sampson County native and the son of free-born African Americans. He was once the principal of the State Colored Normal School, which is Fayetteville State University today. In August 1889, Chesnutt became the first writer who identified as Black to publish a piece in the prestigious *Atlantic Monthly*. Today he is known as one of the nation's most important African American writers.

At EB 60.9 at Turnbull Road, 5.5 miles to the right, rises the 100-foot Cedar Creek Lookout Tower, built in 1934 by the Civilian Conservation Corps. At EB 60.6 one can enter the Bushy Lake State Natural Area, 6,396 acres in Cumberland County, established in 1977 mainly as a bear sanctuary. It is managed by Jones Lake State Park and protects wet pocosin and Carolina bay forest.

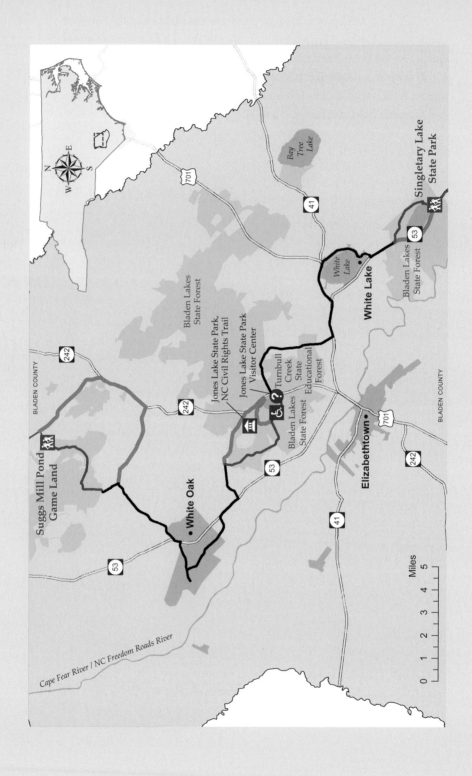

Carolina Bay Country

Suggs Mill Pond Game Land to Singletary Lake State Park

39.2 MILES

Nature welcomes all and embraces all.
La naturaleza nos recibe y abraza a todos.

VIVIANETTE ORTIZ

Carolina bays get their names from the trees that surround them—sweet bay, loblolly bay, and red bay evergreen. While they once were under water, these days the waters have receded and left behind wet, organic soils covered in swampy vegetation, or pocosin bogs. There are 136 named bays and swamps in Bladen County. Cypress trees appear in the coastal landscape. State forests, state parks, White Lake, and one of the oldest residences in North Carolina offer plenty of places to explore near the MST. Watch for trail changes as more natural surface trail is added.

Suggs Mill Pond Game Land covers 11,060 acres in Bladen and Cumberland Counties managed by the North Carolina Wildlife Resources Commission. With help from The Nature Conservancy, the state bought 8,000 of these acres from Canal Industries in 1988. Suggs Mill Pond (also known as Horseshoe Lake due to its shape) is a Carolina bay spanning 600 acres. This unique biome is home to a variety of rare and strange plant species, including carnivorous plants that eastern North Carolina is known for. It is also an important stopover point on the Atlantic Flyway for migrating ducks and birds. Dohn Broadwell is in large part responsible for conserving easements and building impoundments for the migratory birds at Suggs Mill Pond. This game land is closed during hunting season and for controlled burns or logging; during these times, hikers must follow the alternate route.

MST workday volunteers take a break at Harmony Hall Plantation Historic Site. *Photo by Ben Jones; used by permission.*

As the MST leaves Suggs Mill Pond it follows Live Oak Methodist Church Road. The church that gave the road its name was built in 1892 and subsequently damaged by Hurricane Matthew in 2016. At EB 5.4, there are Bethlehem Methodist Church and Cain's Grill, which is popular for breakfast and burgers. At EB 9.1, you will find Camp Bowers and Camp McNeill about two miles north of the MST. These camps are run by the Boy Scouts of America on 1,487 acres of longleaf pine forest. Camp McNeill Cub Scout World shares the same property. At EB 9.4, "bee" on the lookout for Harris Apiaries, in business over thirty years as beekeeper and seller of honey products.

Harmony Hall Plantation Village, 1615 River Road in White Oak, was once a 12,000-acre tract on the Cape Fear River. Now it features one of North Carolina's oldest homes, built around 1760, with the house still on its original foundation (EB 11.2). It was built by Col. James Richardson, and records say that British general Cornwallis commandeered the house during his march from Guilford Courthouse to Wilmington during the Revolutionary War. Richardson enslaved six people, including Simon, who did itinerant preaching, and Judy, who lived to 100 and whose obituary was printed in the newspaper. The house and 2.3 acres of land were given to the Bladen County Historical Society in 1962. In the mid-1980s it was restored, and ninety-seven additional acres were acquired adjoining the Cape Fear River. In 1988, the Historical Society moved a period kitchen and general store to the property and in 1990 also added an early one-room school and a chapel. Harmony Hall has been on the National Register of Historical Places since 1972.

Bladen Lakes State Forest (BLSF) (EB 17.6) sits on 33,670 acres spread over three parcels of land, making it the largest state-owned forest. The forest surrounds, in part, Turnbull Creek Educational State Forest (TCESF), Jones Lake State Park, and Singletary Lake State Park. Most of the forest is in the Game Lands Program, managed by the North Carolina Wildlife Resources Commission. BLSF offers beautiful drives through the wilderness, public hunting areas, and a demonstration trail. Interpretive trails, with environmental exhibits, are open to the public from March through November. Near the BLSF office on NC 242 is an old cemetery. Black bear sanctuary lands are scattered throughout the BLSF. Two pedestrian bridges planned for 2023 will open seven miles of new trail for the MST in Bladen Lakes State Forest and Turnbull Creek Educational State Forest. The trail will connect the state forests' facilities with Jones Lake State Park to establish a twelve-mile corridor of continuous trail through unique ecosystems anchored by two campgrounds and multiple educational exhibits.

Turnbull Creek Educational State Forest (EB 23.7) was established in 1987, covers 890 acres, and is closed mid-November to mid-March and on weekends. In addition to managing the forests of the park, the TCESF also has a historical component, with displays of authentic relics from colonial North Carolina's rich legacy of naval stores, including a turpentine still and metal charcoal cookers. After two bridges are built, the MST in BLST and the TCESF area will be twenty miles off-road.

This segment includes two old fire towers: Cedar Creek Lookout Tower on Turnbull Road in Cumberland County, about a third of a mile from the MST; and the Hampstead Tower at Holly Shelter Game Land on US 17. With modern technology, these towers are no longer needed to spot forest fires. A 1938 US Forest Service manual, *Standard Lookout Structure Plans*, describes towers used not only for fire detection but also for scenic panoramas, accessible to the public, with parking and picnic areas. A few towers along the MST would allow a bird's-eye view. For further reading, find Peter Barr's 2021 book, *Exploring North Carolina's Lookout Towers*.

Hikers experience one of the state's unique Carolina Bays when they take time to savor the four-mile Bay Trail, fishing, boating, or swimming at Jones Lake State Park. *Photo by Ben Jones; used by permission.*

Small towns like Garland in Sampson County have suffered greatly from the loss of jobs and feel "forgotten." Twelve miles north of the MST as it travels through White Lake, Garland lost its largest employer in 2020, the Brooks Brothers factory that made 4,500 classic polo button-down Oxford shirts a day. Garland celebrated the textile plant's reopening by the Garland Apparel Group in July 2021. When possible, remember to support local businesses along the MST!

Jones Lake State Park was the first state park for African Americans and was immediately popular when it opened in the summer of 1939. African American superintendent DeWitt Powell hosted family reunions and church picnics, and on Sunday mornings he allowed baptisms. One of the oldest state parks in North Carolina, it is also on the North Carolina Civil Rights Trail. The park is comprised of 2,208 acres, which include 224-acre Jones Lake and 315-acre Salters Lake . It is located on Highway 242, four miles north of Elizabethtown, and was settled during colonial times. The lake is named for Isaac Jones, who donated the tract of land that became Elizabethtown in 1773. It is one of the best examples of a Carolina bay that is not stream-fed. It is a great park for swimming, boating, fishing, picnicking, camping, hiking, and enjoying the flora and fauna. The Bay Trail is a four-mile loop around the lake; the Cedar Loop is a one-mile journey; and the Salters Lake Trail is one mile, connecting the Bay Trail to Salters Lake.

Camp Chamblee is a beautiful primitive campground perched on a bluff above the dark, meandering waters of lower Turnbull Creek. The forest acres include vault toilets and a well (although as of publication the well was not operating); a Forest Service permit is required. At EB 27.2, the area around the entrance on Sweet Home Church Road is a tree seed orchard managed by BLSF on fields bought by the US Forest Service in the 1930s and 1940s. Just 300 feet past Glen Mar Road (EB 28.1), on the left, Turn Bull Lumber Company specializes in cypress, poplar, and red oak lumber.

Bladen County, established in 1734, is called the "mother of counties" because fifty-five of North Carolina's counties were formed from Bladen's original land. (There were once over 100 counties in North Carolina, but in 1789 some were ceded to Tennessee. North Carolina has consisted of 100 counties since 1911.) Elizabethtown, the Bladen County seat established in 1773, offers tree-lined streets and a small-town feel. The Cape Fear Farmer's Market features local products grown and sold by local farmers. If you're hungry, Melvin's Hamburgers and Hotdogs has been an Elizabethtown landmark since 1938. It serves only burgers and dogs, no fries, and is cash only. Everything about the burgers is the same as the ones Melvin's served when it first opened as a pool room. It draws in locals and tourists, but the long lines move fast as they can complete an order in five seconds. Some say the best bike trail in eastern North Carolina is just south of Elizabethtown, the thirteen-mile trail at Browns Creek Nature Park.

The Revolutionary War Tory Hole Battleground (Battle of Elizabethtown) is in a ravine north of US 701 along the banks of the Cape Fear River, currently Elizabethtown's Tory Hole Park. In the early hours of August 27, 1781, a determined group of seventy-one Patriots surprised and defeated 400 Tory loyalists. The victory permanently weakened Tory power in the Cape Fear region. How did they do it? Sallie Salter, a local woman, was sent into Elizabethtown by the Revolutionaries, on the pretense of selling eggs and socks, to gather information on the Tory positions. Using her information, the Patriots routed the larger force and liberated Bladen County from British influence.

The Cape Fear River, 191 miles of blackwater, flows into the Atlantic Ocean at Cape Fear on Bald Head Island. It originates in the Haw and

Deep Rivers, emptying from Lake Jordan, and is the largest river system in North Carolina, as well as the only major North Carolina river that discharges directly into the Atlantic. It was a major transportation route into the interior in colonial times and made Wilmington a busy seaport. In 1818, the first steamer built in North Carolina, a 100-foot side-wheeler, was launched at Fayetteville and traveled downriver to Wilmington. The Cape Fear runs within a couple of miles of the MST for much of the trail's route from White Oak (EB 9.1) to near Canetuck (Segment 14, EB 21.6), for a total of forty-nine miles. It is one of twenty-five rivers nationwide in the Sustainable Rivers Program.

Brown's Landing lock and dam no. 2, on the Cape Fear River in Elizabethtown, was constructed in 1917. It is one of three dams on the river in Bladen County. (The entire watershed, which extends above Greensboro, contains about 1,100 dams.) The three locks and dams were built to allow commercial navigation but haven't been used since 1995. Rock arch rapids to aid migrating fish passage and fishery resources have been added at dam no. 1 at Rieglewood (also home of a massive International Paper mill) and dam no. 2 in Elizabethtown, restoring American or silver shad, herring, and striped bass. (Early colonists fertilized their fields with shad.) The US Army Corps of Engineers manages the locks and dams. Elizabethtown manages Brown's Landing Park, built on land formerly used for the lock and dam.

For decades, White Lake (elevation sixty-nine feet) has been known as the "Nation's Safest Beach" because of its crystal-clear waters and white sand. Amusement parks, restaurants, and accommodations (a motel, cottage, and campground) dot the lake's shores. The White Lake Water Festival has celebrated the start of the traditional summer season (third weekend in May) for over forty years. Goldston's Beach is a ninety-year-old quintessential family arcade with rides, ice cream, sandwiches, and a souvenir shop. The original Herschell Carousel, built in 1916, is still in operation. Camp Clearwater offers the largest campground and a beautiful waterfront open air chapel. The beach resort is open from mid-May until Labor Day. The NC FFA Center, a five-acre waterfront complex, has hosted summer camps for high school students since the 1930s. The area includes hundreds of acres of blueberries, so in June, buy them freshly picked at roadside stands.

Located on Highway 53 about seven miles from White Lake is Singletary Lake State Park, a Carolina bay open for hiking, fishing, paddling, and picnicking. The lake has a four-mile shoreline and a maximum depth of 11.8 feet. It also provides educational camping opportunities for groups of twenty or more, such as Scouts and 4-H Clubs. The lake's namesake, Richard Singletary, received a land grant in Bladen County in 1729. Colonial settlers in the area relied on subsistence farming along the rivers and creeks. Longleaf pines covered the land and were harvested for turpentine pitch and timber. In 1936, the federal government purchased the future state park land for $4.51 an acre. Three years later, in 1939, it gave the land to the state of North Carolina, and by 1954 that land was a state park. Today, the state park also includes Bay Tree Lake State Natural Area (about thirteen miles north of the main park) and the Turkey Oak Natural Area (133 acres of mostly turkey oak trees that have been left in their natural state for research and education).

Hurricane Matthew

In 2016, Hurricane Matthew dropped a huge amount of rain throughout eastern North and South Carolina. Homes were flooded, roads washed out, crops lost, communities devastated, and hog lagoons and coal ash ponds spilled over into the Cape Fear River Basin. Poor and marginalized communities were hardest hit. Even the MST was impassable. The National Weather Service admonishes, "Don't drown, turn around." Before damage from that storm was cleaned up, it was followed in 2018 by catastrophic Hurricane Florence, which brought days of torrential rains and flooding. It was weeks before damage could be assessed. Examples of rain totals along the MST route include Elizabethtown at 35.9 inches, Jacksonville at 25.3 inches, and Burgaw at 13.6 inches. North Carolina received an estimated 8 trillion gallons of rain! On the coastal areas of North Carolina and the Outer Banks, a nor'easter can bring high tide surge, flooded beaches, and storm-force winds. Hiking along coastal areas at these times should not be attempted, and ferry and automobile traffic may be brought to a halt. Consult the National Weather Service or local weather for storm conditions and predictions.

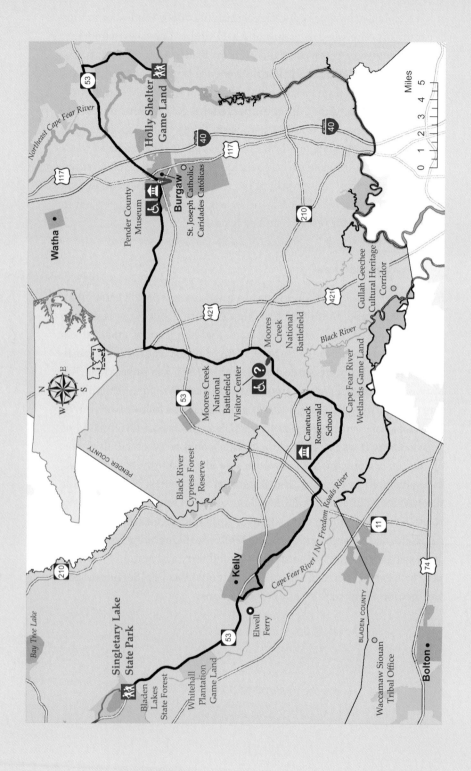

Land of History

Singletary Lake State Park to Holly Shelter Game Land

66 MILES

Returning home is the most difficult part of long-distance hiking.
You have grown outside the puzzle and your piece no longer fits.

CINDY ROSS

These sixty-six miles of history through southeast North Carolina include a Rosenwald School, an old train depot, a river ferry, a national battlefield, and Carolina bays. The area is also known for rich farmland and blueberries. Burgaw locations have been used in movies, and several nearby small communities have intriguing histories.

Whitehall Plantation Game Land (EB 3.8) is 1,663 acres in Bladen County, managed by North Carolina Wildlife Resources Commission. It borders the Cape Fear River on the west side and NC 53 on the east. North Carolina is the "land of the longleaf pine," trees with needles up to eighteen inches long. They were dominant in state coastal forests in colonial times, but by 1920 harvesting and land use changes had pushed the longleaf ecosystem to the brink of extinction. These pines are resilient to storms, fire, and drought, and capture carbon, aiding in the fight against climate change.

Elwell Ferry, on Highway 53 near Carver's Creek on NC 87 (EB 10.1, 0.9 mile off the MST), is a great side trip for those looking to step back in time. The vintage two-car cable ferry shuttles visitors across the Cape Fear River near Kelly. When it first started running in 1905, a ferryboat was poled upriver and then rowed back, all by hand, with space for a wagon and two mules. Daytime ferry service was mostly free thanks to subsidies from the county, but crossers had to pay a quarter on Sundays and fifty cents at night. A cable was installed in the 1930s to guide larger ferries across the 110 yards of river, and in the late 1930s the ferry got a gasoline-powered engine. It was the only way to get between Wilmington and Elizabethtown until 1952.

The Kelly Museum and Historical Society is at EB 12.9. Since 2016 and Hurricane Matthew, the museum has been out of commission and filled with supplies. It sustained further rain damage during Hurricane Florence. Seven miles as the crow flies, to the southwest of Kelly, is the headquarters for the Waccamaw Saponi Indians, who relocated to North Carolina in 1749 and were referred to in the past as the Cape Fear Indians. Known as "People of the Falling Star," they number about 2,000 members, own a small tract of tribal land, and in 1971 became a recognized tribe in North Carolina.

In 1922, the Canetuck Rosenwald School opened with two teachers in western Pender County. Rosenwald schools were dedicated to educating rural Black children during segregation in the Jim Crow South, when public education was out of reach for many. The idea for the schools was conceived by Julius Rosenwald, the son of German Jewish immigrants and the president of Sears, Roebuck and Company, who was inspired by the Jewish concept of *tzedakah* (righteousness and charity). In collaboration with Booker T. Washington, the Rosenwald Fund School Building Program (1912–32) provided funding and support for the construction of 5,300 schools in fifteen states. There were over 813 school buildings in North Carolina, the most of any state. The Canetuck school's rectangular wood-frame building with a clipped gable roof was constructed on four acres behind a row of trees off Route 1104. The Rosenwald Fund provided $800 for the building, local Black Americans raised $1,226, and the remaining $674 came from public funds. The school operated until 1958. Many of the state's Rosenwald schools were demolished or fell into disrepair. Nationwide, an estimated 500 remain. But the Canetuck school and other surviving structures still stand thanks to the dedication of alumni groups, churches, and individuals who purchased and preserved them. Today Canetuck's former Rosenwald school is the Canetuck Community Center.

Nearby

A tributary of the Cape Fear, the Black River flows for sixty-six miles through Sampson, Bladen, and Pender Counties. Along Bladen County's section of the river, in the Three Sisters Swamp, stands an ancient bald cypress that ranks fifth among the world's trees for longevity. It is at least 2,628 years old, dating back to 605 BCE, according to a 2017 survey. The swamp is owned by the North Carolina Nature Conservancy, which believes it includes thousands of 1,000-year-old trees. The oldest stand of trees in the eastern United States, Three Sisters is believed to be one of the great old-growth forests left in the world. Imagine a forest standing just as it did before Europeans arrived. The swamp lies between the SR 1550 bridge and the NC 53 bridge and is only accessible by canoe or kayak: launch at Henry's Landing, a private landing at the NC 53 bridge, or the Wildlife Resources Commission boat ramp. Note that the swamp is near but not on the MST.

Moores Creek National Battlefield (EB 30.8) is one of only two national battlefields in the state and is eighty-seven acres. It was first designated a national military park in 1926. In 1776, 1,000 colonists (a southeastern North Carolina militia) fought and defeated 1,600 British soldiers at the Moores Creek bridge. Muskets in hand, they waited until the Loyalist militia, predominantly made up of broadsword-carrying Scottish Highlanders, attempted to cross the booby-trapped bridge before they pulled their triggers and fired their cannons. The swift battle was a decisive, devastating blow to the British plan to advance toward Wilmington to reinforce Britain's authority in the colony and a first step to revolution against Britain.

There has been a bridge over Moores Creek since 1743, connecting Negro Head Point near Wilmington to Cross Creek (now Fayetteville). A historical marker states, "Old Wilmington and Fayetteville Stage Road, route taken by British and Tory army from Cross Creek to join Lord Cornwallis and Clinton at Wilmington. They were defeated in the battle of this place. 350 were captured as prisoners of war Feb. 27, 1776." Along the trail you will find the only monument to women of the Revolutionary War. It is dedicated in memory of Mary Slocumb, who tended the wounded at Moores Creek.

"This was where the first Revolutionary War battle was fought in North Carolina," said local historian Chris E. Fonvielle Jr. "It was a civil war battle . . . essentially a fight of brother against brother, neighbor against neighbor." Emboldened by their victory, which pushed the Loyalists out of the colony for more than three years, the battle led the Patriots to draft the Halifax Resolves on April 12, 1776, in which North Carolina became the first colony to declare its intention to vote for independence.

The Pender County site of the assault is now staring down a formidable new foe: Mother Nature. Flooding from the Cape Fear River and the Black River has worsened and become more frequent, and historic ("500-year") weather events like Hurricanes Matthew and Florence have inundated the battlefield, sometimes submerging the land in over six feet of water.

Black River Road, also known as Negro Head Point Road, was a main road linking the coast to the interior of North Carolina, and later was the route of the Wilmington and Fayetteville Stage Road. Slave ships would dock at Wilmington and enslaved people were ferried to the head of the Cape Fear River (also where "head" counts were made), then marched along this route ninety miles to Cross Creek, now Fayetteville, where they were auctioned. Mount Misery Road runs near the Cape Fear River not far from Leland—the name comes from the extreme difficulty that laborers had in cultivating this bluff over the northwest Cape Fear. This area, and other parts of Pender, Bladen, Columbus, and Brunswick Counties, is part of the Gullah Geechee Cultural Heritage Corridor, a National Heritage Area managed by the National Park Service. The Gullah and Geechee people who live along the lower Atlantic coast today are descendants of West Africans brought to America against their will and enslaved on the region's rice, indigo, and cotton plantations. The Cultural Heritage Corridor works to preserve and share the history and traditional culture of primarily Gullah people of coastal North Carolina, South Carolina, Georgia, and Florida.

About fifteen miles to the south of Moores Creek Battlefield is Reaves Chapel AME Church, one of the oldest African American and Gullah Geechee buildings in the southeastern part of the state. Edward Reaves, a former enslaved man, donated the land for the church around 1860. Many enslaved people at Cedar Hill Plantation attended the church, including the Pocomoke community and Gullah Geechee peoples, who were experts in rice cultivation when rice plantations lined the banks of the Cape Fear River. With no telephones, the ringing of the church bells announced major events to the community. The building was moved around 1922 and ceased service in 1995. Purchased by the Coastal Land Trust in 2019 and renovated in 2022, it is on the North Carolina Gullah Geechee Greenway–Blueway Heritage Trail. Also a part of the Gullah Geechee Cultural Heritage Corridor are the Poplar Grove Plantation house and grounds, located north of Wilmington on US 17, recognized for growing prized sweet potatoes and peanuts.

The MST shares the Osgood Canal Greenway and Urban Trail in Burgaw. *Photo by Roger Ball; used by permission of Pender County Tourism.*

On Bell Williams Road, Goose Haven Farm (EB 33.5) provides rescue and rehabilitation to abused, neglected, or abandoned animals in the Yamacraw area, named for a small Native American group meaning "great people." On a hot summer day, hikers love sighting Lewis Grocery (EB 37) or the AB Food Mart on US 421 at Piney Woods Road (EB 40.3), with their cold drinks and air-conditioned breakfast and lunch space.

As you enter Burgaw you'll see the Pender County Museum, which preserves the county's history with documents, artifacts, photos, and genealogy. Burgaw, the county seat, is a small town in a picturesque setting with striking architecture and a welcoming nature. While passing through Burgaw take a self-guided walking tour based on the locations from well-known motion pictures and television series (such as *Under the Dome, I Know What You Did Last Summer,* and *Welcome to Flatch*) filmed within Burgaw's downtown area, the courthouse square, and familiar storefronts. The 1850 train station, built by the Wilmington and Weldon Railroad, is the oldest train depot in the state. It contains a transportation museum and is part of the North Carolina Civil War Trails. Economic activity picked up in coastal North Carolina in 1838 with the railroad connecting Wilmington, Weldon, Richmond, and Washington, DC, allowing crops to be sold to new markets and travel to DC in "only" forty-eight hours.

Burgaw hosts the annual North Carolina Blueberry Festival, but you can get homemade blueberry pie, made from scratch with locally grown berries, anytime at Olde Carolina Eatery. The MST travels along rich farmland, which produces plentiful crops of corn, tobacco, soybeans, and cotton. The MST follows the Osgood Canal Greenway and Urban Trail for 2.6 miles through Burgaw.

Ann S. Cottle's book *The Roots of Penderlea: A Memory of a New Deal Homestead Community* summarizes this pathbreaking North Carolina project by combining documentary history and firsthand accounts. According to Cottle, "What started as a vision became a reality in 1934 when, under President Roosevelt's New Deal, Penderlea became one of the nation's first experimental agricultural colonies. Through perseverance, dedication, and cooperation, the original homesteaders and their families built a close-knit community with farms, business enterprises, churches, a school, and civic organizations." The US Department of the Interior purchased 4,500 acres at $6.50 per acre. In 1929 unemployment was 45 percent in North Carolina, so labor was plentiful. Work was done by the Civilian Conservation Corps; wages to clear land were $1.25 per day. One hundred and forty-two homes were planned (1,000–1,400 square feet with electricity, hot and cold water, and a bathroom for $1,200). An unskilled laborer made $0.25/hour and a carpenter $0.75/hour. A farm could be leased for $60 per year, and in 1943 the first farm to be purchased was thirty-nine acres for $2,355 at 3 percent annually for forty years. In 1937 Eleanor Roosevelt visited Penderlea. (The name "Penderlea" is from Pender County and *lea*, meaning "green ground in the woods.")

Watha, a small, quiet community five miles north of Burgaw, is named for Hiawatha, a Native American leader. Watha was home to the first courthouse in Pender County, but in 1926 a devastating fire destroyed much of the town. Scenes in the film *Secret Life of Bees* were filmed in Watha.

Underground Railroad in North Carolina

In the mid-nineteenth century, enslaved Black people made up an estimated 44 percent of eastern North Carolina's population, with about 30,400 free Black people who were skilled artisans. The National Park Service's Underground Railroad Network to Freedom recognizes the routes and people that played a crucial role in helping enslaved African Americans in their pursuit of freedom. Documented sites in the NPS network include colonial towns, plantations, Quaker communities, Union-occupied territories, and freedmen's colonies and settlements. There are a number of designated sites in North Carolina, comprising a statewide trail system, both on land and water, with no beginning or end. The roads, rivers, and ports tell the stories of people who sought freedom and offered shelter during the Civil War. Near the MST, Underground Railroad sites include Guilford County, the Stagville State Historic Site, Tryon Palace in New Bern, and the Freedman's Colony on Roanoke Island (Fort Raleigh National Historic Site).

A 12.6-mile alternate route involves paddling the Northeast Cape Fear River for 4.6 miles and walking 8 miles (see the MST Trail Guide for details). Forget the expression "You can't paddle upstream," for here you can select up or down the river, though navigation can be difficult. A 12.8-mile road route is available for nonpaddlers or if river conditions are unsafe. If you can float the section of the Northeast Cape Fear River in mid-April, it is an excellent place to see blackwater, cypress swamp birds.

Nearby

Down I-40, Wilmington grew as a naval stores port to resupply wooden sailing ships with tar, pitch, rosin, and turpentine. At one time, coastal North Carolina provided two-thirds of the world's supply of naval stores. Wilmington was once called "The Defense Capital of the State" because the city's largest employer, the North Carolina Shipbuilding Company, built 243 cargo vessels during World War II. Wilmington was recognized as an American World War II Heritage City in 2020, the first city to be listed as such. Today it is a major port whose attractions include a fun waterfront, the Battleship *North Carolina* historic site, an annual azalea festival, the Cape Fear Museum, and nearby beaches.

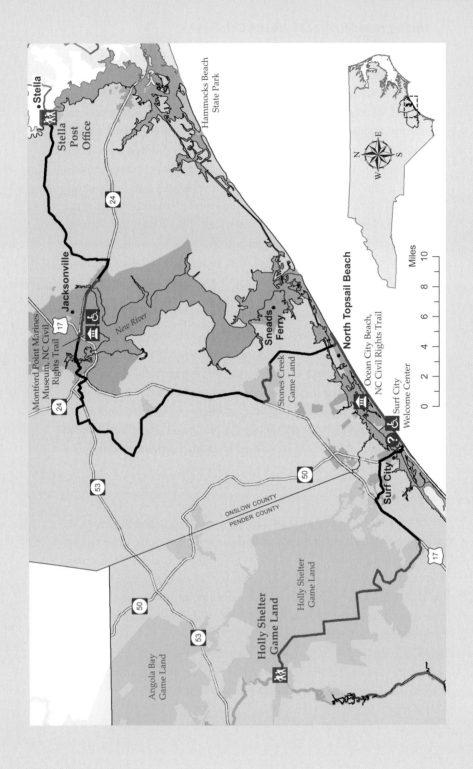

Stella

Stella Post Office

Hammocks Beach State Park

24

Jacksonville

Montford Point Marines Museum, NC Civil Rights Trail

17

24

New River

Snead's Ferry

Stones Creek Game Land

North Topsail Beach

Ocean City Beach, NC Civil Rights Trail

Surf City Welcome Center

53

Surf City

50

ONSLOW COUNTY
PENDER COUNTY

17

Holly Shelter Game Land

Holly Shelter Game Land

50

53

Angola Bay Game Land

Miles

0   2   4   6   8   10

N
W   E
S

SEGMENT 15

The Onslow Bight and Jacksonville

Holly Shelter Game Land to Stella

90.4 MILES

Live in the sunshine, swim in the sea, drink the wild air.

RALPH WALDO EMERSON

The MST travels ninety miles through the Onslow Bight, a shallow bend on the coast between Cape Lookout and Cape Fear known for its ecological diversity. The barrier islands, marshes, wetlands, pocosins, and longleaf pine savannas create an environment that is among the most diverse in the United States and a conservation priority area. Travelers enjoy the beauty of twenty-six-mile-long Topsail Island and the quaint village of Sneads Ferry. This segment's center is the city of Jacksonville (incorporated in 1843) and Marine Corps Base Camp Lejeune. Note that the MST will see several reroutes in coming years.

Holly Shelter Game Land to North Topsail Beach

Holly Shelter Game Land (EB 0–18.9), managed by the North Carolina Wildlife Resources Commission, is public woodlands, wetlands, pine savanna, and lush grasses on 75,000 acres, with areas for hiking, birdwatching, and hunting. The Friends' MST guidebook and FarOut navigational app include good information on hiking this remote and challenging area. Local water is highly tannic and unpredictable. Hunting season is generally September through January 1. There are alligators in the waterfowl impoundments. Of sixty-six species of carnivorous plants found in the

United States, thirty-six occur in southeastern North Carolina. Friends of the MST successfully partnered with The Nature Conservancy and Camp Lejeune to secure funding from the North Carolina Land and Water Fund for the purchase of a 1,600-acre tract of land containing critical longleaf pine savanna and pocosin habitat, to be added to Holly Shelter Game Land. This will allow for the development of five miles of new trail for the MST and remove from its route four miles of unpleasant road walking along Highway 17.

"Holly Shelter was one of the toughest sections of the trail for me," said Graham Zimmerman, a 2020 thru-hiker. "No water sources for nineteen miles took its toll . . . especially considering I was traveling through in August. Leaving the bog and heading into the pine savanna was beautiful. I will always remember reaching the apex of the Surf City bridge and breaking into tears as I saw the Atlantic Ocean. That was an incredibly special moment."

Holly Shelter Game Land is very remote, with sixteen miles between paved roads. The first two-thirds has no shade, but trail angels may help stage water if contacted in advance. There are three other places along the MST with over twenty-two miles between paved roads: hiking through the Smokies, over Bald Knob west of Linville Gorge, and through Harper Creek–Lost Cove Creek west of Grandfather Mountain.

Holly Ridge, in Onslow County, was incorporated in 1941, when Camp Davis opened (1941–45). During World War II, the creation of this antiaircraft army base exploded the population from 28 to 110,000. The small town now promotes itself as the "Gateway to Topsail Island."

The Karen Beasley Sea Turtle Rescue and Rehabilitation Center, 0.5 mile away at EB 26.5, is worth a visit. This all-volunteer hospital cares exclusively for endangered sea turtles. Loggerhead sea turtles, the most widespread turtles in the world, are named for their large heads, which support powerful jaw muscles. Segment 15 has three MST directional poles that make great photo ops—a colorful one is at the Beasley Center. The trail volunteers also had a telephone pole with a three-foot white circle buried deep in the sand to mark where hikers leave the beach on North Topsail Beach, but it was washed away by Hurricane Florence and never found.

In 1955 the iconic Surf City swing bridge over the Atlantic Intracoastal Waterway opened and vacationers heard the weird noise of tires on the grooved surface. The swing bridge was dismantled in 2019. The MST now travels along NC 50, the "Gateway to the Atlantic," over the award-winning

Thru-hikers Moxie and Bald were ecstatic to reach the Atlantic Ocean at Surf City, where Henry "Moxie" Westmoreland poses. *Photo by Charlie "Bald" Milligan; used by permission.*

Surf City Bridge that opened in 2018. Hikers experience the spectacular "Kodak-moment" view as they cross the 68-foot high, 3,800-foot long span with pedestrian-friendly lanes. Everyone who attended the 2019 annual Friends meeting—hosted by Surf City—hiked as a group to the top of the bridge.

Surf City and Topsail Island beaches (EB 28.1–37.7) let eastbound ramblers put their toes into the Atlantic Ocean for the first time. The Surf City Welcome Center and Visitor Information is on the beachfront, adjacent to the Surf City Ocean Pier (built in 1948, rebuilt in 1997, 977 feet long). There is free parking at thirty-five public beach accesses or parks. North Topsail Beach and Onslow County begin about three miles north of the pier. It is about ten miles north to the next beach access with facilities. Topsail got its name from locals watching for the top sail of pirate ships.

While hiking the MST along the shoreline, watch from spring though late summer for areas along the dunes that are staked off. These are protected sea turtle nests. If you are hiking in the early morning, you might see tracks from the ocean to a new nest and back to the water. If you're especially fortunate, you will see a mama turtle nesting or heading home to the ocean. Topsail Island is a sea turtle sanctuary.

On the dune at EB 31.7, you'll see an old rocket observation tower made of white concrete that dates back to the 1940s. Built for the navy's "Operation Bumblebee," it is one of eight towers on the island. Why bumblebee? The secret operation was named after the bee that should not be able to fly yet takes off anyway, much like the secret operation that gave the United States its first strategic surface-to-air missiles. The booster rockets paved the way to creating the ramjet engine, intercontinental ballistic missiles, and the space shuttle. Topsail was a twenty-six-mile barrier island accessible only by boat. In 1942 the project brought water and electricity to the island, as well as roads and the first bridge connecting it to the mainland. On the island's south end, the Assembly Building was constructed for the assembly and storage of experimental missiles; today that facility is the Missiles and More Museum.

Ocean City is a part of North Topsail Beach with a long history. The town of North Topsail Beach was not incorporated until the 1990s, but Ocean City's roots reach back nearly half a century earlier. In the late 1940s, with segregation in full force, a white Wilmington attorney by the name of Edgar Yow approached Samuel Gray of Wilmington and the Chestnut family with an idea. He proposed that they develop the first Black American beach in the South, and they agreed, purchasing six miles of oceanfront property from the federal government on Topsail Island in what became Ocean City. Ocean City Developers Inc. was formed, likely the first interracial corporation at the time, and neighborhood development began. Lots initially sold for $500 to $1,000. The Chestnut family were among the first property owners, and many of their descendants remain in the community today.

In the 1950s, Father Edwin Kirton of St. Mark's Episcopal Church worked with the Chestnut family to bring a summer camp for Black children to Ocean City. The community came together to build a dormitory for sixty children, which still stands today as the Wade H. Chestnut Memorial Chapel. Along with the Ocean City Community Center (near EB 31.9), it is the cultural and social center of the community.

In 1959, Ocean City Developers Inc. built the Ocean City Fishing Pier by one of Operation Bumblebee's abandoned watch towers. Hurricanes Fran and Bertha damaged the pier in 1996, leading to its eventual demolition, but the tower remains. Ocean City was one of the few beaches open to Black Americans in the South until the 1960s. Today the community

Stones Creek Game Lands is northeast of Sneads Ferry, managed by the NC Wildlife Resources Commission. *Photo by Stan Seals; used by permission.*

hosts the Jazz Festival each July, with support from the North Carolina Arts Council. Signs dot each street, recognizing the area's historical significance. In 2022 an official marker designated the town as a site on the North Carolina Civil Rights Trail.

North Topsail Beach to Stella

Topsail Island is considered one of the best North Carolina beaches to find shark teeth, and you might also find a Scotch bonnet shell, the official state shell. And by the way, North Carolina was the first to declare an official state shell. It's also an area where "living shorelines" use bags of oyster shells on marsh banks to curb tideland erosion. As you leave North Topsail Beach, there are facilities at Town Park (EB 38.2) before the 0.5-mile-long High Bridge over the Intracoastal Waterway. "Discover Onslow" at the Onslow County Environmental Education Center on NC 210 just south of Old Folkstone Road (EB 40.6). Rick's Restaurant on the left also sports a large MST directional sign.

Sneads Ferry, located in Onslow County at an elevation of twenty-six feet, began as a rural fishing village when the first settlers arrived in 1728 (EB 42.2; one block off the MST is the post office). That same year, the first ferry in the area was established by Edmund Ennett on the south bank of the New River. This crossing became an important stop on the colonial Post Road connecting Suffolk, Virginia, with Charleston, South Carolina. By 1759, Robert Snead had established a second ferry, this one on the north shore of the New River, and eventually the name of the community changed from Ennett's Ferry to Sneads Ferry. In 1939, the ferries stopped running and were replaced with a swing bridge. Since 2000, the town has experienced consistent growth and development, but it still mostly relies on the seafood and fishing industry. Each year, Sneads Ferry fishermen bring in 385 tons of shrimp, 25 tons of flounder, and 493 tons of other seafood (blue crab, grouper, sea bass, spot, mullet, mussels, clams, oysters, scallops, and more)—that's over 1.8 million pounds of seafood. The annual Sneads Ferry Shrimp Festival in August honors the local seafood industry and is the official North Carolina state shrimp festival.

Along MST Segment 15 are 1800s cemeteries and even a few from the 1700s, some with wooden headstones and wooden slave markers and some with Civil War headstones. When 100,000 acres was purchased by the government in 1941, 639 graves were relocated to form Verona Loop National Cemetery on US 17.

Stones Creek Game Land (4,120 acres) has changed hands over time from privately owned homes and farms to the timberland company Weyerhaeuser, who sold or donated it to conservation and environment entities, with the property now North Carolina Wildlife Resources Commission land. Its eight lakes were formed when dirt was removed to widen US 17. In 2019, North Carolina Wildlife began logging tracts of loblolly pines to restore 131 acres of longleaf pine savannas. They continue efforts to convert additional acreage. Longleaf pines are sources of "heart pine" used for ships, floors, furniture, and turpentine.

Jacksonville, in Onslow County, is the fourteenth-largest city in North Carolina and home to both Marine Corps Base Camp Lejeune (153,439 acres, fourteen miles of beach) and Marine Corps Air Station New River (the Marine Corps' largest airbase and the world's most complete helicopter, tilt-rotor, and amphibious base, 2,600 acres). The city's slogan is "Pardon Our Noise, It's the Sound of Freedom." Jacksonville is blessed with natural beauty enhanced by the New River and its waterways. The New River Inlet was a major trading route from the 1720s to the 1890s.

Sundews are one of the largest groups of carnivorous native perennials found along coastal plain wetlands. They are "flypaper" plants that trap prey in sticky hairs on their leaves. *Photo by Claire Dumont; used by permission.*

Jacksonville history dates to the end of the Tuscarora wars in 1713, when it became a major producer of naval stores, especially turpentine. The 1850s Pelletier House was located on land awarded by a royal grant from King George II of England in 1736. In 1849 the town of Jacksonville was laid out. Big growth came in 1940 with the establishment of Camp Lejeune.

At EB 71 is the Jacksonville City Hall, and Freedom Fountain is on the left. The Jacksonville Onslow African American Heritage Trail is comprised of historical markers and sites throughout Onslow County. Lejeune Greenway (EB 71.1) and Jacksonville Rail-to-Trails Greenway (EB 73) pass Camp Lejeune. Right off the MST is Lejeune Memorial Gardens off Montford Point Road that includes the 9/11 Memorial, the Montford Point Marine Memorial, the Vietnam Memorial, and the Museum of the Marines site. The Beirut Memorial, also located there, honors the 241 killed in Lebanon on October 23, 1983, and 33 who have died from injuries since then.

Nearby

Montford Point (EB 71) is steeped in military and Black history. Prior to 1942, the Marine Corps did not allow African American men to serve in its ranks. That changed on June 1 of that year, when the Corps welcomed Black recruits for the first time, sending them to Montford Point for training. The "Montford Point Marines" faced racism and segregation in the Jim Crow South and as "firsts" charting a new path toward inclusivity and integration of the armed forces. Nevertheless, between 1942 and 1949, 22,609 African American men completed training at Montford Point's Black Boot Camp (today known as Camp Johnson). They went on to play key roles at Iwo Jima, in Vietnam, and in other military campaigns.

PJ Wetzel was the first person to hike the Coastal Crescent route in March and April 2014. His attention to detail, photography, route refinement, and "explorer" approach helped solidify the Coastal Crescent route.

As you leave urban Jacksonville, the last ten miles of road walking become more rural, taking you to the White Oak River and into Carteret County. At EB 78.5, White Oak High School is 3.5 miles north of the MST on Piney Green Road. It has probably the only apiary program in a North Carolina high school, including a pollinator garden, beehives, and a beekeeping class.

You have now hiked through the Onslow Bight.

The Croatan and Neusiok Trail

Stella to Oyster Point Campground

67.3 MILES

Everybody needs beauty as well as bread, places to play in and pray in, where nature may heal, and give strength to body and soul.

JOHN MUIR

For a third of this sixty-seven-mile segment, hikers mostly follow unpaved forest roads through Croatan National Forest. The easternmost twenty-one miles follows the longest hiking trail in eastern North Carolina, the Neusiok Trail, which celebrated its fiftieth anniversary in 2023. Along the entire segment, pick your season carefully to enjoy the diversity of plants and wildlife while being wary of biting insects, dangerous critters, and swampy terrain.

The MST begins Segment 16 at Stella, on Stella Road in Carteret County, at its post office that serves a large, remote rural area. Jacksonville is about ten miles away, a mile west is the Nowhere Café, a half mile away is Midway Methodist Church, and to the east is the White Oak Shores Camping and RV Resort (EB 0.7).

About eight miles south of the MST you'll find Swansboro, the "Friendly City by the Sea," founded in 1783. Located at the mouth of the White Oak River (Weetock to Indigenous Carolina Algonquians), the picturesque waterfront town is home to the annual Mullet Festival. The White Oak River flows past the pristine beaches of Bear Island, home of Hammocks Beach State Park (1,611 acres, established in 1964). The park is just three miles from Croatan National Forest and includes a small harbor next to the Intracoastal Waterway. Bear Island is a four-mile-long, undeveloped barrier island, accessible by a 2.5-mile route via the park's

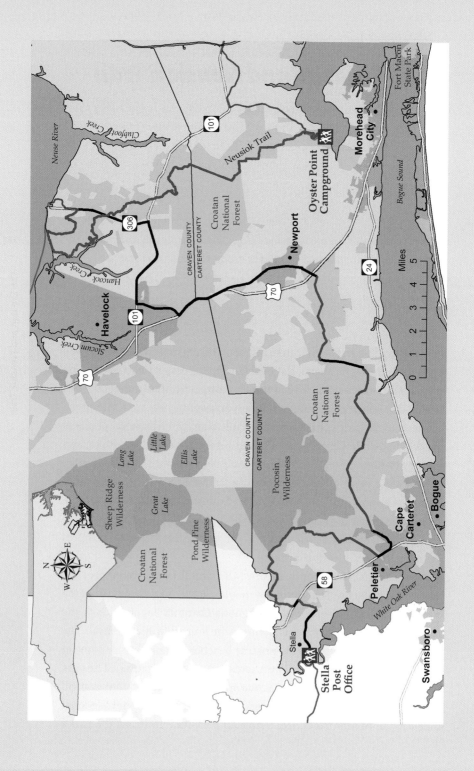

passenger ferry or private ferry, or by paddling a canoe or kayak. It was a coastal park for Black people from 1950 to 1961, when it was owned by the North Carolina Teachers Association (African American teachers), and from 1961 to 1964, when it was Bear Island State Park, designated for African Americans.

The MST goes through the Croatan National Forest for 25.5 miles (EB 3.5–29; established in 1936). In the Croatan Forest between Jacksonville and Havelock, there are not many trails due to the bogs, swamps, pocosins, and biting critters. The word *pocosin* has Native American roots and means "swamp on a hill." These ecosystems were formed as organic matter accumulated over thousands of years, forming a layer of wet, black muck that ranges in depth from several inches at the edge to several feet at the center. The outer rim is covered with pond pine and a thick underbrush of greenbrier and Zenobia, which is found only in pocosins. As you move toward the center of a pocosin, the trees, shrubs, and vines thin, leaving only their roots for footing. Black bears and a number of snakes (including eastern cottonmouth, timber or canebrake rattler, eastern diamondback rattler, and Carolina pygmy rattler) call these areas home. But hikers are more likely to encounter biting insects like gnats, yellow flies, and mosquitoes.

In the 160,000-acre Croatan National Forest, which the MST borders for several miles, are three wilderness areas: Sheep Ridge Wilderness, Pond Pine Wilderness, and Pocosin Wilderness.

From EB 18.9 to 20.1, you'll see groundwater monitoring installations. The North Carolina Division of Environment and Natural Resources regulates the disposal of wastewater and residuals generated by cities, towns, and industry, as well as by activities like groundwater remediation. The monitoring installations help determine how much pollution the Coastal Plain wetlands can absorb.

The MST comes into the small community of Peletier, established in 1996, then continues in the Croatan Forest for over twenty miles on forest roads through longleaf pines, crosses US 70 (EB 27.7), and crosses the Newport River at EB 28.5. Next stop is the Newport Historical Museum and Battle of Newport Barracks Civil War Memorial Park (EB 29.2). The museum and park commemorate the largest battle in Carteret County. Union troops had occupied the Newport Barracks since 1862, but Confederate troops attacked on February 2, 1864, in an attempt to retake control. The battle, spread over three engagements, lasted four hours and resulted in the death of eleven soldiers. The Union troops were forced to retreat to Beaufort, but not before they burned the bridges into town.

Gene and Sue Huntsman, long active with the Carteret County Wildlife Club, are founders of the Neusiok Trail. *Photo by David Wild; used by permission.*

Nearby

Located in Havelock, Marine Corps Air Station Cherry Point was built in 1941 and today encompasses about 29,000 acres. It is home to the Second Marine Aircraft Wing and has more than 9,000 square miles of dedicated airspace for military, civilian, and commercial air traffic. When NASA still had a space shuttle program, it used the air station's extra-long runways as emergency landing sites.

When reflecting on North Carolina's strong military history and numerous training bases like the Marine Corps Air Station, it is important to know about therapeutic hiking programs for veterans. These programs provide support for veterans transitioning from their wartime experiences through long-distance outdoor expeditions—to "walk off the war."

Havelock and the northern half of the Neusiok Trail are in Craven County, formed in 1705 and named for the Earl of Craven, one of the Lords Proprietors. At EB 42.2 the Neusiok Trail crosses NC 306 at a parking area, and at EB 52.4 it crosses a trailhead on NC 306. At EB 44.1 is the Pine Cliff Equestrian Trailhead.

The Neusiok Trail was built in 1971–76 through miles of difficult swamps, bogs, salt marshes, and pine forest lands. It is maintained by the Carteret County Wildlife Club and the US Forest Service and Croatan National Forest. Gene and Sue Huntsman, with PhDs in fishery biology and botany, respectively, are considered its visionaries. Funding

Two hikers speed along Neusiok Trail boardwalk to complete the twenty-one-mile trail in a day. *Photo by Jerry Barker.*

was provided by the Wildlife Club, the US Forest Service, the American Hiking Association, and state funds, with several remote lumber drops by Marine helicopters. It is the longest hiking trail in eastern North Carolina, at twenty-one miles, and was made into a dedicated part of the MST in 1990. Hikers may encounter wildlife, including black bears and alligators, along with mosquitoes, flies, and ticks. Several miles of boardwalks help in the wettest areas, but they sometimes are unusable due to flood waters and storm damage (one bog bridge is 322 feet long). On the bright side, you'll enjoy wildflowers, woodpeckers, pine savannas, bald cypress, sandy paths, and some gentle country road walking. You definitely don't want to forget your bug spray on this hike, and sunscreen, water, and food are also necessities. Look out for bald cypress knees that can trip a hiker, and wear blaze orange during hunting season.

Three backcountry campsites are available along the Neusiok Trail: Copperhead Landing Shelter (EB 49.6), Dogwood Camp Shelter (EB 55.9), and Blackjack Lodge Shelter (EB 65). All three sites have water. Some hikers prefer to hoof it through the twenty-one miles in a day and avoid critters by hiking in early spring or late fall. The Neusiok Trail ends at Oyster Point Campground.

Dave Whitlow, longtime trail maintainer of the Neusiok Trail and Croatan Task Force leader, told of the ship stores industry that was big in the Neusiok area—tar, pitch, and turpentine. That was followed by the liquor-making and moonshine activity in the area. The hooch was called CCC, for Craven County Corn. You can still see the remnants of a couple of the still sites. "The legend that I was told," Dave said, "was Al Capone came to the area looking for a piece of the action and was promptly run off."

Thru-hiker "Beerdra" Smith encountered Segments 15–17 under challenging conditions in 2018: "Because of Hurricane Florence and Hurricane Michael, I did a ton of road walking around the Croatan and Neusiok due to flooding and damage even six weeks after the storms, but I was determined to finish. The craziest things on my extended road walk were the dead fish along the road! No water in sight but huge fish lay dead everywhere. The saddest sights were the hundreds of homes with all their water-soaked belongings piled by the side of the road, and on the coast the number of completely destroyed homes was surreal." Beerdra highly recommends a detour into Beaufort (pronounced BOW-fort), which she says "is adorable and good for resupply."

SEGMENT 17

Down East North Carolina

Oyster Point Campground to Cedar Island Ferry

47.9 MILES

Take me to the ocean. Let me sail the open sea. To breathe
the warm and salty air and dream of things to be.

ERICA BILLUPS

229

Down East North Carolina

The folks in Carteret County call this part of North Carolina "Down East." Everyone knows the Outer Banks, but few know the "inner banks," with their sounds, marshes, and estuaries. Estuaries are zones where fresh water and salt water mix and constitute a crucial but delicate ecosystem upon which much marine life depends. North Carolina is proud of its 322 miles of shoreline as well as 12,008 miles of estuarine coastline. Currently, the forty-eight-mile route is all on road shoulders, but a reroute might soon put eight miles on natural trail. The route is also biked by some. You'll be welcomed by the people in small villages along the Core Sound.

The Iroquois-speaking Tuscarora Indians were the Native inhabitants of the area and lived between the Neuse and Pamlico Rivers. The white colonists who arrived as early as 1706 were mostly of German, Scotch-Irish, French, and English descent, but they came from northern American colonies rather than from Europe directly. Similarly, in 1791 Rhode Island Quakers migrated to the area, where they settled on the north side of the Newport River.

At EB 5.0 you cross Harlow Creek and may notice how straight it is. From 1795 to 1828 this was the Harlow Creek Canal, hand dug by enslaved labor, to create a boat route from Beaufort to New Bern.

The MST passes many churches, especially along the road segments of eastern North Carolina. Churches have been generous in permitting

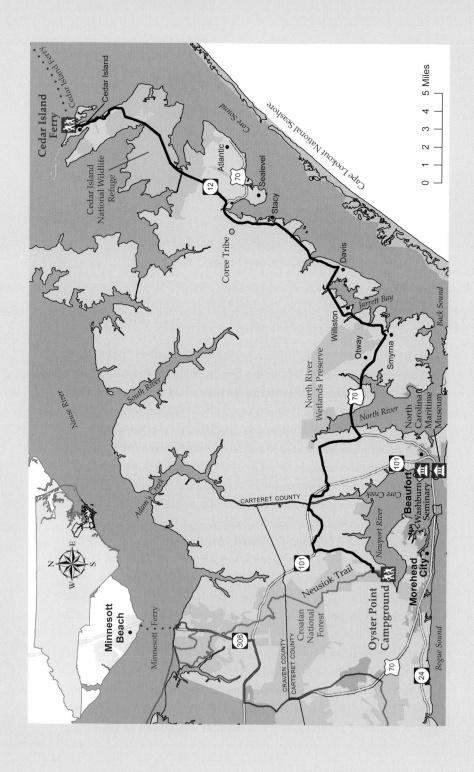

On NC 101 in Carteret County, the MST crosses Core Creek and the Atlantic Intracoastal Waterway. *Photo by Stan Seals; used by permission.*

hikers to get water from their spigots, and some allow camping and/or day-hiker parking. They have been true "trail angels." Along this segment, for example, from EB 1.5 to EB 46.2 there are nine churches, and six—Baptist, Freewill Baptist, Missionary Baptist, Community, Pentecostal Holiness, and United Methodist—offer water for hikers. Another great spot for a break, 200 yards from EB 8.0, is Core Creek Methodist Church on Hardesty Loop Road, on the Atlantic Intracoastal Waterway. Small churches historically have been community gathering places, with Sunday a day for rest, faith, family, and friends.

Beaufort, established in 1713, the fourth-oldest town in North Carolina, is the Carteret County seat. From the MST intersection at US 70 (EB 15.1), Beaufort is about five miles and Morehead City (with some designated MST) is about nine miles. Beaufort attractions include an educational visit to the North Carolina Maritime Museum, the Beaufort Pirate Invasion, and New Year's in the Park with a Pirate Drop. The Old Burying Ground dates to the early 1700s, and among the notable people buried there is Capt. Otway Burns, who served in the War of 1812 and has a cannon marking his grave.

Each October, Morehead City hosts the North Carolina Seafood Festival on its waterfront. The largest three-day festival in North Carolina, it features a wide variety of seafood prepared in familiar and surprising ways, as well as music, dancing, arts and crafts, and the Flounder Fling. Side trips from Beaufort and Morehead City give access to Fort Macon, Shackleford Banks, and the Cape Lookout Lighthouse via taxi boats, and to the beaches of the Crystal Coast. Cape Lookout National Seashore was established in 1966. Wild horses roam the nine-mile-long Shackleford Banks barrier island, protected by law, and limited to 130 horses since 1997.

Not far from Atlantic Beach is Fort Macon State Park, which opened in 1936. The park features a restored Civil War fort, an impressive coastal education center, and a pristine beach perfect for swimming, surf fishing, and relaxing in the sun. At the eastern tip of Bogue Banks, the park is almost entirely surrounded by water and offers a rare bit of undeveloped coastal beauty.

At EB 20.7, the MST passes the entrance to North Rivers Farm, a 6,000-acre restoration project managed by the North Carolina Coastal Federation. It is the largest restoration project of its kind in the country, aiming to revert the farmland back to its original natural state of forested, freshwater, and tidal wetlands. This will improve the water quality downstream and eventually open the estuaries back up to shell fishing. The North Carolina Trails Program worked with the Coastal Federation to route the MST through the North River Wetlands Preserve. Eight miles of MST trail were dedicated in 2017, but a western access point for thru-hiking has not yet been established. However, the federation and Friends are currently working with adjacent property owners to help connect this segment of the MST through the preserve.

As the MST heads east on US 70, it passes the small Carteret County communities of Bettie, Otway, Smyrna, Williston, Davis, Stacy, and a little off the MST, Sealevel and Atlantic. When you cross the North River Bridge the first community is Bettie. Otway (EB 19.4), an unincorporated community located in the Straits Township in Carteret County, calls itself the hub of the Down East region. With a population of over 400, it has several businesses, including the Otway Bed and Breakfast, located on six acres with four rooms furnished with antiques. The towns of Otway and Burnsville in the West, are named for War of 1812 privateer and later North Carolina state senator Otway Burns.

Smyrna's population is over 500, and like these other communities, it advertises its best weather months as April, May, and October (EB 21.4). Williston, population 220, is near Jarrett Bay. US 70 and the MST make a ninety-degree left turn at Davis, population 440, but a right turn leads to Davis Ridge, formerly an all-Black community of farmers and mullet fishermen, whose homes and fields were devastated by the great 1933 hurricane. Davis Shore Provisions represents fifty-three local artists and bakers with Down East charm. Davis is just blocks from Core Sound (White Oak River Basin) and Davis Shore Ferry Service to Cape Lookout National Seashore.

More Oysters than Pearls

Yes, you're in oyster country. Oysters were historically plentiful in North Carolina waters and were traded for other supplies. After the Civil War, they were sold for cash up the East Coast. The war on oysters started when unsustainable harvesting depleted oyster beds, and development, timbering, and agricultural use degraded habitat. Agencies and businesses are working hard to restore healthy oyster reefs along the coast. Oyster shell recycling is one such successful step. Oyster beds can provide homes for up to 300 species of plants and animals. Throughout this segment look for sites on the North Carolina Oyster Trail, which features forty sites with wild and farmed oysters.

Back on the Trail

Continuing east on US 70 is the community of Stacy, population 245. As you cross Salter's Creek you'll find the intersection of US 70 and the southern terminus of NC 12. Follow NC 12 to the Cedar Island ferry; NC 12 continues 136 more miles to Corolla.

Follow US 70 to the community of Sealevel, about a mile off the MST, right on the water, with 450 inhabitants. Early settlers called this area Hunting Quarters. Considered one of the lowest-elevation communities in North Carolina, it is the terminus of US 70. Check out Hoop Pole Creek Nature Trail and Old Tater Barn Picker's Trading Post. The last village before entering Cedar Island Refuge is Atlantic, population 608, about 3.5 miles from the MST. Here is the Marine Corps Outlying Field Atlantic, a military airport of the US Marine Corps. Commercial fishing has long been the main industry that supports the community. Today, Luther L. Smith and Son Seafood is the only remaining fish house in operation there, and Drum Inlet Marina offers a full-service harbor.

Shackleford Banks is the western endpoint of the Cape Lookout National Seashore, a fifty-six-mile stretch of coastline between Beaufort Inlet and Ocracoke Inlet. The settlement of Diamond City once sat on the eastern end of Shackleford Banks, but the San Ciriaco hurricane of 1899 caused many of its approximately 500 residents to leave, and by 1902 the community was deserted. Many Ca'e Bankers (*Ca'e* is the local brogue for "Cape") floated their homes to Morehead City, establishing a neighborhood on the sound called the Promise Land.

Carteret County's Cedar Island National Wildlife Refuge (EB 38.7–44) spans 11,000 acres of irregularly flooded, brackish marsh that are home to salt grass, saltmeadow hay, and black needlerush. The spartina salt marshes in the intertidal wetlands are predominately saltmarsh cordgrass. North Carolina's 220,000 acres of salt marshes are threatened by rising sea levels, and the state could lose over 30 percent of them by 2060. This will harm tourism, fish and birds, protection from storm surges, and water quality. The wildlife refuge also includes 3,480 acres of pocosin and woodland areas, mostly populated by live oak and loblolly, longleaf, and pond pine. In addition to the plant life it supports, the refuge is a site of incredible biodiversity, with 270 species of birds (many of them migratory), 91 species of amphibians and reptiles, and 35 species of mammals. The earliest land purchase was in 1964.

After completing his thru-hike in the heat of summer in 2019, Henry Westmoreland exclaimed, "I will never forget my first sight of Cedar Island National Wildlife Refuge as I crested the High Bridge—nothing but unspoiled wetland on either side of the road as far as I could see, to the horizon in front of me and to either side. It was awe inspiring and left me speechless, except to pray, thankful for being there to experience it." The bridge over Thorofare Channel Bay, built in 1953, is 3,000 feet long.

About three miles before reaching the ferry you cross John Day Ditch, a hand-dug ditch about two miles long for the purpose of keeping Day's cattle from straying off his property. In 1927, he owned about 1,000 cattle, and some of their offspring still roam the island. A right turn down Lola Road takes you to Pilgrim's Rest Baptist Church and the Silas Lupton Cemetery, with three graves dating from between 1839 and 1918.

Not many trails include two ferry rides to complete a hike. The 2.5-hour Cedar Island Ferry (toll; reservations recommended; 800-BY-FERRY or www.ncferry.org) connects the mainland to Ocracoke Island. Another ferry runs daily year-round between Ocracoke and Hatteras, forty minutes each way, with a pedestrian ferry operating during summer months. Cedar Island is a low-lying piece of land, so heed hurricane warnings—remember, cows were washed off the island in a 2019 tropical storm.

The Outer Banks

Cedar Island Ferry to Jockey's Ridge State Park

81.9 MILES

The seashore is . . . a most advantageous point
from which to contemplate this world.

HENRY DAVID THOREAU

NC Highway 12 stretches just inside the ocean dunes from the southern tip of Ocracoke Island to Hatteras Island, across Oregon Inlet on the magnificent three-mile-long Basnight Bridge, through Whalebone Junction, to Nags Head, and on to Jockey's Ridge State Park. The shoreline is continuously being reshaped—every tide a new beginning. The Outer Banks are a place of extremes and very susceptible to the effects of climate change, with sea-level rise being the most critical. Cape Hatteras has four park campgrounds, open seasonally: Ocracoke, Cape Point, Frisco, and Oregon Inlet. This segment is not only a tourist destination but also a haven for outdoor folks. It is internationally known as a winter birding destination, and a hike from the ferry at Cedar Island to Jockey's Ridge will round out a large list of the birds you can see in North Carolina. Peak bird time along this stretch of the coast is October through February.

Cedar Island Ferry to Cape Hatteras Lighthouse

Segment 18 covers a total distance of eighty-two miles or 7 percent of the entire MST, with sixty-six miles on beaches, nine on other trails, and six on roads and bridges, plus two ferry rides. Who could have picked a better eastern terminus of the MST than atop the highest of Jockey's Ridge sand dunes, the highest dunes east of the Mississippi River?

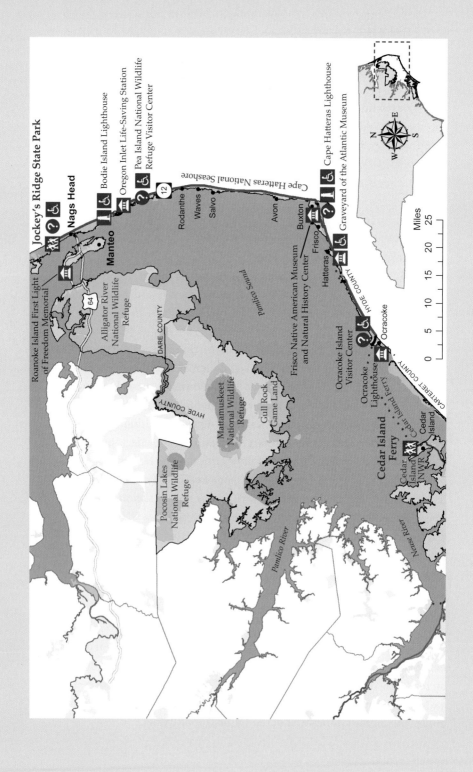

While the big three birding sites along the seashore (Pea Island, Bodie Island, and Oregon Inlet) are deservedly the spots most tourists frequent, the start of this segment in winter can be an amazing birding experience. The morning ferry ride from Cedar Island to Ocracoke can yield a great number of species, and for those hardy enough to stand at the front of the ferry in winter, you can get close looks at common and red-throated loon, long-tailed duck, bufflehead, red-breasted merganser, brant, and many other species of ducks and waterbirds.

How many lighthouses are there in North Carolina? While there are 18,600 in the world, there are only seven in North Carolina: from south to north, Oak Island, Bald Head Island, Cape Lookout, Ocracoke, Hatteras, Bodie Island, and Currituck Beach. Opened in 1817, Old Baldy Lighthouse on Bald Head Island in the Cape Fear River is the state's oldest. It is 110 feet high with 108 steps and can only be reached by boat or air. Each lighthouse has a distinctive paint pattern and light sequence to allow mariners to recognize it from all others during the day and night as they sail along the coast. There is another one thirteen miles off the Hatteras cape—the Diamond Shoals Lighthouse. It operated from 1966 to 2001 but since 2012 has been privately owned.

The Cape Lookout Lighthouse is in Carteret County, in the Cape Look-out National Seashore, on Shackleford Banks, known as the Southern Outer Banks. It opened in 1859 at 163 feet high with 207 steps. Its light was fully automated in 1950 and is only one of a few that operates during the day. It is reachable by boat or ferry and open for climbing from May to September.

The Ocracoke Lighthouse is North Carolina's oldest operating light-house and the nation's second-oldest. It is not open for climbing. The first lighthouse was built in 1798, replaced in 1820 due to shifting sands, and replaced again by the present seventy-five-foot-tall tower that shines fourteen miles out to sea. The three lighthouses along the MST route—Ocracoke, Cape Hatteras, and Bodie Island—will be described in more detail as we hike north along the Outer Banks.

Did you know Hyde County doesn't have a stoplight? This county is located along the Pamlico Sound and includes Ocracoke Island. Hyde County was established in 1705 and is the second-least populous county in North Carolina. Since 1950, three ferries have served Ocracoke. MST hikers routinely use the Cedar Island and Hatteras ferries, but there is also an NCDOT ferry from Swanquarter. Ocracoke is approximately sixteen

The must-visit 1822 Ocracoke Lighthouse is 600 yards off the MST.
Photo by Jerry Barker.

miles long and, except for the village of Ocracoke, is part of Cape Hatteras National Seashore.

Early settlers called themselves "hoi toiders"—their brogue for "high tiders." Now the locals sometimes call tourists "dingbatters" because of the silly questions they ask. In the summer a tram runs through the village, but it can also be biked and, of course, walked. Sites to visit while on the island include the British Cemetery, the lighthouse, Springer's Point Nature Preserve, the annual fig festival, the pony pens, and the miles of beach. Silver Lake Harbor is dotted with boats, shops, and restaurants, and Community Square is a busy information center. You can catch a ride (for a fee) to nearby Portsmouth Island.

Springer's Point Nature Preserve is 124 acres donated by the Coastal Land Trust—a peaceful Ocracoke point near where the pirate Blackbeard (a.k.a. Edward Teach) often anchored his ship to hide out or lay low. It was here that Blackbeard's sixty-four-foot sloop *Adventurer* was attacked by Lt. Robert Maynard and his two small sloops on November 22, 1718. Blackbeard was killed in the battle, and his headless corpse is rumored to be buried in a mass grave somewhere on the island. More than 300 years after his downfall, Blackbeard continues to fascinate residents and visitors alike. Today, you can find all things Blackbeard and pirate at Teach's Hole, a museum and pirate specialty shop. Another tall tale in the area is that of businessman Sam Jones, who built his Ocracoke home and buried his horse standing up near Springer's Point so he could ride it after his death.

On the northern tip of Portsmouth Island, which is visible from Ocracoke's southern end, the once-thriving village remains, preserved by volunteers and the National Park Service. Nestled near where Ocracoke Inlet meets the Pamlico Sound, Portsmouth Village offers visitors true seclusion, as well as a fascinating history. Explore the village on foot and get a glimpse into the past in its old homes, post office, lifesaving station, one-room schoolhouse, and Methodist church. Low-lying sand dunes and tall grasses line the ocean beach, and scattered all around are dozens of perfect, untouched seashells. It's a great place to find the elusive Scotch bonnet, North Carolina's state shell. Mosquitoes and biting flies also occupy the island, so be prepared.

At EB 1.2, past off-road vehicle (ORV) ramp 72 on the right, is NPS parking for the North Carolina Coastal Land Trust's Ocracoke Wetlands Preserve. On the left, you'll find a monument for the US Navy Loop Shack Hill. The walkway allows hikers to experience the delicate marsh and hammock environment and Loop Shack Hill (used for military training from 1943 to 1946 and from 1951 to 1972). The Ocracoke Preservation Society donated the twenty-four-acre tract. At EB 4.5 is access to the Ocracoke Campground and Hammock Hills Nature Trail. This 0.8-mile forest trail is good for families and children, as well as birdwatching and fishing.

Visit the Ocracoke Pony Pens (EB 7.8) with wild ponies that are direct descendants of shipwrecks. The first Spanish explorers (1565) skirted the coastline transporting coffee, sugar, general supplies, and Spanish mustangs, which were instrumental work horses for the new settlements as well as modes of transportation for the explorers once onshore. In the 1730s, Ocracoke settlers discovered them and their beneficial help to the new communities. The horses are much smaller than modern horses, with bulky frames, small legs, and distinctive wild manes and tails. Don't pet or feed the horses, or enter the pony pen; failure to follow these rules will result in an NPS fine.

A half mile east of the Pony Pens at North Beach Access is the Great Swash. Long ago this was the Hatteras Inlet, and now it's an excellent place to put a kayak into the sound. Hunting has been an important part of life on these islands since the days of the first European settlers, with the main targets being ducks and geese, sold to restaurants in the East.

The Migratory Bird Act of 1917 ended market hunting. Members of the Green Island Club, formed in 1923 at the north end of Ocracoke, hunted for sport instead.

At over eighty miles long and fifteen to twenty miles wide, Pamlico Sound is the largest sound on the East Coast, stretching from Portsmouth Island and the Cape Lookout National Seashore to Manteo and the Dare County mainland. *Sound* is a regional term for a saltwater lagoon. The Pamlico has an average depth of five to six feet and is fed by the Neuse and Pamlico Rivers (the latter of which is the estuary of the Tar River) as well as by three ocean inlets.

Cape Hatteras National Seashore, which measures 75.8 miles and stretches from Hatteras Inlet to Bodie Island in Dare County, was the first national seashore, as well as the first area of the MST designated by North Carolina State Parks. It recorded 2.8 million visitors in 2022. Cape Point Campground is the largest campground in the park. It is next to the ocean, one mile from the MST and the Hatteras Lighthouse. Sand and wind require longer than normal tent stakes, and insect netting and repellant will enhance your camping experience.

The Lost Colony and More Coastal Histories

Was the "Lost Colony" really lost? The Croatoan Archaeological Project seeks to answer this question and many others related to the history of Croatoan (modern-day Hatteras Island) and its inhabitants. Evidence indicates that the 1587 party of 117 British colonists first landed on Hatteras, encountered friendly Natives, but found the sand too dry and moved to Roanoke Island. At the Cape Creek archeology site, about a mile from the Hatteras Lighthouse, artifacts and shell mounds have been identified. The current research is to determine if some or the entire 1587 colony was not "lost" but instead resettled from Roanoke Island to Hatteras. John Lawson in 1700 observed "blue-eyed Indians" indicating blended race (see Scott Dawson's *The Lost Colony and Hatteras Island*, 2020). The Hatteras Public Library / Community Building and the Hatteras Island Ocean Center in Hatteras Village display for the public's perusal all artifacts found on the island related to the research.

There are more than 3 million shipwrecks under the ocean waters around the world. The Graveyard of the Atlantic Museum, in Hatteras Village next to the ferry docks, shares the maritime history of the Outer Banks and documents the more than 2,000 shipwrecks off the state's coast (free admission). The Outer Banks played a role in the Civil War and both World Wars. When the Union captured Confederate forts at Hatteras Inlet in August 1861, it created one of the first safe havens for escaping enslaved people. The Hôtel d'Afrique was part of the Underground Railroad and is located at a site near the museum. During World War II, German submarines sank so many of the Allies' tankers and cargo ships that the waters became known as "Torpedo Junction." Several shipwrecks are visible at low tide in the "Graveyard of the Atlantic." The remains of the *Laura A. Barnes*, a 1921 schooner, can be seen in front of the museum.

In 2006, a shipping container full of Doritos fell overboard, and the lost cargo washed up on Hatteras Island. Locals "salvaged" the shipwrecked snacks and feasted on the Nacho Cheese, Spicy Nacho, and Cool Ranch fare. The tastiest disaster along the Outer Banks is remembered in the museum.

Back on the Trail

As you hike the beaches of Hatteras, you might encounter closures due to federally protected threatened or endangered species, including the piping plover (there were only thirty-nine pairs in North Carolina as of 2020) and sea turtles. Safety concerns are many: strong ocean currents, rip currents and jellyfish, breaking waves along the shore, sun and heat, hot and blowing sand, dehydration, thunderstorms, mosquitoes, spiny plants, overwash on NC 12 during hurricanes, nor'easters, and other storms; evacuations; closed facilities; lack of cell signal; and road danger for hikers and bikers. Hikers need to be prepared, alert, and willing to take refuge for safety. But the powerful swells and unpredictable ocean waves make the Outer Banks an attractive place for surfing and wind sports. Surfers come from all over to paddle out at Cape Hatteras, Rodanthe (a favorite site is S-Curves), Nags Head, and Kill Devil Hills. Windsurfers, kiteboarders, kayakers, paddle boarders, and parasailers congregate in the shallow sound-side waters around Frisco, Buxton, and Avon. These areas are internationally known as some of the best sound-based board sport locales in the world.

The Frisco Native American Museum and Natural History Center is about two-thirds of a mile from the ocean. It opened in 1987 in a 100-year-old building that has served as a general store, post office, and shell shop. Visit the Billy Mitchell Airport, named after a local who was a pilot in World War I. It is managed by the National Park Service and the North

Sunlight beams onto the Open Ponds Trail through Buxton Woods Coastal Reserve. *Photo by Stan Seals; used by permission.*

Carolina Department of Aviation, with no night landings or take-offs. Mitchell was a US Army general and a major proponent for creation of the US Air Force.

The MST leaves the beach near ORV ramp 49, heads through the Frisco Campground, and travels 3.4 miles along Open Ponds Trail in Buxton Woods Coastal Reserve. This is a 1,725-acre conserved maritime forest (the largest in North Carolina and the largest contiguous tract of its kind on the Atlantic coast) with ancient oaks, pines, wax myrtles, grapevines, and wildlife edged by dunes and beaches, south of the Hatteras Lighthouse. The reserve is also home to the world's only maritime shrub swamp. Buxton Woods totals 3,000 acres and is Hatteras Island's major source of groundwater recharge.

Buxton Woods sits on a series of relic sand dunes running east to west. A shrub thicket of live oak and red cedar dominate the coastal edge of the area, and the maritime evergreen forest farther inland protects the dune ridge from erosion. The surprisingly high elevation of the dune ridges allows visitors to take in breathtaking views of the coast and forest. The

"Lookout Loop" trail, off Old Doctor's Road, is a great example of a dune ridge's remnants. Buxton Woods is part of the North Carolina Game Lands program, so hunting is allowed seasonally.

The eight villages of Ocracoke, Hatteras, Frisco, Buxton, Avon, Salvo, Waves, and Rodanthe are not part of the national seashore, but each has an intriguing story. How they got their names and their historic beginnings is revealed as hikers move north. Sandy Bay is just south of Frisco, with views of sound and ocean, shallow water for kids, lots of sailors and kiters, and paved parking. A hiker might stop at a village for supplies or a snack break and get to know the locals. Off Sand Street in Salvo, the wreckage of the *Pocahontas* is occasionally visible. Buxton (population 1,500) hosts an annual Hatteras Island Arts and Crafts Guild Show. After the Great Atlantic Hurricane of 1944, only twelve homes were left standing in Avon.

At EB 25.7 you might pass gravesites of British soldiers killed in World War II near the North Carolina coast. The *San Delfino*, a British tanker ship, was destroyed by German torpedoes in 1941, and the body of an unknown sailor washed ashore on the beach at Buxton. He was buried nearby in Buxton Woods by villagers. One last body from the HMS *Bedfordshire* washed up a few days later on Hatteras Island, and residents buried him beside the *San Delfino* sailor. A right on Lighthouse Road takes you to Cape Point Campground and to excellent shelling and surf fishing at Cape Point (ORV ramps 43 and 44).

Cape Hatteras Lighthouse to Jockey's Ridge State Park

Located on the Cape Hatteras National Seashore, the Cape Hatteras Lighthouse stands at 198.5 feet, making it the tallest brick lighthouse in the country and the second-tallest in the world. Known as "America's Lighthouse," it signals boaters to stay away from the Diamond Shoals, underwater sandbars that reach twenty miles out into the Atlantic Ocean from Cape Hatteras. The current lighthouse was built and first used in 1870, and the iconic candy-cane pattern on its exterior was added in 1873. The light beams can be seen from more than twenty miles away. In 1999, as the Atlantic Ocean eroded the barrier island and inched closer to the beacon, the lighthouse was transported 2,900 feet inland over the course of twenty-three days at a cost of $11.8 million. The lighthouse is open for climbing from mid-April to Columbus Day. Visitors climb 166 feet up 257 steps (of 269 total steps).

The Cape Hatteras Visitor Center is open year-round. Also check out the two-floor Museum of the Sea, which is located in the Cape Hatteras Lighthouse Double Keepers' Quarters and has exhibits focusing on Outer Banks history and local natural history. Sometimes you will see the term *light station*, which describes the total property and multiple outbuildings. Two US commemorative postage stamps have featured the lighthouse: a 1972 two-cent stamp for the National Park Centennial and a 1990 twenty-five-cent stamp for the US Lighthouse Service's Bicentennial.

The *G. A. Kohler* shipwreck remains are usually on the beach, but how much is exposed, at any given time, is up to the sand and wind. It sank in a hurricane in 1933 and may be visible on the beach at ramp 27, four miles south of Salvo. The ship was salvaged for iron during World War II.

Two miles before Salvo, on the sound side, is No Ache Island, a soothing name for an inhospitable place. According to the US Postal Service, the Salvo post office is the second-smallest post office in the country at eight feet by twelve feet (the smallest is in the little town of Ochopee, Florida). Following tradition, the post office building is portable, moving according to the postmaster, who purchases it from the last postmaster and then transports it to their private residence. It was listed on the National Register of Historic Places in 1993.

Chicamacomico Historic Site commemorates a lifesaving station that operated from 1874 to 1954 and was considered one of the best maritime sites on the East Coast. The first lifesaving station in the state, it is credited with some of the greatest rescues on the Outer Banks. The five open buildings are in the village of Rodanthe and can be visited from Easter to Thanksgiving. Interesting trivia: the beach here is the easternmost point of North Carolina. Avon Village was known as Kinnakeet (a Carolina Algonquian word for "that which is mixed") in its early years, when it was a thriving fishing and boat-building community. But when the post office came in 1883, it got the new name, possibly after the famed English river.

Between Avon and Salvo was Little Kinnakeet Lifesaving Station, built in 1874, transferred to the National Park Service in 1954 before permanently closing in 2022. It was just north of the Kinnakeet beach access. Rodanthe, Waves, and Salvo make up the settlement of Chicamacomico (a Native word roughly translating as "sinking down sand"). Rodanthe is known for celebrating "Old Christmas" on January 7, an Orthodox Christian custom brought over by the original settlers who used the "old style" Julian calendar. There was once a natural wetland area called Aunt

Phoebe's Marsh, but it is now covered by an abandoned theme park and waterslide. The Inn at Rodanthe is a vacation rental, easy to spot on its oceanfront perch, and is the house from the 2008 film *Nights in Rodanthe.*

The MST continues on the beach along Rodanthe. On the sound side, the 2.4-mile Jug Handle Bridge opened in 2022 and stretches from northern Rodanthe, just past the beach access at Green Point (near EB 50.6) to the southern portion of the Pea Island National Wildlife Refuge. The bridge includes 352 155-foot-long pilings. It's close to the *Pappy Lane* shipwreck in Pamlico Sound near Rodanthe, identified in October 2017 as a World War II troop transport.

The Captain Richard Etheridge Bridge on Pea Island over New Inlet (EB 56.9, completed in 2018) is narrow and busy, but the beach may be an option at low tide. It is helpful to have access to tide tables. Etheridge was keeper of the Pea Island Life-Saving Station from 1880 until his death in 1900. Born into enslavement on Roanoke Island in 1842, he became an officer in the Union army's Buffalo Soldiers.

Pea Island National Wildlife Refuge, north of Rodanthe and south of Oregon Inlet, includes over 5,000 acres of maritime forests and marshlands and twelve miles of beach. Established in 1938 as part of the National Wildlife Refuge System by the US Fish and Wildlife Service, the land was set aside to protect and provide habitat for migratory birds (greater snow geese, various waterfowl, shorebirds, wading birds, and raptors) and endangered and threatened species (loggerhead sea turtles). It was also intended to provide opportunities for the public to enjoy wild spaces. Pea Island is managed as part of the North Carolina Coastal Plain Refuge Complex and administered through the Alligator River National Wildlife Refuge.

The refuge, with impoundments for improved habitat—such as the 390-acre North Pond—provides sanctuary for nearly 400 species of migratory birds. It is one of the best, if not the best, place for birdwatching in the state and is a prized spot on the North Carolina Birding Trail. The map for the refuge is dotted with quirky names such as Cat, Hog, Goat, and Goose Islands; Blackmar Gut; Pauls Ditch; Dulls Point; Ira Lump; and Loggerhead Hills.

The *Oriental* shipwreck is located directly across from the Pea Island Visitor Center (EB 59.4). The steam engine sticks out of fifteen to twenty feet of water (depending on the tides) about 100 yards from shore, with strong currents rushing around it. It resembles a boiler and is also known as "The Boiler Wreck." This was a 210-foot federal transport tanker that sank on May 16, 1862, while carrying Civil War supplies from New York to South Carolina, along with personnel who helped free enslaved people. The Pamlico Sound town of Oriental (previously known as Smith's Creek) was named after the steamship.

Saving Lives

In 1874, the US Life-Saving Service added to its growing network of life-saving stations by establishing seven stations along the Outer Banks, strategically located at the most dangerous spots for vessels in the Atlantic Ocean. The Ocracoke station is located in Ocracoke Village east of the present Coast Guard Station near Silver Lake. The Little Kinnakeet station was located north of Avon Village and is owned by the National Park Service. The Pea Island Life-Saving Station was formerly located across from the Pea Island National Wildlife Refuge headquarters. Remnants of its stone foundation can be seen near the parking area. Rodanthe's former cookhouse has been refurbished and relocated to Collins Park in Manteo as the Pea Island Cookout Museum. Some of the former stations now are private residences or stores, but most were destroyed in storms or by fire.

Just before crossing the Basnight Bridge, you'll pass the Pea Island Life-Saving Station No. 177, the only station completely manned by a crew of African Americans (from 1880 to 1948) and the first in America with a Black keeper, Richard Etheridge.

The original station at Kill Devil Hills was moved to Corolla in 1986. Now restored, it is home to Twiddy and Company's real estate office. The second Kill Devil Hills station, built on the original foundation, is now a private home. The original Kitty Hawk station (1874–1915) was located near Mile Post 4½ on Beach Road; the second station, built in 1915, is now a private home.

Back on the Trail

The 2.8-mile-long Marc Basnight Bridge over Oregon Inlet connects Hatteras Island to Bodie Island. It is named for Dare County's state senator from 1984 to 2011, who was also senate president pro tempore from 1993 to 2010. The bridge opened in 2019, replacing the Bonner Bridge, and is the third-longest continuous segmental concrete box girder unit in North America, with nine major spans of 350 feet. The new bridge highway deck includes an extra ten-foot-wide area, suitable for

From the Bodie Island Lighthouse you can see the expanse of Outer Banks marsh and ocean horizon. *Photo by Danny Bernstein; used by permission.*

MST hikers to use (with caution) but may also be used as an additional lane when Hatteras Island residents are forced to evacuate. Between the 1920s and 1963, ferries operated across the ever-changing channels of Oregon Inlet. In 1934, the North Carolina Highway Commission began subsidizing runs. NC 12 became a numbered state highway in 1963. At the north end of the bridge is the Oregon Inlet Fishing Center, known for charter boat fishing.

A violent and destructive hurricane hit the Outer Banks in 1846, slicing through the land between Bodie Island and Pea Island. A ship named the *Oregon* was caught in Pamlico Sound during the storm, and when the weather cleared, the ship's crew went to the mainland to announce the creation of a new inlet separating Hatteras Island from the rest of the Outer Banks. To this day, the new inlet is known as Oregon Inlet.

Bodie (pronounced "body") Island Lighthouse is located south of Nags Head, one mile from EB 71. The first lighthouse was built in 1847 on fifteen acres purchased for $150 (property boundary markers are still visible), but within two years it was leaning and was soon abandoned. A new structure was built in 1859, then blown up by retreating Confederate troops in 1861. Today's 150-foot-tall lighthouse was completed in 1872 with the familiar black-and-white horizontal stripes. It is seasonally open for climbing (for a fee) with the restored keeper's quarters used as a year-round visitor center. It's 214 steps to the top.

Bodie Island—which is no longer an island—extends from Oregon Inlet to Whalebone Junction, where US 64/158 enters the Outer Banks. Whalebone Junction, one of the Outer Banks' major landmarks, is located in Nags Head and is where US 64, US 158, and NC 12 converge. This is the end of Cape Hatteras National Seashore and the beginning of Nags Head, with the Whalebone Cape Hatteras Visitor Center near the US 64 intersection. Bodie Island's habitat was badly damaged in the early 1900s from overuse by hunting clubs; building of dikes and impoundments; grazing by cattle, sheep, ponies, and pigs; and burning of marshes. These activities were banned in the mid-1930s. From 1937 to 1941 over 2,500 CCC/WPA workers built dune fences for erosion control, and in the 1950s dunes and flats were planted with hundreds of trees and acres of beach grasses, sea oats, salt meadow grass, and smooth cordgrass.

From the lighthouse, cross the expansive grassy area to a viewing platform for spectacular vistas of a large saltwater marsh that's great for birding. Wading birds, many seasonal waterfowl, American avocet, and black skimmers are commonly seen. The nearly one-mile Bodie Island Dike Trail is just south of the visitor parking lot, another great spot for birding (whimbrel and red knot between peak and offseason, skimmers and least terns in the summer; and waterfowl, like loons and scoters, in the winter).

Jennette's Pier—which the MST goes under at EB 76.7—is about 400 yards north of US 64 and has its own history, first as a wooden fishing pier and now as a concrete one, run by the State of North Carolina through the North Carolina Aquarium system. Pier manager Mike Remige told *Star News Online* that the pier, established in 1939, was reborn in 2011. The pier still allows fishing but also has many educational exhibits inside. Numerous conservation efforts have been incorporated into its operation, including the three wind turbines that produce much of its electricity. Across NC 12 from the pier, Sam and Omie's has been in business since 1937, exuding a barefoot and "beachy" atmosphere and serving tasty dishes morning, noon, and night.

Nearby

Allen Poole, MST task force leader for the Outer Banks, notes that many good venues are on Roanoke Island, in Manteo. The Outer Banks History Center is a good source of information about the Outer Banks, as is the National Park Service's office for Cape Hatteras National Seashore. The

Outer Banks Visitors Bureau can provide you with further information about the area. Manteo, on Roanoke Island, is not on the MST route, but it is worth visiting. Sites include the Roanoke Marshes Lighthouse, Manteo Waterfront, *Elizabeth II* vessel, North Carolina Aquarium, and Fort Raleigh National Historic Site.

Consider visiting the Nags Head Woods Preserve, a 1,400-acre maritime forest with a ridge of ancient sand dunes, and an extensive marsh system on the western Roanoke Sound side. Hike the eight trails (including one built to the accessibility standards of the Americans with Disabilities Act) that total over eight miles, visit the butterfly garden, or enjoy weekly programs during the summer. This was the site of a thriving village through the 1930s, and artifacts remain of village life. Some of the trees may be hundreds of years old. The preserve is open dawn to dusk every day, one mile from the beach/MST and US 158 in Kill Devil Hills at MP 9½.

Between May and September, sea turtles come ashore to lay their eggs on more than 300 miles of beach in North Carolina. This is also peak season for beachgoers, so visitors must do all they can to protect the nests and future sea turtle populations. During this time, driving at night is banned on the beaches. If you're walking on the beach after dark, you should refrain from introducing any artificial light, such as from a flashlight or cellphone, as this can confuse newly hatched turtles. At Cape Hatteras alone, five species of sea turtles (loggerhead, leatherback, hawksbill, green, and Kemp's ridley) use the beaches for nesting. But sea turtles aren't the only ones at risk—nesting birds such as piping plovers, American oystercatchers, Wilson's plovers, least terns, gull-billed terns, and common terns should not be disturbed during their nesting seasons.

Jockey's Ridge State Park, located in Nags Head in Dare County, covers 427 acres, making it the smallest state park in North Carolina. Established in 1975, it was the most visited state park for seven years (2015–2021, with 1.8 million visitors in 2021). Jockey's Ridge is the tallest living sand dune on the Atlantic coast, and it's perfect for kite flying, sandboarding, sightseeing, and sunset viewing. From the top, you can see from the ocean to Roanoke Sound. Just when you expected to finish the Mountains-to-Sea Trail at sea level, you have to climb back up 90 to 100 feet to the imaginary finish line—the most natural incline a hiker has faced since Moore's Knob in Hanging Rock State Park. Photos can be taken at the MST Terminus Monument.

Jockey's Ridge State
Park ranger Jennifer
Cox celebrates with
thru-hiker Cedric
Turner-Kopa on his
"cool" November 19,
2020, completion.
*Photo by Cedric
Turner-Kopa; used by
permission.*

It's always exciting to finish a hike, be it a beautiful day hike or a 1,175-mile thru-hike. Graham Zimmerman characterized reaching Jockey's Ridge at the end of his 2020 thru-hike as "a punctuation to what became the experience of my lifetime. Reflecting on the trail has become a daily meditation for me. My trek was a deeply human experience, from seeing the natural beauty of our state . . . to the people I met along the way."

The state park visitor center includes a museum and 360-foot board-walk featuring exhibits on the dune's ecology. Mobility-impaired visitors who call twenty-four hours in advance may be able to reserve a ride on an all-terrain vehicle to the dune's highest point. Kitty Hawk Kites, the largest hang-gliding school in the world, offers lessons in the park. Because of the wind resource, Jockey's Ridge was the first North Carolina state park to install a wind turbine power generator. When renovations to the visitor center are completed in 2023, Friends of the MST will install the trail's new Eastern Terminus Monument.

The dunes at Jockey's Ridge formed 3,000 to 4,000 years ago and served as an important landmark for mariners. According to legend, the dunes get their name from early inhabitants who caught and raced wild ponies in the area. The eastern end of the MST is at the highest point

Jerry Barker celebrating on MST's eastern terminus at Jockey's Ridge State Park. *Photo by Johnny Massey; used by permission.*

on the dunes, but because of the unique ecology of the area, the highest point is constantly shifting. In 1973, portions of the dunes were slated to be flattened for residential development, but Carolista Baum saved them by planting herself in the path of the bulldozer and shutting down the operation. She formed the People to Preserve Jockey's Ridge, and the community fought nearly two years before the North Carolina State Parks system bought the land in April 1975. In her honor, the park's address is 300 West Carolista Drive. Later the National Park Service declared the dunes a national natural landmark.

On the sound side of the park, visitors can enjoy sunbathing, wading, paddling, and walking a one-mile trail to wetlands, grassy dunes, and maritime thickets where birders can catch sight of flycatchers, warblers, and sparrows, and a variety of waterfowl, including threatened American oystercatchers.

Nearby

Kill Devil Hills and the Wright Brothers National Memorial are 4.4 miles north of Jockey's Ridge State Park. Wilbur and Orville Wright came to the Outer Banks in 1900 because the area was described as a mile wide and clear of trees for sixty miles. The Big Kill Devil Hill, the location of the Wright Brothers Monument, built in 1932, is the ninety-foot sand dune where the Wright brothers conducted some 1,000 glider flights. The 428-acre national memorial, established in 1927, honors the first human flight of twelve seconds, 120 feet, at 10:35 a.m. on December 17, 1903. The memorial includes a visitor center, the First Flight Airstrip, and a monument. Did you know the Wright brothers returned in 1908 and Orville flew with their mechanic, Charles Furnas, the first American passenger in a powered airplane?

Does the MST go near the Currituck Beach Lighthouse? Not close for a hiker, but it is only thirty-one miles north of Jockey's Ridge State Park, on the Northern Outer Banks. The lighthouse, 162 feet high, was built in 1875 with a million red bricks, which were left unpainted to distinguish it from the southern lighthouses. Currituck Beach Lighthouse is in Historic Corolla Park and was recently added to the National Register of Historic Places. Just north, roaming freely among the dunes and on the beach on the northernmost Currituck Outer Banks, are the Corolla wild horses, whose Spanish mustang ancestors were brought over nearly 500 years ago. North Carolina designated the colonial Spanish mustang—Corolla's wild horses and others like them—as the official state horse in 2010.

The End of the Trail

Travel is fatal to prejudice, bigotry and narrow-mindedness.

MARK TWAIN

Mountains-to-Sea Trail hikes always come to an end—at the end of a day, at the end of a weekend, or at the Tennessee border or the Atlantic Ocean. There are tender feet, gear to stash away, and clothes to wash. But through it all are the hidden gems you've uncovered, friends you've made, memories to savor and stories to tell and retell. More history, culture, and interesting sites remain to be discovered and shared, more than a single book can contain, so I hope you take many journeys on this special route that snakes its way through our state.

You are invited to help others enjoy the magic of hiking in the North Carolina mountains, Piedmont, or coastal plain by becoming a member of Friends of the Mountains-to-Sea Trail, volunteering for trail-building and maintenance, and purchasing an NC MST license plate or MST gear. Helpful information is available at MountainsToSeaTrail.org.

Acknowledgments

The book was made better by friends' willingness to proofread segments of the book. My deep thanks to Don Bergey, Jeff Brewer, Marcia Bromberg, Chris Corn, Carl deAndrade, Fred Dietrick, Mark Edelstein, Carla Gardner, Jim Hallsey, Susan Hester, Bob Hillyer, Paul Hosier, Alan Householder, Randy Johnson, Ben Jones, Johnny Massey, Steve Metcalf, Steven Mierisch, David Parker, George Poehlman, Allen Poole, Carolyn Sakowski, Bill Scott, Tim Supple, Robert Trawick, and Germaine Yahn. Bill Reaves aided in preparing photographs. The nineteen MST segment maps were skillfully prepared by Curtis Belyea.

This book involved many contributors of history and culture near the MST. These folks have varied connections to the MST and thus helped present a comprehensive look at the 1,175-mile corridor. I express my sincere thanks and recognition by naming them here. Please accept my apology to anyone whom I inadvertently left out.

Aram Attarian, Dan Auman, Brian Baker, Erin Baker, Cathy Barr, Boykin Bell, Greg Bell, Mary Bengtson, Denise Bishop, David Bland, Jake Blood, Larry Blythe, Bill Boyarsky, Bill Brown, Derrick Brown, Terri Buckner, Danny Burnstein, Anne Cassebaum, Rick Chatham, Dottie Cooke, Chris David, G. Olivia Dawson, Joel Deaton, Brandon Dillman, Tara Dower, Claire "Marmot" Dumont, Hussein El-Genk, Stuart English, Frances Ferrell, Mike Fischesser, Chris Fonvielle Jr., John French, Julie "Jester" Gayheart, Joy Greenwood, Peter Hampson, Aaron and Lexie Harris, Meredith Henry, Susan Hester, Alan Householder, Gene and Sue Huntsman, John Blackfeather Jeffries, Steph Jeffries, Steven Joines, Angelina Jumper, Arthur Kelley, Cathy Kinlaw, Alexa Lawrence, Howard Lee, Joe Liles, Les Love, Amanda Lugenbell, Dana Matics, Donnie Rahnàwakęw McDowell, Joe McClernon, Bill Meador, Mark "Explores"

Miles, Craig Miller, Kaye Miller, Charlie "Bald" Milligan, Chuck Millsaps, Jason Murrell, Helen Norman, Mike Parker, Brantley Partin, Austin Paul, Joseph Paul, John Pepin, Phil Pinski, Tammy L. Proctor, Ethan Rehder, Corey Roberts, Bill Sadler, Beverly Scarlett, John Schelp, David Schwartz, Gregory Scott, Stan Seals, Keith Sidden, Curtis Smalling, Deirdre "Beerdra" Smith, Richard Smith, Lisa "Conundrum" Speas, Edward "Skip" Stoddard, Keith Taylor, Cedric Turner-Kopa, John Underhill, Doug Veazey, Don Walton, Walt Weber, Henry "Moxie" Westmoreland, Dave "Finder" Whitlow, David Wild, Christine Wilson, Harry Wilson, Ben Wittenberg, Greg Yahn, and Graham Zimmerman.

Friends of the Mountains-to-Sea Trail staff were immensely helpful and responsive, as they are to each and every hiker seeking advice. Thank you, Betsy Brown, Jim Grode, Elizabeth Hipps, Ben Jones, Brent Laurenz, and Sherry Seagroves.

Acknowledgments

Bibliography

INTRODUCTION

Bernstein, Danny. *The Mountains-to-Sea Trail across North Carolina: Walking a Thousand Miles through Wildness, Culture and History.* Mount Pleasant, SC: History Press, 2013.

De Hart, Allen. *Hiking North Carolina's Mountains-to-Sea Trail.* Chapel Hill: University of North Carolina Press, 2000.

Grode, Jim, ed. *Great Day Hikes on the North Carolina's Mountains-to-Sea Trail.* Chapel Hill: University of North Carolina Press, 2020.

Houskeeper, Heather. *A Guide to the Edible and Medicinal Plants of the Mountains-to-Sea Trail.* 2014.

Ward, Scot. *The Thru-Hiker's Manual for the Mountains-to-Sea Trail of North Carolina.* 3rd ed. Lexington, KY: C.R.A.S.H. Publications, 2012.

SEGMENT 1

Bernstein, Danny. *Carolina Mountain Club: One Hundred Years.* Asheville, NC: Carolina Mountain Club, 2023.

Brulliard, Nicholas. "A Liking for Lichens." *National Parks*, National Parks Conservation Association, Spring 2020, 24–25.

Bryson City–Swain County Chamber of Commerce. "Great Smoky Mountains National Park: Mingus Mill." GreatSmokies.com. Accessed July 2020. https://www.greatsmokies.com/mingus-mill/.

Buncombe County Register of Deeds. "As Long as the Grass Shall Grow: A History of Cherokee Land Cessions and the Formation of Buncombe County." BuncombeCounty.org, September 17, 2021. https://www.buncombecounty.org/Governing/Depts/register-of-deeds/default.aspx.

Coates, Carol. "A Belated Mother's Day Story." *Living on the Diagonal* (blog), May 16, 2019. https://livingonthediagonal.com/tag/lufty-baptist-church/.

Decker, Sarah Jones. "Coming into Focus: George Mesa's Legacy." *A.T. Journeys*, Summer 2021, 24–31.

Discover Life in America. "Smokies Species Tally: How Many Kinds of Life Inhabit Great Smoky Mountains National Park?" DLIA.org. Accessed December 2020. https://dlia.org/smokies-species-tally/.

Eastern Band of the Cherokee Indians. "Take a Journey to the Home of the Eastern Band of Cherokee Indians." VisitCherokeeNC.com. Accessed September 2020. https://visitcherokeenc.com/eastern-band-of-the-cherokee/.

High Country of North Carolina. "Blue Ridge Parkway Wildflowers." HighCountryHost.com. Accessed September 2020. https://highcountry host.com/Blue-Ridge-Parkway-Wildflowers-found-in-the-NC-High -Country.

Kays, Holly. "The Untold Story: Smokies Seeks to Showcase History of African-Americans in the Park." *Smoky Mountain News* (Waynesville, NC), August 21, 2019. https://smokymountainnews.com/archives/item/27510 -the-untold-story-smokies-seeks-to-showcase-history-of-african-americans -in-the-park.

National Park Service, Great Smoky Mountains. "Synchronous Fireflies." Last updated July 13, 2021. https://www.nps.gov/grsm/learn/nature/fireflies .htm.

Weber, Walt. *Trail Profiles and Maps: From Clingmans Dome to Mount Mitchell and Beyond.* 3rd ed. Asheville, NC: Carolina Mountain Club, 2018.

Whisnant, Anne Mitchell. "Routing the Parkway, 1934." Driving through Time: The Digital Blue Ridge Parkway, digital collection. Documenting the American South, University of North Carolina at Chapel Hill Libraries, 2010. https://docsouth.unc.edu/blueridgeparkway/overlooks/competing _routes/.

SEGMENT 2

Steurer, Peter M. *History of the Carolina Mountain Club, Commemorating the 80th Anniversary: 1983–2003.* Carolina Mountain Club, October 2003. https://www.carolinamountainclub.org/view/assets/uploadedAssets/CMC -HistoryBook.pdf.

US Forest Service. "National Forests in North Carolina." FS.USDA.gov. Accessed September 26, 2022. https://www.fs.usda.gov/nfsnc.

Whisnant, Anne Mitchell. "Black History on the Blue Ridge Parkway: Places, Stories, and New Research." YouTube video, 31:00, posted by Blue Ridge Parkway Foundation on June 3, 2021. https://www.youtube.com/watch?v= M9owDb8pcS4.

SEGMENT 3

Ambler, A. Chase, Jr. *Rattlesnake Lodge: A Brief History and Guidebook.* Booklet. 1994. https://www.rattlesnakelodge.com/.

Anderson, Alan. "The Trees of Mount Mitchell." In "The Wisdom of the Forest." Unpublished manuscript, 1997. Black Mountains Program,

Southern Appalachian Highland Conservancy. http://main.nc.us/BMCP/mitchell.html.

Inscoe, John C. "Michaux, André." In *Dictionary of North Carolina Biography*, edited by William S. Powell, vol. 4. Chapel Hill: University of North Carolina Press, 2016. https://www.ncpedia.org/biography/michaux-andre.

Jeffries, Stephanie B., and Thomas R. Wentworth. *Exploring Southern Appalachian Forests: An Ecological Guide to 30 Great Hikes in the Carolinas, Georgia, Tennessee, and Virginia.* Chapel Hill: University of North Carolina Press, 2014.

Jones, Rebecca. *African Americans and the Blue Ridge Parkway.* Historic Resource Study, National Park Service, August 2009. https://irma.nps.gov/DataStore/DownloadFile/629763.

SEGMENT 4

Chavez, Karen. "Foothills Conservancy Permanently Protects Rare Southern Appalachian Mountain Bog Land." *Asheville (NC) Citizen-Times*, January 9, 2020. https://www.citizen-times.com/story/news/2020/01/09/rare-mountain-bog-land-forever-protected-western-north-carolina/2834942001/.

Jarvis, Robin. "Most People Have Long Forgotten about This Vacant Ghost Town in Rural North Carolina." OnlyinYourState.com, September 15, 2018. https://www.onlyinyourstate.com/north-carolina/mortimer-ghost-town-nc/.

———. "Thousands of Daffodils Fill a Ghost Garden at the End of This Spring Hike in North Carolina." OnlyinYourState.com, March 15, 2019. https://www.onlyinyourstate.com/north-carolina/daffodil-flats-linville-gorge-nc/.

Lael, Ralph I. "The Brown Mountain Lights." Pamphlet. Self-published, 1965.

Minick, Jeff. "What Lies Beneath." *Smoky Mountain Living*, October 1, 2017. https://www.smliv.com/stories/what-lies-beneath/.

Reuben, Aaron. "Appalachian Atlantis: The Lost Mountain Utopia of Fonta Flora." *Our State*, September 30, 2019. https://www.ourstate.com/appalachian-atlantis-the-lost-mountain-utopia-of-fonta-flora/.

Robbins, Zach. "Steels Creek Falls—Pisgah National Forest, NC." HikingUpward.com. Accessed summer 2020. https://www.hikingupward.com/PNF/SteelsCreekFalls/.

Washburn, Mark. "Where Did Mysterious Mountain Lights Go?" *News and Observer* (Raleigh, NC), July 9, 2016. https://www.newsobserver.com/news/state/north-carolina/article88661217.html.

SEGMENT 5

Delia, Ann. "Ground Cedar's Explosive Spores." School of the Greenwood, February 13, 2013. https://www.schoolofthegreenwood.org/single-post /2016/02/13/Ground-Cedars-Magnificent-Spores.

Grandfather Mountain Stewardship Foundation. "What Is Grandfather Mountain?" Grandfather.com. Accessed September 26, 2022. https:// grandfather.com/about-grandfather-mountain/what-is-grandfather -mountain/.

Jones, Rebecca. *African Americans and the Blue Ridge Parkway.* Historic Resource Study, National Park Service, August 2009. https://irma.nps.gov /DataStore/DownloadFile/629763.

Keefe, Susan. *Junaluska Speaks, Oral Histories of a Black Appalachian Community.* Jefferson, NC: McFarland, 2020.

National Park Service. "History of the Linn Cove Viaduct." Blue Ridge Parkway, NPS.gov. Last updated November 19, 2019. https://www.nps.gov /blri/learn/historyculture/linn-cove-viaduct.htm.

SEGMENT 6

Brown, Joe. *Brown Ancestors: Brauns Abstammung, 1430 to 2012.* Clemmons, NC: Haystack, 2012.

LivingPlaces.com. "Rockford Historic District, Rockford." Accessed summer 2020. https://www.livingplaces.com/NC/Surry_County/Rockford /Rockford_Historic_District.html.

North Carolina Historic Sites. "Horne Creek Farm." August 12, 2021. https:// historicsites.nc.gov/all-sites/horne-creek-farm.

SEGMENT 7

Dillon, Tom. "From the Mountains to the Sea." *Wildlife in North Carolina,* April 1981. https://digital.ncdcr.gov/digital/collection/p16062coll4/id /12268.

Forsyth County Public Library, North Carolina Collection. "Pilot Mountain . . . A Brief Illustrated History of Our Best Known Landmark . . . Including a True Account of the Battle of Pilot Mountain That Never Happened." Blog post, March 24, 2017. https://northcarolinaroom.wordpress.com /2017/03/24/pilot-mountain-a-brief-illustrated-history-of-our-best-known -landmark-including-a-true-account-of-the-battle-of-pilot-mountain-that -never-happened/.

Fitts, Mary Beth. "Trowel Blazers: Sauratown Woman." *Women of the OSA* (blog). North Carolina Office of State Archaeology, September 1, 2019. https://archaeology.ncdcr.gov/blog/2019-09-01/trowel-blazers-sauratown.

Grogan, Emily. "The History of the Sauratown Trail from Hanging Rock State Park to Pilot Mountain State Park." Sauratown Trails Association,

SauratownTrails.org, July 12, 2005. http://sauratowntrails.org/history
.html.

Hanging Rock State Park Expansion. "Background." Accessed September 26,
2022. https://hangingrockexpansionmasterplan.wordpress.com/about
/background/.

O'Donnell, Lisa. "Old Structures Remind Us of Pilot Mountain's Past." *Winston-
Salem (NC) Journal*, April 24, 2013, updated April 9, 2019. https://
journalnow.com/.

SEGMENT 8

Commemorative Landscapes of North Carolina. "Battle of Clapp's Mill,
Burlington." Documenting the American South, University of North
Carolina at Chapel Hill Libraries. Accessed summer 2020. https://
docsouth.unc.edu/commland/monument/839/.

Lewis, J. D. "The American Revolution in North Carolina: Summerfield."
Carolana.com, 2009. https://www.carolana.com/NC/Revolution
/revolution_summerfield.html.

SEGMENT 9

Abernethy, Michael D. "Life on the River: The Haw River's Past, Present and
Future." *Times-News* (Burlington, NC), January 10, 2015.

Cassebaum, Anne Melyn. *Down along the Haw: The History of a North Carolina
River*. Jefferson, NC: McFarland & Company, 2011.

Classical American Homes Preservation Trust and the Richard Hampton
Jenerette Foundation. "Ayr Mount." ClassicalAmericanHomes.org. Accessed September 26, 2022. https://classicalamericanhomes.org/sites
/ayr-mount/.

Haw River Assembly. "Natural and Cultural History of the Haw River."
HawRiver.org. Accessed September 2020. http://hawriver.org/about-the
-river/history/.

Haw River Trail. "Land Trail Maps: Sellers Falls." TheHaw.org. Accessed October 2020. https://www.thehaw.org/land-trail/land-trail-maps/sellars-falls/.

Johnson, Herman C. *Rafting 250 Miles down the Haw River to the Sea*. Self-published, 2021.

Laying the Foundation for Preservation. "Gibsonville Prison Farm." Accessed
August 2020. https://gibsonvilleprisonfarm.wordpress.com/.

Occaneechi Band of the Saponi Nation. http://www.obsn.org.

SEGMENT 10

Carolina Country. "Getting to Know Margaret Nygard and the Eno
River." October 2018. https://www.carolinacountry.com/departments

/departments/tar-heel-lessons/getting-to-know-margaret-nygard-and-the
-eno-river.

Durham County Library. "Margaret Nygard, Champion of the Eno." *And Justice for All: Durham County Courthouse Art Wall.* Accessed June 2020. http://andjusticeforall.dconc.gov/gallery_images/margaret-nygard-champion-of -the-eno/.

Eno River Association. "Ribbons of Color along the Eno River: The History of African Americans and People of Color Living on the Eno." *Eno River Journal* 10, no. 1 (2021).

———. "Ribbons of Color along the Eno River: The History of People of Color Living on the Eno." *Eno River Journal* 10, no. 2 (2022).

———. "The Search for Fish Dam Road." EnoRiver.org. Accessed November 2020. http://enoriver.org/fishdam/index.htm.

Miles, Mark. "Exploring the Old Durham Pump Station at Eno River State Park." *Mark Explores* (blog), December 15, 2019. Used by permission. https://markallmywords.com/2019/12/15/exploring-durham-pump -station/.

———. "Hiking through Wildflowers on George Pyne Trail at Penny's Bend." *Mark Explores* (blog), August 9, 2020. Used by permission. https://markallmywords.wordpress.com/2020/08/09/hiking-george-pyne-trail-at -pennys-bend/.

North Carolina Mutual Life Insurance Company. "History." NCMutualLife .com. Accessed September 2020. https://www.ncmutuallife.com/history/.

Open Durham. "Fairntosh." OpenDurham.org. Accessed July 2020. https:// www.opendurham.org/buildings/fairntosh.

Shain, Taylor, dir. *The Eno River Is My Lifeline: The Scarlett Family Story.* "Beverly Scarlett—a Short Documentary" on YouTube, 5:09, posted by IHearttheEno on August 31, 2020. https://www.youtube.com/watch?v= IWEh7HxVYtg.

Wake County Register of Deeds. "Wake County Enslaved Persons Project." WakeGov.com. Accessed August 2021. https://www.wakegov.com /departments-government/register-deeds/wake-county-enslaved-persons -project.

SEGMENT 11

North Carolina Wildlife Federation. "The Butterfly Highway." NCWF.org. Accessed October 2021. https://ncwf.org/habitat/butterfly-highway/.

Smallwood, James Edgar. "History of Dams and Mills at Milburnie, NC." Restoration Systems, Neuse River Restoration Milburnie Dam Removal, March 2018. https://milburniedam.com/wp-content/uploads/2018/05 /History-of-Milburnie-Dam.pdf.

Sumner, Perry W. "Wildlife Profiles: Virginia Opossum." North Carolina Wildlife Resources Commission, January 1995. https://www.ncwildlife.org /Portals/0/Learning/documents/Profiles/opossumvirginia.pdf.

Triangle Land Conservancy. "Bailey and Sarah Williamson Preserve." TriangleLand.org. Accessed September 2020. https://www.triangleland .org/explore/nature-preserves/williamson-preserve.

Wake Audubon Society. "Anderson Point Park." WakeAudubon.org. Accessed September 2020. https://www.wakeaudubon.org/initiatives/conservation /anderson-point-park/.

SEGMENTS 11A–16A

Inge, Leoneda. "African American Legacy in New Bern." North Carolina Voices: Civil War series, North Carolina Public Radio, June 20, 2011. https://www.wunc.org/post/african-american-legacy-new-bern.

Johnston Community College. "About Howell Woods." Howell Woods Environmental Learning Center. Accessed September 2020. https://www .johnstoncc.edu/howellwoods/about/index.aspx.

Miller, Adrian. *Black Smoke: African Americans and the United States of Barbecue*. Chapel Hill: University of North Carolina Press, 2021.

Tryon Palace. "History: The Public School in New Bern." TryonPalace.org. Accessed September 27, 2022. https://www.tryonpalace.org/the-palace -historic-homes/new-bern-academy-museum/history.

SEGMENT 12

Bentonville Battlefield State Historic Site. "American History I: Lesson Guides." North Carolina Historic Sites, 2014. https://files.nc.gov/dncr -historicsites/eleventh_grade_lesson.pdf.

North Carolina Department of Natural and Cultural Resources. "Legendary Percy Flowers, 'King of the Moonshiners.'" *This Day in North Carolina History* (blog), August 2, 2016. https://www.ncdcr.gov/blog/2014/08/02 /legendary-percy-flowers-king-of-the-moonshiners.

North Carolina Historic Sites. "Bentonville Battlefield: History." HistoricSites .NC.gov. Accessed September 27, 2022. https://historicsites.nc.gov/all -sites/bentonville-battlefield/history.

North Carolina State Extension. "North Carolina's Forest and Forest Products Industry by the Numbers." Accessed October 2020. https://content.ces .ncsu.edu/north-carolinas-forest-and-forest-products-industry-by-the -numbers.

SEGMENT 13

Gullah Geechee Cultural Heritage Corridor Commission. "About." GullahGeecheeCorridor.org. Accessed September 27, 2022. https:// gullahgeecheecorridor.org/about/.

Kinlaw, Cathy Faircloth. *White Lake: A Historical Tour of the Nation's Safest Beach*. Self-published, AuthorHouse, 2015.

Bibliography

Robinson, Justin. "Suggs Mill Pond Game Land." Take A Hike! Accessed
    summer 2020. https://sites.google.com/site/hikingnc/home/locations/
    nc/fayetteville/suggs-mill-pond.
Wright, Emiene. "How the 'MLK of Jones Lake' Made This NC Park an Island
    of Equality." *Cardinal & Pine*, February 7, 2022. https://cardinalpine.com
    /story/how-the-mlk-of-jones-lake-made-this-nc-park-an-island-of-equality/.

SEGMENT 14

Brown, Naomi P. "Restoration Begins for Historically Black Church in
    Brunswick County." North Carolina Public Radio, December 28, 2021.
    https://www.wunc.org/arts-culture/2021-12-28/restoration-begins-for
    -historically-black-church-in-brunswick-county.
Cecelski, David. "The Road to the Cape Fear: Susan Johnson's Diary, Part 8."
    DavidCecelski.com, November 30, 2018. https://davidcecelski.com/2018
    /11/30/the-road-to-the-cape-fear-susan-johnsons-diary-part-8/.
Cottle, Ann S. *The Roots of Penderlea: A Memory of a New Deal Homestead Com-
    munity*. Wilmington: University of North Carolina Wilmington, 2008.
Rose, Mariel. "Pocomoke: A Study in Remembering and Forgetting."
    Ethnohistory 45, no. 3 (Summer 1998): 543–73. https://www.jstor.org
    /stable/483323.
Serrano, Nicholas. "Canetuck Community Center" In *SAH Archipedia*, edited
    by Gabrielle Esperdy and Karen Kingsley. Society of Architectural His-
    torians and University of Virginia Press, 2012. https://sah-archipedia
    .org/buildings/NC-01-141-0059.

SEGMENT 15

Fontana, Pat. "The Lasting Legacy of Ocean City Beach." *Topsail Magazine*,
    July 16, 2021. https://www.topsailmag.com/the-lasting-legacy-of-ocean-city
    -beach/.

SEGMENT 16

Rich, Brad. "Coastal Sketch: Gene and Sue Huntsman." CoastalReview.org,
    May 13, 2016. https://coastalreview.org/2016/05/14383/.

SEGMENT 17

Cecelski, David. "Our Coast's People: Late Daughter of David Ridge."
    CoastalReview.org, February 11, 2022. https://coastalreview.org/2022/02
    /our-coasts-people-last-daughter-of-davis-ridge/.
Green, Mark. "John Day's Ditch." *Southern Greens* (blog), July 19, 2012. http://
    southerngreens.blogspot.com/2012/07/john-days-ditch.html.

US Fish and Wildlife Service. "Cedar Island National Wildlife Refuge." FWS
.gov, August 20, 2020. https://www.fws.gov/refuge/cedar_island/.

SEGMENT 18

Brennan, Emily. "The Archaeology of Roanoke: The Lost Colony." *Digging
into Archaeology* (blog), Archaeology in the Community, June 14, 2017.
https://www.archaeologyincommunity.com/digging-into-archaeology/the
-archaeology-of-roanoke-the-lost-colony.

Carr, Dawson. *NC 12: Gateway to the Outer Banks*. Chapel Hill: University of
North Carolina Press, 2016.

Croatoan Archaeological Society. "Croatoan Archaeological Project."
CASHatteras.com. Accessed September 27, 2022. http://www.cashatteras
.com/Products.html.

Economic Development Partnership of North Carolina. "Trip Ideas: Walk in
Blackbeard's Footsteps in North Carolina." VisitNC.com. Accessed August
2020. https://www.visitnc.com/story/uwdF/walk-in-blackbeard-s-footsteps
-on-the-coast.

National Park Service, Cape Hatteras. "Cape Hatteras Light Station." NPS.gov.
Accessed September 2020. https://www.nps.gov/caha/planyourvisit/chls
.htm.

Ocracoke Township Tourism Development Authority. "Portsmouth Island."
VisitOcracokeNC.com. https://www.visitocracokenc.com/visit-portsmouth
-island/.

Stover, Douglas. *Pea Island Life-Saving Station, Rodanthe, North Carolina, Coast
Guard Station #177*. Historic Resource Study, National Park Service, 2008.
https://www.nps.gov/parkhistory/online_books/caha/life_saving_hrs.pdf.

Thiel, Rita. "New Trail in the Works from Ball Field to Loop Shack Hill."
Ocracoke Observer, October 30, 2018. https://ocracokeobserver.com/2018
/10/30/new-trail-in-the-works-from-ball-field-to-loop-shack-hill/.

Wagner, Adam. "Can NC Highway 12 Withstand Climate Change in Outer
Banks?" *News and Observer* (Raleigh, NC), August 1, 2021.

———. "NC 12 Was Brainchild of OBX Real Estate Developer." *News and
Observer* (Raleigh, NC), August 5, 2021.

Index

Page numbers in italics refer to illustrations.

Index

Index

Other **Southern Gateways Guides** you might enjoy

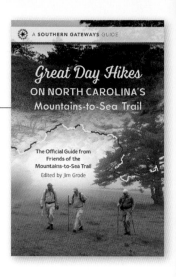

Great Day Hikes on North Carolina's Mountains-to-Sea Trail

FRIENDS OF THE MOUNTAINS-TO-SEA TRAIL
Edited by **JIM GRODE**

The official guide to the best day hikes of the Mountains-to-Sea Trail

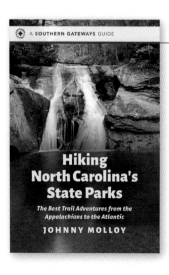

Hiking North Carolina's State Parks

The Best Trail Adventures from the Appalachians to the Atlantic

JOHNNY MOLLOY

The perfect companion to hiking the wonders of North Carolina's state parks

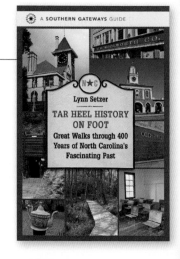

Tar Heel History on Foot

Great Walks through 400 Years of North Carolina's Fascinating Past

LYNN SETZER

Day-tripping through our state's vibrant history

Available at bookstores, by phone at **1-800-848-6224**, or on the web at **www.uncpress.org**